A SOCIAL BASIS FOR PREWAR JAPANESE MILITARISM

PUBLISHED UNDER THE AUSPICES OF
THE CENTER FOR JAPANESE AND KOREAN STUDIES,
UNIVERSITY OF CALIFORNIA, BERKELEY

RICHARD J. SMETHURST

A Social Basis for Prewar Japanese Militarism

The Army and the Rural Community

UNIVERSITY OF CALIFORNIA PRESS
Berkeley · Los Angeles · London

University of California Press
Berkeley and Los Angeles, California
University of California Press, Ltd.
London, England
Copyright © 1974, by
The Regents of the University of California
ISBN 0-520-02552-0
Library of Congress Catalog Card Number: 73-84385
Printed in the United States of America

To Satsuki

If boys enter grammar school at six, high school at thirteen, and graduate at nineteen, after which from their twentieth year, they spend a few years as soldiers, in the end all will become soldiers and no one will be without education. In due course, the nation will become a great civil and military university.

YAMAGATA ARITOMO, 1873, from Roger F. Hackett, *Yamagata Aritomo in the Rise of Modern Japan, 1838–1922* (Cambridge, 1971), p. 65.

. . . if we think toward the future and correctly guide reservists, who will number three million in another six or seven years, and the nation's youth, we can control completely the ideals of the populace and firm up the nation's foundation. By continuing to promulgate educational orders like the recent one, we can permeate education and the local government with the ideal that good soldiers make good citizens.

TANAKA GIICHI, 1913, from letter to General Terauchi Masatake, quoted in Inoue Kiyoshi, *Taishōki no seiji to shakai* [Politics and Society in the Taisho Period] (Tokyo, 1969), p. 369.

Party politics is like a three-cornered battle and interrupts the flow of events. Only one party can hold power at any time. Thus, the work of leading our seventy million fellow citizens under the throne as a truly unified and cooperating nation in both war and peace, however you think about it, has been assigned to the army. The navy has but limited contact with the populace. Only the army, which touches 200,000 active soldiers, 3,000,000 reserve association members, 500,000 to 600,000 middle school students, and 800,000 youths, has the qualifications to accomplish this task.

UGAKI KAZUSHIGE, 1925, from *Ugaki Kazushige nikki* [The Diary of Ugaki Kazushige] (Tokyo, 1968–1971), I, pp. 497–498.

CONTENTS

ACKNOWLEDGMENTS

Since I began this study in a graduate seminar at the University of Michigan with the encouragement and guidance of Professors Roger F. Hackett and Umetani Noboru, a number of organizations and individuals have helped me. I would like to thank the Foreign Area Fellowship Program and the University Center for International Studies of the University of Pittsburgh for essential financial support over the years.

Many people have aided me in my search for research materials in Japan and the United States. I am particularly grateful to Professor Ishida Takeshi of Tokyo University's Institute of Social Science, Mr. Takahashi Masae of the Misuzu Publishing Company, Professor Hattori Harunori of Yamanashi University, Mr. Yamaguchi Hirotoshi, formerly of the Yamanashi Prefecture Board of Education, Professor Matsushita Yoshio of Kōgakuin University, the staffs of the Anjō City Library, of the Meiji Newspaper Repository, Press Center, and Institute of Social Science Library, all of Tokyo University, of the East Asian Libraries of the University of Michigan and Columbia University, and of the Library of Congress, and to all of my interview and questionnaire respondents. I am also indebted to a number of scholars who read and criticized all or part of this manuscript: Carol N. Gluck, Christopher E. Lewis, and Professors Evelyn S. Rawski, Thomas G. Rawski, and Richard Sims. Finally, I would like to single out three people without whose help this manuscript could not have been written: Mr. Kamikawa Rikuzō, Japanese language teacher and counsellor; and Professors Morioka Kiyomi, sociologist of Tokyo University of

Education, friend and respected teacher, who (among other contributions to my scholarly development) led me to my case study communities and through my earliest interviews, and Mae J. Smethurst, for
encouragement, long suffering patience, and seemingly endless research
and editorial assistance.

INTRODUCTION

Most writers discussing the events which led to Japan's participation in World War II have written as if they believed that the government and more particularly its military wing operated in a vacuum separated from the populace at large. For example, scholars have lucidly described and analyzed the Manchurian Incident and the February 26th Incident and the decision for war in 1941, but few have attempted to show comprehensively what allowed the "mainstay officers" and the "young officers" and the "control faction" the freedom to act at these moments in Japanese history and seemingly to ignore public opinion. Some scholars have discussed the army's attempts to educate the public in military values, but all of these works concentrate only on the views and efforts of the central planners and do not touch on the important question of the local educational process. Still others have mentioned the peace preservation laws, police suppression, and censorship, but in doing so have treated practices performed largely by civilians, the Home Ministry's "thought police," that affected much more the small group of city-based intellectuals who opposed the events leading to war (or wished they had) than the bulk of the population.[1]

---

1. For fascinating accounts of military politics in Japan in the 1930s, see James B. Crowley, *Japan's Quest for Autonomy: National Security and Foreign Policy, 1930–1938* (Princeton, 1966); Hata Ikuhiko, *Gun fashizumu undōshi* [A History of the Military Fascism Movement] (Tokyo, 1962); and Takahashi Masae, *Shōwa no gumbatsu* [The Showa Military Clique] (Tokyo, 1969). Two older, but still interesting works are Richard Storry, *The Double Patriots* (London, 1957); and Kinoshita Hanji, *Nihon fashizumu shi* [A History of Japanese Fascism], 2 vols. (Tokyo, 1949–1951). For works touching briefly and impressionistically on the army's efforts to militarize the public, see Fujiwara Akira, *Gunjishi* [A Military History] (Tokyo, 1961), especially pp. 150–152; Fukuchi Shigetaka, *Gunkoku Nihon no keisei* [The

Hannah Arendt wrote that dictatorships do not succeed without popular bases of support; history does not record examples of modern despots or despotic oligarchies establishing themselves against the majority's will.[2] Although I wish to avoid the difficulty of determining to what extent Japan's wartime government was in fact dictatorial, I think Arendt's statement can apply to prewar Japan and its government. If we are to interpret accurately the implementation and success of the policies of the military segment of Japan's government, we must analyze its roots in the whole society. The Japanese army was able to guide its nation's destinies in the wartime era because it molded an obedient rural following before the crisis decade of the 1930s and continued to solidify what one observer called its "electoral constituency" thereafter.[3] The object of this book is to describe and analyze how between 1910 and 1945 officers like General Tanaka Giichi created or utilized four national organizations in order to ensure military popularity, spread a nationalistic ideology, and build the army a solid basis of support. Tanaka's goal was to use Japan's thousands of hamlets as the army's agrarian "cells." He achieved this end by establishing the organizations' branches in every community in the nation and by preempting the existing rural social order.

The most important of the four organizations was the Imperial Military Reserve Association (*Teikoku zaigō gunjinkai*). Tanaka established it in 1910, and by 1936 it had 14,000 branches and enrolled three million volunteers between the ages of 20 and 40, half of whom had never served on active duty. Tanaka and other officers, such as General Ugaki Kazushige, helped unify the Greater Japan Youth Association (*Dainihon seinendan*) in 1915, created youth training centers (*seinen kunrenjo*) in 1926, and founded the Greater Japan National Defense Women's Association (*Dai nippon kokubō fujinkai*) in the 1930s. These complementary organizations, subordinate to the reservists at the local level, added another nine or ten million people to the army's network. The officers steadily insinuated the branches of the organizations into the community framework of "village Japan" so that the army's military and patriotic ideals became an important

Formation of Militaristic Japan] (Tokyo, 1959), especially pp. 95–115, 212–248; and Inoue Kiyoshi, ed., *Taishōki no seiji to shakai* [Politics and Society in the Taishō Period] (Tokyo, 1969), especially pp. 376–401. *The Asahi Journal's Shōwashi no shunkan* [Moments in Shōwa History] (Tokyo, 1966) contains accounts of police suppression; see especially I, pp. 43–51, 186–194, 222–239, 258–266, and II, pp. 343–356.

2. Hannah Arendt, *The Origins of Totalitarianism* (Cleveland, 1958), p. 306.

3. Attributed to Tokutomi Sohō in R. P. Dore and Tsutomu Ōuchi, "Rural Origins of Japanese Fascism," in James W. Morley, ed., *Dilemmas of Growth in Prewar Japan* (Princeton, 1971), p. 197.

layer of the rural value system. This effort to strengthen military ties with farm communities stemmed from the obsessions of Tanaka, Ugaki, and their mentor, Yamagata Aritomo, with national unity, and from an excessive but real fear that this unity was threatened by mass movements and Western ideologies in the twentieth century. The officers' drive to produce "civilian soldiers" was intensified by their perception of Japan's strategic military needs to mobilize the whole populace—not just a few soldiers—at a time when Japan and the other nations of the world were entering the modern era of total war. Yamagata, Tanaka, Ugaki, and their successors wanted to build a rich and militarily powerful Japan.[4]

Tanaka and Ugaki established branches and subbranches of their organizations in every agricultural village (*mura*) and hamlet (*buraku*) and used long-standing internal social stratification, cooperation, cohesiveness, and sanctions against nonconformity for army purposes. In other words, the army leaders did not search for new methods to build their rural support; they looked to village conventions instead. The branches of each organization recruited officials from the existing village leadership and reflected the community's internal stratification. They also obtained local, not national or army, financing. Like purely local organizations, they used social pressure to attract members, and they gained virtually 100 percent enrollment of eligibles. And, even though they carried out military and patriotic duties, the branches performed many community services as well. Each local branch became a microcosm of the hamlet and village as a whole. It achieved the army's goal of local acceptance by functioning as an age-group organization for the appropriate villagers. In other words, the army's success at building rural support was based on its use of each villager's parochial commitment to the hamlet's social order and to the hamlet itself as the center of his world.

The army's branches absorbed traditional community functions so thoroughly that members did not always perceive themselves as reservists, youth association members, or defense women when they performed the duties of these groups. One Japanese villager informed the author that in his community reservists officially ran the local volunteer fire department as one of their military activities. When pressed to recall whether or not he thought of himself as a reservist when he fought fires, the respondent could only answer, "Hmmm, what should I say? I guess I never really thought about it very much. Everyone [my age] belonged to both [the reservist branch and the

4. Richard J. Smethurst, "The Creation of the Imperial Military Reserve Association in Japan," *Journal of Asian Studies,* xxx, no. 4 (1971), pp. 815–828.

fire department], and I did too." He went on to say (as did many other villagers) that reservists were the "mainstays" (chūken) of his community. But neither he nor any of the other ex-reservists could say whether reservists became mainstays because they served as reservists or because they were already the community's healthiest men, in the physical prime of their lives, and happened also to be reservists. The army's organizations were so totally integrated into the nation's hamlets and villages by the 1930s that loyalty to the army and loyalty to the hamlet and village had become synonymous.

Tanaka and Ugaki were not content to build this "indirect" form of mobilization; they also wanted to win the active support of the villagers, support based on a patriotic commitment to national and martial values. Thus they introduced into their local "curriculum" patriotic and military duties, as well as the soldier's ethos (gunjin seishin), an amalgam of village, family, warrior, and national values centered on the emperor. Their intent was to reinforce the combined impact of the hamlet and village service and the patriotic and military duties by inculcating an ideology which included paternalistic and community as well as soldierly and nationalistic values. Tanaka's ideal nationalist would practice the local virtues of self-subordination to group interests, diligence, conformity, and acceptance of the authority of fathers and social superiors, and the national virtues of bravery, obedience to officers, reverence for the emperor, and even xenophobia. Tanaka wanted rural people to identify national values with locally important values and thus to strengthen the village social order and build national unity at the same time. The end product of Tanaka's and Ugaki's efforts was the creation of "national villagers." A national villager was a person who supported military and national goals because of an identification with his hamlet and a commitment to its values. He was also one who developed a new positive identification with the emperor and the army, the symbols of Japan's unity.

Many scholars have discussed the growth of superhamlet and national outlook among Japanese farmers, whose local identification remained strong; but to Tanaka and Ugaki national outlook was inadequate.[5] Tanaka and Ugaki wanted to produce "nationalistic"

5. See John Embree, Suyemura: A Japanese Village (Chicago, 1964), pp. 170, 187, 201, 303; Suzuki Eitarō, Nihon nōson shakaigaku genri [Principles of Japanese Rural Sociology] (Tokyo, 1940), pp. 337–339; Shiota Shōbē, "Tochi to jiyū o motomete" [In Search of Land and Freedom], Shōwashi no shunkan, I, pp. 114–122; Fukutake Tadashi, Nihon sonraku no shakai kōzō [The Social Structure of Japanese Villages] (Tokyo, 1959); Erwin H. Johnson, "Status Changes in Hamlet Structure Accompanying Modernization," in Ronald P. Dore, Aspects of Social Change in Modern Japan (Princeton, 1967), pp. 170–177.

national Japanese who served their nation by serving their army and emperor. Their aim was the molding of citizens who were loyal villagers *and* adherents of the nationalistic "soldier's ethos." Tanaka and Ugaki's ideal "hamlet soldier" practiced, even in civilian life, the five basic virtues of the *Imperial Rescript to Soldiers and Sailors:* decorum, courage, loyalty, obedience to emperor and superiors, and bravery. He obeyed officers, officials, landlords, and other superiors filially, as he obeyed his father. In the rural tradition, he worked hard, productively, cooperatively, and in docile and obedient unity. He performed all of these virtues in the name of the emperor and his unique nation and army. In other words, the ideal national villager's job was to follow the soldier's ethos, the combination of warrior values, paternalism, "ruralism," "emperorism," and national uniqueness and even superiority.[6]

An understanding of the emperor's position in prewar Japanese thinking is crucial to an understanding of the army's nationalism because it was the emperor who provided the focus of the soldier's ethos and the cherished unity. To millions of products of the civil and military educational systems, the emperor was not merely the supreme symbol of the state, the Japanese equivalent of the American flag; he was also the semi-divine father figure of a cohesive Japanese *völkisch* community that excluded outsiders. Japanese nationalism, not unlike the German cultural and linguistic form propounded by the disciples of Herder, Fichte and Hegel, was an ethnic nationalism based on "Japaneseness" in a homogeneous and long-isolated society. It thus differed from the French brand, which depended on residence in the nation-state. To the Japanese military nationalist, one was either a

---

6. Tanaka was a prolific writer on the soldier's ethos, especially for reservists. For example, see Kawatani Yorio, *Tanaka Giichi den* [The Biography of Tanaka Giichi] (Tokyo, 1929); *Tanaka Giichi denki* [The Biography of Tanaka Giichi], 3 vols. (Tokyo, 1960); Hosokawa Ryūgen, *Tanaka Giichi* (Tokyo, 1958); Tanaka, *Tanaka chūjō kōenshū* [The Collected Speeches of Lt. Gen. Tanaka] (Tokyo, 1916); Tanaka, *Taisho kōshoyori* [From a High and Clear Place] (Tokyo, 1925). Tanaka published over 300 articles in *Senyū* [Comrades in Arms], *Wagaie* [Our Family], *Taishō Kōron* [Taishō Review], and *Teikoku seinen* [Imperial Youth] between 1910 and 1925, many on the subject of the soldier's ethos. See also Ugaki Kazushige, *Ugaki Kazushige nikki* [The Diary of Ugaki Kazushige], 3 vols. (Tokyo, 1968–1971), especially I., pp. 519–523 and 547–550. And see Tanaka Giichi, "Kokumin kyōroku o nozomu" [Requesting the Cooperation of the Populace], *Senyū*, 20 (1912), pp. 11–13; "Osorubeki shisō no appaku," [The Frightening Ideological Pressure], *Senyū*, 93 (1918), pp. 8–12; "Guntai kyōiku shikan" [A Personal View of Military Education], *Tanaka chūjō kōenshū*, pp. 58–113; "Zaigō gunjin no kokoroe" [Rules for Reservists], *Tanaka chūjō kōenshū*, pp. 114–122; Ugaki, "Shidanchōkai dōseki ni okeru rikugun daijin kōenyoshi" [A Summary of the Army Minister's Speech to the Division Commanding Generals], *Senyū*, 232 (1929), pp. i–vi.

member of the unique Yamato people, or an outsider. If one was a member, he was Japanese forever, no matter where he migrated, lived, or had been born. If one was not a member, he could never become Japanese even if he looked, spoke, and acted in every way like a Japanese. The emperor was believed to be a descendant of the divine progenitor of this unique group, the sun goddess; he was therefore viewed as mystical father-priest-leader of the people and as the fountainhead of Japanese ethnicity. When one spoke of *chū*, loyalty to the emperor—as all of the interview respondents in this study did—he referred to more than political obedience to the state and its symbol. The term encompassed all of the user's feelings about unique Japanese ethnicity, the ideas of filial piety to a national father figure in a paternal society, of "feudal" dependence on a benevolent lord, and of reverence, love, and awe of a man-deity (*arahitogami*). In short, the nationalist held a deeply emotional attachment to the emperor. One might best describe the attitude of Japanese to the figure who unified their nationalism as similar to that of a loyal, filial, nationalistic, and religiously devout Britisher to his employer, father, king, *and* God. All of the symbols and major documents of prewar Japan—the rising sun flag, national anthem, Constitution, *Imperial Rescript to Soldiers and Sailors, Imperial Rescript on Education,* and declarations of war and peace—referred to or emanated from the emperor, not the state, government, or people. The emperor was Japanese sovereignty, and one sang praises and shouted banzais to him, not to the flag, Constitution, or political system. When one spoke of his emotional attachment to Japan or of his nationalism, he generally did so by mentioning his feelings toward the emperor. The interview data to be presented in Chapter V indicate that while the respondents' primary orientations in the 1930s focused on their families and hamlets, they simultaneously became fervently patriotic and nationalistic and developed deep emotional feelings toward the emperor, who personally commanded the army and navy. When one served his hamlet, he served his emperor, army, and nation; when one served the emperor, army, and nation, he served the hamlet. It was the emperor who combined all of the cohesive hamlet and village groups into a national unity.[7]

It was at the hamlet and village or rural areas that the army had its

---

7. For translations of the two rescripts, see Arthur Tiedemann, *Modern Japan* (New York, 1962), pp. 107–114; Takahashi Masae, *Ni-niroku jiken* [The February 26 Incident] (Tokyo, 1965), *passim* and especially pp. 134–137 (Takahashi presents a provocative discussion of officers' perceptions of their relationship to the emperor); Embree, *Suyemura*, p. 303; John W. Hall, "A Monarch for Modern Japan," in Robert E. Ward, *Political Development in Modern Japan* (Princeton, 1965), pp. 11–64; and Inoue Kiyoshi, *Tennōsei* [The Emperor System], (Tokyo, 1966), pp. 110–119.

greatest success in building a social basis for militarism and inculcating nationalistic values. In the agricultural community, cooperation was essential to one's livelihood, and everyone who was eligible did join the army's organizations. Cities, however, lacked the social integration, cohesion, and sanctions necessary to local and national unity, and over two-thirds of the urban eligible did not join. The army organized factory branches to use paternalistic labor-management relations as the basis of an urban "hamlet" and never abandoned the hope that they might somehow organize urban areas, but they also recognized and used their rural advantage. In fact, the military's nationalistic ideology, the soldier's ethos, the beliefs that officers wanted to spread to all Japanese, stressed values found primarily in agricultural villages and towns. Tanaka and Ugaki included the emperor-centered nationalistic and martial ideas of the Field Marshal Yamagata's *Imperial Rescript to Soldiers and Sailors* in the ethos and also emphasized the family and group values of the nation's hamlets and villages. The two generals amalgamated these beliefs into their ethos, not only because they believed in them and wanted all Japanese, both rural and urban, to believe in them, but also because Tanaka and Ugaki apparently realized that an emphasis on family and hamlet *and* national values would make militarism and nationalism more palatable to rural Japanese, that is to the majority. As late as 1935–1940, three-fifths of the population lived in towns and villages, and more than half still supported themselves by fishing and farming, in spite of continuous urbanization. Japan was a predominantly agrarian society, and rural success secured for the army a solid basis of support.

The major part of this study will be based on data collected in a number of rural communities, particularly in the town of Anjō in Aichi Prefecture, in the villages of Ōkamada, Futagawa, Mitsue, and in the town of Katsunuma in Yamanashi Prefecture. Discussions of the activities of the army's organizations in these communities will be presented as case studies of the military's efforts at the socialization of civilians. The local materials are drawn from a collection of unpublished Anjō materials, from interview and questionnaire information gathered mostly in the towns and villages listed above, and from a few local youth association histories, such as the two volumes from Anjō. The interviews and questionnaires are especially important because of the dearth of other local documentation; many of the materials that were not destroyed by American strategic bombing were burned by order of the reserve association's national headquarters in August, 1945, or were sold as wastepaper after the war.

Before I turn to an investigation of the army's use of the existing social structure of rural Japan to spread its ideals and win popular support, I will introduce the national leaders, their motivations, efforts, and policies, and the milieu in which they operated in establishing the system for military socialization. The first part of the book will treat the work of one part of the military elite in building the four massive organizations. The work of establishing them was not performed by all of Japan's modern military leaders, only by officers in its most important single part, the Choshu faction of Field Marshal Yamagata Aritomo, creator of Japan's modern army, police and local government system and its successors. These men, almost all ex-samurai from that feudal domain in Western Japan which took the lead in overthrowing the old regime in the 1860s, had a strong commitment to building national unity. Other military men were also concerned with national unity but played a less active role in creating it because of inadequate perseverance or means. What distinguished Yamagata and his followers from most other officers was not so much their belief in a structured and military-dominated Japan, but their power and their commitment to total war planning and political activity. Yamagata and his three closest officer-protégés, Katsura Tarō, Terauchi Masatake, and Tanaka, all served as prime ministers between 1889 and 1929 (a total of 15 of the 40 years), and Ugaki Kazushige made an ill-fated effort to form a cabinet. Only one general that headed the government before 1937 was not a member of the Choshu faction.[8]

Yamagata and his followers built their socialization system for civilians in the face of ever increasing threats to national unity when Japanese society entered the modern world and became gradually more complex and diversified. From the beginning of his career, Yamagata had recognized the need for national unity against hostile external and internal threats, but the dangers to unity before 1900 were minimal because the authoritarian feudal legacy provided a basis for societal integration. But as Japan entered the "demonic" modern world and as even poor farmers and fishermen became literate and more cosmopolitan, this legacy had to be shored up. Thus Yamagata's protégés, Tanaka and Ugaki, established their system to mold "national villagers" and to fight modernizing Japan's inevitable and increasing diversity. The two officers wanted the material benefits of modernization, but not many of its intellectual and social fruits.

---

8. Tokinoya Katsu, ed., *Nihon kindaishi jiten* [An Encyclopedia of Modern Japanese History], (Tokyo, 1960), pp. 682–689. The one exception was Kuroda Kiyotaka of Satsuma who headed the second modern cabinet in 1888–1889. Yamagata replaced Kuroda as Prime Minister in December, 1889, and no non-Choshu general formed a government until Hayashi Senjūrō in 1937.

These military men were not alone in their compulsion to maintain unity. Many civilian leaders, particularly civil bureaucrats, local government and school officials, landlords, and industrialists feared the same trends and cooperated with the army in the development of its social basis. They too had interests in maintaining local and national social order, and this civilian support, especially at the village and factory level, helped the army achieve success.

Finally, I wish to point out that the army broadened and deepened its efforts as the dangers to unity became greater, but the belief in the need for a cohesive national social order and all of the elements of its rural system—the ideology, the national leadership, the organizations, and their local impact and method of acceptance—had their roots in the mid-nineteenth century and did not change or become significantly harsher or more authoritarian even during World War II. Although historians often look at modern Japan in terms of pendulum swings from Meiji authoritarian oligarchy to Taisho democracy to Showa fascism, if one periodizes not in terms of who held the prime minister's chair, but rather of what groups held real power, both central and local, or in terms of the nature of rural society and the army's impact on it, he will find more continuity than transformation in Japan's last one hundred years. Japanese farmers had become "national villagers" by 1943, but their lifestyle and hamlet-centered orientation had not changed dramatically since the 1920s or even the 1870s. Even stringent and dictatorial wartime mobilization caused far fewer alterations in rural than in urban society. Life in a Japanese hamlet was both as free and as authoritarian in "democratic" 1926 as it was in "fascist" 1943. The social basis for militarism was nurtured, but its development did not encounter abrupt modification of policy or effect.

I

YAMAGATA ARITOMO, TANAKA GIICHI AND THE FOUNDING OF THE RESERVIST ASSOCIATION

On November 3, 1910, the emperor's fifty-eighth birthday, most of the illustrious figures in Japan's late Meiji-Taisho military establishment, including four imperial princes, two field marshals, and both the Army and Navy Ministers, gathered in the garden of the Tokyo Officers' Club for the opening ceremony of the Imperial Military Reserve Association.[1] At exactly 3:30 P.M., the 1160 honored guests, officers, and regional representatives sang the imperial anthem and then listened while Major General Oka Ichinosuke, a protégé of Yamagata Aritomo and a future Army Minister, read a few opening remarks. After Oka finished his short speech, the chairman of the new organization, Army Minister Terauchi Masatake, a Choshu-born Yamagata protégé, strode to the rostrum and presented a proclamation calling on reservists to exalt and spread the uniquely Japanese warrior spirit, to increase cooperation, to apply themselves to their own work, and to become models of good citizenship in their home communities. The third speaker was the honorary president of the *zaigō gunjinkai* and added the prestige of the imperial family to the occasion and the organization. He was Prince Fushimi, the scion of a branch of the imperial family, who had been a Yamagata associate since their joint trip to Moscow for the tsar's coronation in 1896. After the prince stepped away from the rostrum, the seventy-two-year-old, but still im-

---

1. *Teikoku zaigō gunjinkai sanjūnenshi* [The Thirty Year History of the Imperial Military Reserve Association] (Tokyo, 1944), pp. 46–49; *Tanaka Giichi denki* (Tokyo, 1960), I, pp. 411–412.

posing figure of the builder of Japan's modern army, Field Marshal Yamagata himself, rose from his chair and moved forward to enjoin the new organization's members to fulfill their duties:

We soldiers . . . must humbly master our warrior code, assiduously polish our military technique, and become the pillars of the national army.

When we return home, we must influence the younger generation with our virtue, become model citizens, and not hesitate to take on the task of serving as the emperor's strong right hand.

We reservists, reverently receiving our president's princely message, must carry out our organization's primary aims and fulfill the ideal that all citizens are soldiers. Not only must we repay our obligation to the emperor, but we must also make our nation prosper.

This is my admonition to all reservists at this opening ceremony.[2]

Following the elder statesman's short talk, the ceremony closed with a few remarks from General Oka, the band's rendition of the imperial anthem, and finally three banzais each for the emperor and Prince Fushimi. This late fall gathering, dominated by officers from the old feudal domain of Choshu, marked the end of five years of planning and negotiations.

Between 1906 and 1910, a small group of Yamagata subordinates and their colleagues conceived and established the reserve association to extend military influence into the civilian society. Of the nine key planners aside from Yamagata, who took no active role in the establishment of the reserve association other than to give his blessing, five were from Choshu: Tanaka, the so-called "father of the reserve association," Terauchi, Major General Nagaoka Gaishi, Colonel Sugano Shōichi, and Navy Commander Yoshikawa Yasuhira. At least three of the four others—Oka, Lieutenant Colonel Kojima Sōjirō, Yamagata's aide-de-camp, and Colonel Kawai Misao, a close friend of Tanaka's from their school days at the military academy—were closely affiliated with the Choshu faction leaders.[3] Yamagata's Choshu clique planned, founded, and ran the central organization of the army's civilian socialization system from its conception in 1906. The late Meiji creation of the centralized reservist association marks an important dividing line in the Choshu officers' efforts to build national unity and spread military values. Not only was it the army's last attempt to expand its influence through primarily military organizations—the zaigō gun-

---

2. *Sanjūnenshi*, pp. 48–49.

3. *Sanjūnenshi*, pp. 27–37, 76; Ijiri Tsuneyoshi, ed., *Rekidai kenkanroku* [A Chronological Record of Officials] (Tokyo, 1967), pp. 360–434; Hosokawa Ryūgen, *Tanaka Giichi* (Tokyo, 1958), p. 23; Roger F. Hackett, *Yamagata Aritomo in the Rise of Modern Japan, 1838–1922* (Cambridge, 1971), p. 268.

jinkai enlisted only those men who passed the conscription physical examination and were eligible for active service, it was also the army's first effort to educate civilians, for one-half the members enrolled even though they had never served on active duty. It was also Yamagata's final venture in building national unity, and it was his Choshu follower, Tanaka Giichi's first. To aid our understanding of the army's socialization system for civilians, we will discuss in this chapter (1) what in their experience, education, and contemporary environment impelled Yamagata, Tanaka, and their generational go-betweens, Katsura and Terauchi, and the others involved to use the conscription and reservist systems to spread the ideals of the soldier's ethos and national unity, (2) how they planned to utilize them, and (3) what first steps they took.

YAMAGATA ARITOMO, NATIONAL UNITY AND THE CONSCRIPTION SYSTEM

According to his biographer, Roger F. Hackett, Yamagata Aritomo from very early in his career felt "impelled by a desire to erect a strong, unified imperial order and [was] driven by the conviction that the free play of political forces was detrimental to this end."[4] He was obsessed with building a national unity founded on "the ancient ideal of a warlike spirit focused on loyalty to the emperor, and on patriotism" because of his education, experience, and perceptions of the dangers facing Japan both before and after he became a key figure in the Meiji government.[5] Yamagata grew to manhood in an extremely authoritarian and hierarchical society during an era of national crisis. Born into a Choshu fief warrior family in 1838, Yamagata learned in school, at home, and at play values that emphasized obedience, bravery, duty, loyalty, unity, and status—the bushido values he wrote into Japan's modern military ideology. Until the age of thirty, the focus of most of his actions was his obligatory service to the lord of Choshu domain; by the late 1860s his loyalty was to the symbol of national unity, the emperor. No matter what resentments Yamagata may have felt because lower samurai status slowed his upward mobility, his feudal upbringing and personal sense of duty must have made it difficult for him to advocate building an open society after Japan joined the modern world in 1868.

More important to the development of his obsession with unity than

---

4. Hackett, *Yamagata Aritomo*, p. 102.

5. Matsushita Yoshio, *Meiji gunsei shiron* [Historical Essays on the Meiji Military System] (Tokyo, 1956), I, pp. 33–34.

the quarter of a century Yamagata inhabited a hierarchical and restrictive feudal world were the dramatic experiences he and his generation of educated Japanese faced after 1853. When Yamagata was only fifteen, foreign warships visited his secluded country and forced her rulers to sign humiliating treaties. Over the next decade and a half, the foreigners returned again and again; some desecrated the imperial country by becoming residents, and barbarian ships even shelled the fortifications of Yamagata's own Choshu domain. At the same time, plots, counterplots, assassinations, and civil war marked the years before Yamagata and his colleagues in the Meiji government came to power in 1868. Yamagata, educated during this era in the nationalistic Confucianism of Yoshida Shōin on the one hand, and within a circle of fervent, emperor-serving compatriots—the "men of sincerity" of the 1860s—on the other, probably realized even before the Tokugawa downfall that strong, highly structured government, national wealth, and military power were the means to solving Japan's external and internal crises. Unity not only worked to eliminate domestic rifts, it also allowed Japan to face the foreigners from strength. Yamagata's fervor for strong central power and conformity must have been reinforced by his involvement in creating Choshu's "modern" army, his role in leading it to victory in 1868, and his part in helping to direct the new government and army for a half century thereafter.

One cannot forget that the 1868 leaders who remained in power during the Meiji period shared Yamagata's desire for unity, at least until almost the end of the century. Even the dissidents, who fell from power in the 1870s and 1880s, and most of the Meiji oligarchs' other opponents agreed with the government—with the single caveat that power be shared with them. The critics also wanted to build a strong, rich, and emperor-centered Japan capable of defending itself against the Western threat.

What distinguished Yamagata from his fellow restoration leaders both in and out of power was the fervor with which he pursued unity and his ability to build it. All of the Meiji oligarchs had similar pre-1868 warrior backgrounds, but Yamagata had been more deeply involved in martial affairs than most and was one of the few who chose to continue serving in the military. Almost all of the others enlisted in the civil side of government. It has been argued that military men of all nations tend to be more concerned with internal unity than their civilian compatriots. Officers believe domestic order and stability are essential to fulfilling their duty of national defense. Yamagata was no exception; his deep involvement with the Choshu army before 1868, and his choice of a military career afterward, both reflected and reinforced his obsession with unity. This interest in turn impelled the field marshal to establish the machinery to create and insure an orderly society. He took the lead in building an army that operated independently of civilian control while influencing civil government both at the national and local level (in the latter case, through the power to conscript). Yamagata also served in important civil positions from which he was able to build unity. Rather than confine his activities to the narrowly military, he and many of his protégés after him involved themselves in politics both during their terms of active duty and afterward. Yamagata was particularly concerned with those aspects of government which had a direct and immediate influence on local Japan. Thus, while Itō Hirobumi, the most important of the civil oligarchs, wrote a constitution, the main immediate impact of which was on literate public opinion and those concerned with central power, Yamagata involved himself with conscription, local government, the police, education, and local reservist organization. And then, once he had stated an interest in spreading his brand of central influence into local areas, Yamagata alone left behind a large coterie of well-placed military and civilian followers to carry on his work.[6]

Yamagata's first major step in building national unity focused on imperial and military values was the establishment of a potentially universal male conscription system. His system for recruiting soldiers, enforced from 1873, broke the warrior monopoly on military service by broadening the class origins of the army and by giving all Japanese males an active duty right and obligation. The establishment of conscription thus not only helped to build Japan a modern fighting machine, it also widened the military's social base. Yamagata and his successors, particularly General Katsura Tarō in the 1890s and Tanaka in the early 1900s, came to view the conscription system as more than a means for recruiting and training soldiers for war. They saw the draft as a way of building unity and commitment to national goals through the education of civilians in military values, through the soldier's ethos. Their plan, as it evolved around the time of the 1894–1895 war with China, was to give intensive military, spiritual, physical and patriotic education to as broad a cross-section of twenty-year-olds as possible, and then to send them back to civilian society to serve as community examples of diligence and good behavior. Katsura and Tanaka believed that the ideals emphasized in army training—unity, cooperation, and hierarchy through the comraderie and discipline of

---

6. Hackett, *Yamagata Aritomo*, pp. 1–155; Oka Yoshitake, *Yamagata Aritomo* (Tokyo, 1958), pp. 1–51; Samuel P. Huntington, *The Soldier and the State: The Theory and Politics of Civil Military Relations* (Cambridge, 1957), p. 66.

the company; simplicity, frugality, and hard work through a Spartan lifestyle and rough physical exercise; and loyalty, obedience, and conformity through the inculcation of emperor- and officer-centered patriotism—not only formed good soldiers, but also molded "village mainstays" (kyōtō no chūken) for local Japan. It was in this vein that Tanaka echoed Yamagata's 1873 statement and called the army the "final national school." He thought that the best educated citizens inevitably were those who had served on active duty in the army and had absorbed these values. "All citizens are soldiers" meant not only that all citizens had a legal obligation to serve in the military, but also that they had to be educated to be like soldiers all of the time. To Tanaka, the conscription system helped build this crucial aspect of a social basis for militarism.[7]

These Choshu officers believed that the army, of all national organizations, best trained and indoctrinated young Japanese. But this "final national school" did not succeed in becoming the major instrument for achieving the military's goals. Even though all young men at the age of twenty or when their exemptions ended took the conscription physical examination, the army drafted only a small percentage of young Japanese before 1937. Because of budgetary limitations on the number of divisions and thus on training facilities, the total number of peacetime personnel never exceeded 300,000 before the end of 1937. Throughout this period only 12 to 16 percent of Japanese twenty-year-olds, and only 25 to 35 percent of those who passed the physical examination, "went to the barracks." Moreover, the annual percentage actually decreased between 1916 and 1936. Available statistics indicate that the number of draft eligibles rose from about 600,000 to 800,000 during these two decades, whereas the number called to active duty remained fairly constant: 100,000 before 1919, 130,000 until the 1925 elimination of four divisions, and then around 100,000 after that. The "aggressive, imperialistic" Japanese army contained, in the year before the China incident of 1937, at most 250,000 officers and men, and was one of the smallest armies in the world at the time.[8]

---

7. Tanaka Giichi, "Guntai to chihō to no kankei," [The Relationship of the Army to the People], Senyū, 7 (1911), pp. 9–14; "Subekaraku hōsei kinchoku no han o shimese" [Become Models of Integrity], Senyū, 18 (1912), p. 2; "Kokumin no kyōroku o nozomu," Senyū, 20 (1912), pp. 11–13; "Kokumin to guntai" [The People and the Army], Tanaka chūjō kōenshū (Tokyo, 1916), pp. 56–57; Tanaka Giichi denki, I, p. 399; Hackett, Yamagata Aritomo, pp. 59–67; Fujiwara Akira, Gunjishi (Tokyo, 1961), pp. 53–59; Malcolm Kennedy, The Military Side of Japanese Life (Boston and New York, 1924), pp. 51–52; Sasaki Ryūji, "Nihon gunkokushugi no shakaiteki kiban no keisei" [The Formation of the Social Basis of Japanese Militarism], Nihonshi kenkyū [Studies in Japanese History] 68 (1963), pp. 1–30.

8. Rikugun daijin kambō, Rikugunshō tōkei nempō [The Annual Army Ministry

THE GROWTH OF LOCAL RESERVIST ORGANIZATIONS

Yamagata and his senior protégé, Katsura, recognized the inadequacies of the conscription system for civilian education even before the Sino-Japanese War, and they decided to cast their net more widely by making major changes in the draft regulations in 1889. These changes led in turn to the establishment of a series of local and independent martial and reservist organizations. Before 1889, the conscription law included so many draft exemptions that almost all men with education or wealth stayed out of the army. Because of these loopholes, Katsura wrote, the army lost its best potential soldiers. These people, for the most part from the village ruling class, learned to disdain the army and in turn influenced their "natural" followers, the village-ruled, to dislike the military. Katsura's solution, apparently at the urging of the German military adviser, Major Meckel, was to eliminate most exemptions and simultaneously to introduce a one-year volunteer officer candidate system for graduates of middle or higher schools. By this innovation, the educated landlords' sons served only one year on active duty, and then returned home as second lieutenants. Their families' tenants concurrently served three years (later two) at the barracks and returned home as enlisted men. By these innovations Katsura aimed to identify the military's elite, the officer corps, with the village's, the landlord class, and thus increase army prestige and at the same time reinforce both military and village order.[9]

According to Sasaki Ryūji, a Japanese scholar working with documents for the now nonexistent Yana County in eastern Aichi Prefecture, Katsura achieved greater success than he expected because of what was initially the grass roots' development of local martial societies (shōbudan). The landlord-officers, Sasaki writes, saw the new one-year volunteer system as beneficial to themselves as well as to the army. They believed it provided one more means of reinforcing

---

Statistical Yearbook], 1925, pp. 10–11; 1935, pp. 10–11; Iijima Shigeru, *Nihon sempeishi* [A History of Troop Selection in Japan] (Tokyo, 1943), pp. 467–468; K. Inahara, ed., *Japan Yearbook, 1934*, p. 223; *Rikukaigun gunji nenkan* [The Army and Navy Military Affairs Yearbook], 1938, pp. 721–724; *Teikoku oyobi rekkoku no rikugun* [The Armies of the Empire and the Powers] (Tokyo, 1936), Appendix I; Kennedy, *The Military Side of Japanese Life*, p. 306; Ōtsuka shigakkai, *Shimpan kyōdoshi jiten* [A New Encyclopedia of Local History] (Tokyo, 1969), pp. 248–249.

9. Tokutomi Iichirō, *Kōshaku Katsura Tarō den* [The Biography of Prince Katsura Tarō] (Tokyo, 1917), I, pp. 401, 448; Sasaki, "Shakaiteki kiban," pp. 1–5; Ernst L. Presseisen, *Before Aggression: Europeans Prepare the Japanese Army* (Tucson, 1965), pp. 123–124; Fujiwara, *Gunjishi*, p. 54; Ōishi Shinzaburō, "Chōheisei to ie" [The Conscription System and the Household], *Rekishigaku kenkyū* [Studies in Historical Science], 194 (1956), pp. 1–12.

their own social and political control. Some of the more innovative among them then made the system even more effective by building community military organizations in which they served as leaders and their enlisted men-tenants as followers. These martial societies, and, a few years later, reservist groups (*zaigō gunjindan*), which the army quickly supported and encouraged, performed patriotic, relief, military, and community service duties in conjunction with nonmember village men of authority and prestige. The societies conducted ceremonies to show respect for the imperial family, to remember the war dead, and to honor the families whose sons fought in the two wars during 1890 to 1910 (more often than not, sons of poor or middle income families). They also contributed money and labor to the families of war casualties, helped the families of those on active duty both during the wars and in peacetime, and even gave patriotic education to women. And local reservists carried out military training for youth group members to emphasize martial ideals, especially discipline and obedience, and performed all manner of local construction and repair projects and disaster relief. Sasaki concludes that these activities plus the army's success in the two wars fulfilled Katsura's vision. The local societies raised military prestige, reinforced the respect villagers naturally felt for their local leaders, strengthened unity and productivity, and slowed the growth of dissident movements.[10]

Eastern Aichi had no monopoly on local martial and reservist organizations in the decades around 1900. With army encouragement, similar organizations sprung up all over Japan. Local veterans' groups had been formed in some areas as early as 1877 by returned veterans from the wars to suppress the Akizuki, Hagi, and Seinan uprisings against the government (ironically, Tanaka had participated in one of the rebellions); but those fulfilling the aims of Katsura and local leaders appeared of course only after the 1889 revision of the conscription regulations. One such group was formed in 1892 in Ashikaga City, just north of Tokyo. Leaders of this reservist unit stated that their goals were "to study the soldier's ethos, to cultivate a vigorous nature, to reform public morals, to enhance the prestige of the military, and to become models for the general public." The officials of two others, formed several years later in Inako Village in Mie Prefecture and in Hakodate, outlined the members' duties, which included local youth group leadership, help to families of men on active duty, public works, fire fighting, and cooperation with the local police. These examples, in addition to those of Professor Sasaki of Yana County, indicate how

---

10. Sasaki, "Shakaiteki kiban, " pp. 9–19.

a number of communities established local martial and reservist groups which performed the same duties as the branches of the national organization did after 1910. By 1906, because of army encouragement, there were over 4,000 and by 1910, over 11,000 such local groups which made community and civilian socialization in military and patriotic values one of their major duties.[11] It was on this foundation that Tanaka, with the support of Yamagata and Terauchi and when Katsura served as Prime Minister, built the central institution of the system under study, the Imperial Military Reserve Association.

YAMAGATA'S NONMILITARY EFFORTS
TO CREATE UNITY

Although these two efforts, the conscription system and autonomous local reserve groups, represent the Choshu faction's major attempts at extending military influence into the local civilian scene before Tanaka became one of its front line leaders, they represent only a part of Yamagata's nineteenth century efforts at building national unity. At the same time Yamagata built his conscription system and encouraged the spread of local reservist groups, he took three other steps toward building and maintaining national unity. Yamagata created a centralized police force, which placed primary importance on the spread of national governmental influence and the suppression of political heterodoxy; he formed a centralized "local autonomy" system of government; and he helped introduce a nationalistic content into the school curriculum.

Yamagata, when he became Home Minister in 1885, reorganized the police to bring them closer to rural society and make them better able to detect and suppress political dissidence. In the decade before he tackled this task, the police, theoretically under central government control, actually functioned as independent prefectural forces. The regional authorities organized their policemen into army-like garrisons of one hundred or so officers each, rather than into stations at the town and village level. Yamagata immediately dispersed the policemen to local branch stations or to village-level police boxes and brought government influence and surveillance closer to the grass roots of the still basically agrarian Japanese society.

Yamagata also knew that once political subversion developed, it would have to be crushed and that it was more likely to occur in

---

11. *Sanjūnenshi*, pp. 10–13, 19–24; Sasaki, "Shakaiteki kiban," pp. 6–23; Murata Kikugorō, ed., *Teikoku zaigō gunjinkai mohan bunkaishi* [A History of Imperial Military Reserve Association Model Branches] (Kawagoe, 1927), pp. 1–364.

urban, and particularly metropolitan Tokyo, than in rural Japan. Thus, in addition to spreading his police net, he also established harsh and restrictive measures to crush any movement that challenged unity as he perceived it. The 1887 regulations severely limited the citizen's, and particularly the Tokyoite's, freedom to petition the government, to assemble, to demonstrate, and finally even to reside in the capital. One of his most famous actions as Home Minister was the enforcement of the 1887 Peace Preservation Ordinance under which, with five days' notice, he ordered 570 "dangerous" people to leave the capital for three years. It is not surprising that the two other pre-1932 Prime Ministers most remembered for their suppression of political extremists (as they defined them) were two of Yamagata's most important followers, Prime Minister Katsura in 1905 and 1910, and Prime Minister Tanaka in 1928.[12]

While he was still Home Minister, Yamagata, with the advice of the German Albert Mosse, created a local government system which attempted to balance community autonomy with central control (although the scale leaned toward the latter). The system's purpose was to give rural communities enough self-rule to reinforce the existing hierarchical political order and to stimulate patriotism and national identity by encouraging villagers to believe the government trusted them. At the same time, the system circumscribed local independence to protect communities from party politics and subversive ideologies. Under the 1888–1890 laws, villages and towns elected their own mayors and assemblies, although they did so in the context of stringent prefectural and Home Ministry control. Cities had even less say in choosing their chief executives: the three major cities before 1898 had virtually no governmental autonomy whatsoever.[13] It was undoubtedly Yamagata's confidence in the spiritual and political health of rural Japan and his belief in the village as the locus of a traditional unity and cooperation which he wanted to enlist for national goals, that influenced him to give rural commuities more autonomy than urban ones.

The final and again concurrent nonmilitary effort at stimulating support for national goals was Yamagata's and Education Minister Mori Arinori's establishment of ethical education in the school system in the next to last decade of the nineteenth century. During his 1885–

---

12. Hackett, *Yamagata Aritomo*, pp. 101–107; Hyman Kublin, *Asian Revolutionary: The Life of Sen Katayama* (Princeton, 1964), p. 204; Shiota Shōbē, "Chian ijihō no bōi" [The Tyranny of the Peace Preservation Law], *Shōwashi no shunkan* (Tokyo, 1966), I, pp. 43–51.

13. Hackett, *Yamagata Aritomo*, pp. 107–115; Kurt Steiner, *Local Government in Japan* (Stanford, 1965), pp. 37–38; 44–48.

1889 tenure in office, Mori laid the institutional foundations for modern, patriotic education by his reforms in ethical and teacher education, and in 1890, shortly after he became Prime Minister, Yamagata sponsored the writing of the *Imperial Rescript on Education,* which set the basic values of that education. The *Rescript* espoused such ideals as working for collective national, not individual goals, reverence for the emperor, and obedience to those in authority. Beginning from this decade, elementary school children heard the *Rescript* read at periodic school ceremonies and spent part of each week learning about the virtues of cooperation, self-sacrifice, Japan, and even of her military. Their teachers were well trained to give this kind of education. Not only did they study highly patriotic and militaristic normal school curricula—many normal school presidents were retired officers—but they also participated in a special conscription program for the graduates of teachers' colleges. The army exempted teachers from the normal two-year service obligation and instead called them to the colors for six months of intensive military training and indoctrination. The army's aim was to send the teachers back to their charges full of zeal to help the army educate civilians its way.[14] The police, self-government, and educational systems so important in creating national unity—and so closely related to the movement to tie the military into rural Japan and to reinforce the local social order—provided part of the foundation and some of the precedents for the development of increased national identity and societal integration in the twentieth century. But, as we shall see in Chapter III, neither the police nor the schools set up their basic units at the hamlet level, nor were policemen and teachers recruited for service in their own hamlets. Thus, as important as schools were in the dissemination of patriotic and nationalistic values, and as crucial as the police were to the maintenance of order, these two organizations were not integrated into the hamlet's social order and did not become as important in mobilizing local support for national purposes as the army's system did.

TANAKA GIICHI AND THE
RESERVE ASSOCIATION

In the opening decade of this century, Yamagata withdrew from official political life and was replaced by his military and civil protégés. The most important of the elder statesman's military disciples in the efforts to maintain and extend national unity were: General Katsura, Prime

---

14. Arthur Tiedemann, *Modern Japan* (Tokyo, 1962), 113–114; Fujiwara, *Gunjishi,* p. 55; Herbert Passin, *Society and Education in Japan* (New York, 1965), pp. 86–91.

Minister three times between 1900 and 1912 and an enthusiastic sup-
pressor of dissident political movements; General Terauchi, Army
Minister from 1902 until 1911 and later Prime Minister; and our
second key figure, Tanaka Giichi. Colonel Tanaka became in this
period the foremost architect of military-centered national unity; it was
he who took the initiative and created the centralized national reserve
association.[15]

Tanaka became one of Yamagata's three key military followers even
though his early years did not mark him as a man chosen to play
such an important role. He was born the son of a poverty-stricken,
low-ranking warrior in the castletown of Hagi in 1863, a quarter of a
century after his mentor. Although Tanaka was blessed with Choshu
birth, his father, unlike Yamagata, did not play a significant role in the
pre-Meiji Restoration events; thus Tanaka did not benefit from being
the son of even a moderately important Choshu figure. Moreover,
poverty and antigovernment rebellion characterized his youth. Tanaka's father barely supported the family in the 1870s by making paper
umbrellas, and in 1876, the thirteen-year-old Tanaka fought in Mae-
bara Issei's Hagi Rebellion against Yamagata's government. Pardoned
because of his young age, Tanaka studied diligently, served briefly as
a school teacher, entered the military academy, and graduated in 1886
as a lieutenant of infantry.

Despite these youthful disadvantages, Tanaka's talent and military
and political views enhanced his army career and brought him to
Yamagata's attention before the end of the century. In 1898, by grad-
uating from the War College, Tanaka, like Ugaki Kazushige and most
Taisho-Showa period generals, guaranteed himself a place in the army's
elite. Only the brightest of the army's young lieutenants and captains
matriculated at the War College, where they studied broad military
matters: logistics, mobilization, administration, strategic planning, and
foreign societies, languages, and military systems. War College graduation was so important to entry into the army's managerial class, i.e.,
into its upper echelons, that only six of eighty-nine generals after
1915 had not attended the college.[16] All of the officers concerned with
planning and running the organizations in the army's socialization
system had War College degrees. Men with broad training in the
political side of warfare, in the need for national mobilization, were

---

15. *Tanaka Giichi denki*, I, pp. 400–402, 414, 426, 429; Kuroda Kōshirō, *Gensui
Terauchi hakushaku den* [A Biography of Field Marshal Count Terauchi] (Tokyo,
1920), pp. 412–413; Hackett, *Yamagata Aritomo*, p. 145.
16. Matsushita Yoshio, *Nihon gumbatsu no kōbō* [The Rise and Fall of the
Japanese Military Clique] (Tokyo, 1967), III, pp. 297–305.

the ones most likely to be concerned with establishing civilian foundations for their army.

After graduation in 1898 Tanaka continued to distinguish himself. Captain Tanaka, a Russian language officer, received a timely study assignment to Russia for four years. In 1904–1905, when the Russo-Japanese War broke out, he became a key staff officer in Manchuria and was able to utilize the expertise gained from his experiences in the enemy's capital. Between 1905 and 1910, while he rose in rank from lieutenant colonel to major general, Tanaka took the lead in writing a comprehensive national defense plan, in revising the army's training techniques and manuals, and in forming the nationally unified reserve association.[17]

Tanaka's rapid rise in rank and influence, despite his undistinguished family origins, can be attributed only to his having received the patronage of Yamagata. Since not all Choshu officers automatically became the field marshal's close protégés (there were one hundred Choshu general grade army officers between 1868 and 1926, but only four important Yamagata military successors), his success must have come through his talent, his political acumen, and his views on national unity and popular support for the military as well as his Choshu origins. Early in his career Tanaka began expressing views similar to those of Yamagata. In doing so, he suggested both the advantage Japan had over other modernizing nations and her dilemma; Tanaka believed that Japan had closer military-civil ties and stronger popular support for the military than most countries, but, at the same time, that these ties and this support were in constant danger of destruction. Tanaka first stated this idea in 1886 when, as a lieutenant just graduated from the military academy, he wrote that while the Japanese army maintained strong bonds between officers and enlisted men, a still tighter relationship was necessary. In order to cultivate this kind of union, he asserted that officers should live in the barracks with their subordinates. He equated this necessity with army-populace unity on the grounds that enlisted men—invariably drafted and not career soldiers —were really civilians. Building a social basis for militarism began in the final national school, he wrote later, and until that school guaranteed its own unity, the army could not form it elsewhere. In 1902, after Tanaka returned from Russia, he reported that the Russian army's major weakness was its lack of communication between officers of noble birth and common soldiers of peasant stock. Tanaka believed that this alienation was comparatively absent, but not impos-

17. Hackett, *Yamagata Aritomo*, pp. 234–235; Fujiwara, *Gunjishi*, pp. 108–115; *Tanaka Giichi denki*, I, pp. 370–382; Hosokawa Ryūgen, *Tanaka Giichi*, pp. 32–73.

sible, in Japan. After the Russo-Japanese War, Tanaka concluded that Japan won the war because her officers and enlisted men worked together and because her people supported the army with pride and respect; the Russians lost because of rebellion at home and class antagonisms at the front. Tanaka believed these dangers had to be avoided in Japan. When Tanaka expressed his feelings about the needs of strengthening unity and avoiding division in Japan, he found a ready audience among Choshu faction leaders; Yamagata was, after all, a long-time advocate of national unity and probably the most powerful man in Japan, and Terauchi was Army Minister.[18]

When Lieutenant Colonel Tanaka returned from Manchuria in 1905 (he went as a major in 1904), he was assigned to serve as a staff officer in the Army Ministry in Tokyo; he received as one of his assignments the unification and expansion of the army's system for bringing the army in contact with local Japan which his mentor had begun. Because of the key army positions Tanaka held from 1905 until his retirement in 1925, and because of his powerful backing, he took the lead in the founding of three crucial institutions in the system of indoctrination for unity: the establishment of a unified reserve association, of reservist factory branches, and as we shall see in Chapter II, of a national youth association. As president of the Seiyūkai political party in 1925, he encouraged the creation of a fourth, the youth training center system. Although Tanaka received much help in his efforts, it is difficult to downgrade the role that this one Choshu officer and Yamagata protégé played in building the organs of civilian indoctrination in military values.[19]

Tanaka's first goal in consolidating and extending the existing instruments of military socialization was the unification of the thousands of local reserve organizations into a national association. As early as 1898, before leaving for St. Petersburg, Tanaka had expressed his feelings about the need for combining local reservists' clubs under army and navy control. Local groups were important for stimulating patriotism, but, without central guidance, there existed the possibility

---

18. Tanaka, "Kokumin to guntai" *Tanaka chūjō kōenshū*, pp. 2–6, 56–57; *Tanaka Giichi denki*, I, pp. 403–408; Hosokawa, *Tanaka Giichi*, pp. 25, 35–36, 47; Kawatani Yorio, *Tanaka Giichi den* (Tokyo, 1929), pp. 131, 143.

19. *Sanjūnenshi*, p. 76. Of the 918 pages in Kawatani's biography of Tanaka, 213 describe the general's role in organizing the reservist and youth associations. Two chapters of Tanaka's latest biography are devoted to Tanaka's efforts in this regard. See Chapter Six, "Teikoku zaigō gunjinkai no sōritsu" [The Founding of the Imperial Military Reserve Association] *Tanaka Giichi denki*, I, pp. 398–450, Chapter Ten, "Taishō to seinendan" [The General and the Youth Association], I, pp. 592–628.

of independent and divisive actions or of the local organizations becoming nothing but drinking clubs for veterans. To ensure that
all local branches adopted proper attitudes toward the army and indoctrination, to make certain that the local groups did not abandon
their activism after the patriotic fervor of the Russo-Japanese War
died down, and to extend reservist educational activities to those men
who passed the conscription physical examination, but did not serve
on active duty, Tanaka decided that some kind of direct army control
was necessary.[20]

But Tanaka and his fellow planners faced several problems that had
to be solved before the local organizations could be unified. To begin
with, only Yamagata and Terauchi among the army's top-ranking
generals agreed with Tanaka's broad view of reservist goals. Thus he
had to overcome the feelings of those other officers and civilians who
believed that the proposed unified reserve association should be aimed
solely at post-service training and the emergency recall of ex-servicemen
and, accordingly, should be limited in membership to veterans and
tightly controlled from the center. Many of these men saw no need to
spread military values to civilians. The existing system, they stated,
had worked successfully in two wars, so why change now? Tanaka
overrode these officers' narrow views of reserve association goals and
made the association a social educational organ. Nevertheless, their
objections forced him to overemphasize overt control and downgrade
the role of nonveterans when he established the *zaigō gunjinkai* in
1910. To pacify his critics, he announced in 1911 that the quarter of
the members who had never served on active duty and had not been
trained would be gradually phased out of the association; in actuality,
by 1920, these "civilians" comprised over half of the organization's
army enlisted men. Tanaka won this and other battles because he
persisted in playing a continual role in the reserve association, while
other, more doctrinaire officers lost interest.[21]

After overcoming these objections, Tanaka and his colleagues had
to grapple with the problem of centralization and army supervision.
How could they unify and command the organization so as to estab-

---

20. *Tanaka Giichi denki*, I, pp. 399–400; *Sanjūnenshi*, pp. 25–44.

21. Tanaka, "Kokumin to guntai," *Tanaka chūjō kōenshū*, pp. 48–54; *Sanjūnenshi*, pp. 36–39, 43; Kikoshi Yasutsune, "Honkai setsuritsu no shūshi o gokai suru
nakare" [Do Not Misunderstand the Reasons for Establishing This Association],
Senyū, 14 (1911), pp. 3–4; Terauchi Masatake, chairman's proclamation, *Senyū*,
22 (1912), p. i; Kurose Yoshikado, announcement by assistant chairman, *Senyū*, 29
(1913), p. i; Kawatani, *Tanaka Giichi den*, p. 131; *Tanaka Giichi denki*, I, pp. 401–
402, 426–427; Hori Shika, *Saishō to naru made Tanaka Giichi* [Tanaka Giichi until
He Became Prime Minister] (Tokyo, 1928), p. 127.

lish nationwide uniformity and maintain control and, at the same time, allow enough initiative from below to present at least the facade of the association's independence and to ensure a large membership? This dilemma was similar to the one Yamagata faced when writing the local government laws two decades earlier. They finally decided to establish the *zaigō gunjinkai* as a private association, legally supervised (*kanshi*), but not commanded, by the army minister. It was not until 1936 that the organization became official (*chokurei dantai*), but even then the service ministers directed (*kantoku*), and did not legally command, local reservist branches. In establishing the association as a private one, Tanaka aimed at avoiding the accusation of having created a militarily-controlled civilian organization, and he reiterated several times the need for reservist "independence." In spite of his efforts, however, most outside observers must have realized that the primary purpose for unification was to bring the local groups under army control and that Tanaka had done just that. Few could mistake the reserve association's chain of command for that of an "independent" organization. The chain of command led directly to the Tokyo central headquarters, staffed by both retired and active duty field grade and general officers, and then to the Infantry Section of the Military Affairs Bureau of the Army Ministry, to which the minister delegated authority. Many Army Ministry and General Staff (and after 1914, navy) positions automatically involved the holder in reservist affairs. Moreover, Tanaka assigned intermediate responsibility for directing local reservists to regional army headquarters—the seventy-four army regimental areas (after 1925, fifty-seven) scattered around the country for conscription and training purposes. The regimental commander (*rentaichō*) in each region had responsibility for training local draftees and, of course, for commanding his regiment; the area commander (*rentai shireikan*) supervised the district's conscription system and reservist affairs. The details of the structure of the *zaigō gunjinkai* changed somewhat between 1910 and 1945, but the principle of military control under the guise of "supervision" over an "independent" reserve association remained constant.[22]

In spite of this overt control from above, individual reservists and local branches were allowed an increment of independence—member-

22. *Senyū*, 1 (1912), pp. 56–61; *Teikoku zaigō gunjinkai gyōmu shishin* [A Directory of Imperial Military Reserve Association Affairs] (Tokyo, 1929), pp. 89–90; "Teikoku zaigō gunjinkai no gaiyō," [Essentials of the Imperial Army Reserve Association], *Kaikōsha kiji* [The Army Officers Journal], April 1937, p. 83; *Rikukaigun gunji nenkan*, 1936, pp. 503, 512–520, 562–583; *Sanjūnenshi*, pp. 293–298; Matsumura Shōin, "Teikoku zaigō gunjinkai kiyaku kaisei ni tsuite" [Concerning the Change in Imperial Military Reservist Association Rules] *Kaikōsha kiji*, April 1933, pp. 132–135.

ship was voluntary and branches chose their own leaders, within certain limitations, at least. Tanaka insisted that membership be voluntary in order to persuade the public that the army was not trying to
mobilize civilian support by coercing young men and especially those
with no active duty experience to join its organization. In practice,
this led to a process in which rural youths joined almost without exception because of the pressure of community solidarity, while urban
youths joined much less frequently. By the 1920s rural membership
represented at least 80 percent and urban under 40 percent of the
eligibles.[23] Tanaka found very quickly (if he did not know from the
beginning) that reservist membership was high in communities where
group cohesion was strong, low where it was not. The *zaigō gunjinkai*,
therefore, emphasized village, hamlet, and family unity and cooperation in its ideology not only as a way of building national unity and
cooperation, but also as a way of guaranteeing its high rural membership percentage. Membership for eligibles remained voluntary until
the war period of 1937 in order not to appear coercive and because
of the leaders' confidence in rural support.[24]

Tanaka introduced a system for the "grass roots" selection of leaders to enhance the facade of local autonomy. As in the case of voluntary enrollment, Tanaka's plan was safe in rural areas since the members tended to choose from the traditional elite. Village and town
branches were subdivided into hamlet or hamlet-cluster subunits. The
hamlet members chose their subunit chief and assistant chief, who in
turn selected the branch officials. The reserve branch selection process
worked like all other hamlet and village deliberations—not through
open discussion and Western-type voting procedures, but by the grad-
ual achievement of a consensus of opinion. The hamlet leaders emphasized local as well as military needs in choosing their branch
leaders. They considered community activism and high status on the
part of the candidate to be as important as high military rank, and
this reinforced the meshing of community and reserve branch structure. The fully developed rural reserve branch was as much a community organization as a national one. Tanaka's insistence on individual choice in joining the reserve branch and on local independence
in the selection of the leaders, helped create a successful rural *zaigō
gunjinkai*.[25]

23. See Table 7 in Chapter Three.
24. "Teikoku zaigō gunjinkai no gaiyō," p. 90.
25. *Senyū*, 1 (1912), pp. 56–61; *Teikoku zaigō gunjinkai gyōmu shishin*, pp. 97–
100; Tanaka, "Tokuni kōryo o yōsuru jūyō mondai," *Senyū*, 96 (1918), pp. 13–15;
Senyū, 13 (1911), pp. 56–59; Matsumura, "Teikoku zaigō gunjinkai kiyaku kaisei ni
tsuite," p. 132.

City branches served the army well in a number of ways even though many eligibles did not join. The voluntary membership and election system did lead to low enrollment but, at the same time, to zealous members and leaders as well. Most city members joined, in the absence of community pressure, because of belief in the organization's goals and ethos. They tended to be themselves, and to select as leaders, men with a firm commitment to military and nationalistic goals. Urban branches (factory branches excepted) did not help the reservists expand their foundations of support, but they guaranteed that the support they did receive was firm and even occasionally overly zealous. An inordinately large number of reservist political activists in the 1930s belonged to or led city-based units. When the reservists attacked Professor Minobe Tatsukichi and his 'Emperor Organ Theory' in 1935, the single most active group of members was from Tokyo, the association's least successful area of recruitment. In other words, although urban reservists were fewer in number than their rural counterparts, they gave the army more earnest and active support, on at least one occasion threatening the military and *zaigō gunjinkai* leadership itself from the right.[26]

Because of the narrow base of urban success Tanaka began searching within half a decade for an urban alternative to the cooperative farm village as the basis for *zaigō gunjinkai* branches. He found it in factory branches, branches formed from men eligible for membership and working in a certain factory, mine, or office, rather than from those living in a particular neighborhood. Tanaka's inspiration for factory branches was not of Japanese origin; on a 1914 trip abroad to investigate reservist and youth groups in Europe and America, the German Chief of Staff, Erich von Falkenhayn, lectured Tanaka on the efficacy of factory branches. Tanaka reported Falkenhayn as saying that Germany's military strength was based partly on the spiritual and industrial strength gained from organizing reservist branches in the nation's factories. The German general believed that soldier-workers worked harder, produced more, and obeyed the factory's rules more often than their nonmilitary coworkers. One can imagine Tanaka's favorable reaction to Falkenhayn's suggestion. Here was a

26. See Richard J. Smethurst, "The Military Reserve Association and the Minobe Crisis of 1935," in George M. Wilson, *Crisis Politics in Prewar Japan* (Tokyo, 1970), pp. 1–23; *Shōwa jūnen ni okeru shakai undō jōkyō* [The Circumstances of Social Movements in 1935] (Tokyo, 1937), *passim*. This annual report, published by the Police Bureau of the Home Ministry, contains reports of political activities conducted by urban reservists for every year from 1933 to 1939. See also copies of the Home Ministry's *Shisō geppō* [Monthly Ideology Report] and *Tokkō geppō* [Monthly Thought Police Report] for the same period.

way to increase productivity for government goals and at the same time check that which threatened national unity—labor organization and unrest and "subversive" ideologies (*aku shisō*) in an era of increasing unionization, strikes, and imported, individualistic ideas. Moreover, most Japanese companies in this same period were adopting techniques for dealing with their employees which used the traditional family-centered, particularistic, paternalistic approach rather than the more universalistic, contractual, individual-oriented Western ones. Thus reservist factory branch "familism"—with its soldier's ethos roots—and company paternalism could help each other increase company and national production, maintain group rather than individual orientation in urban areas, and play a role in extending military influence into the "asphalt roots" of civilian society. The establishment of factory branches in 1914 was particularly timely because Japan did not yet have a large "permanent proletariat," people who had lived and worked in the city for several generations. Most urban workers still had rural roots in cooperation, unity, and the family; and Tanaka, needless to say, wanted to preserve "Japan's advantage." Factory branches, first set up in 1915, numbered 257 by 1926, and 567 by 1937.[27]

Tanaka and his fellow planners not only had to pacify army and civilian critics, they also had to allay navy misgivings. The Navy Ministry assigned Choshu-born Commander Yoshikawa to Tanaka's group of planners; nevertheless, the navy feared the creation of a unified reserve association. Naval officers believed it would become an army-dominated, political pressure organization which would give the army extra leverage in its competition with the navy for funds and power. The navy brass reasoned that the army had taken the initiative in the planning and thus would control the headquarters. Moreover, most of the members were surely to be former soldiers because there were so many more of them. The army was not only four times larger than the navy, but the ground force recruited its enlisted men almost entirely from among draftees who served only two years on active duty. The volunteer sailors served five years. Thus, soldiers returned home with three more years of reservist eligibility than sailors. After several years of negotiations between Terauchi and Tanaka on the one hand, and Navy Minister Saitō Makoto and his assistant, Admiral

---

27. *Tanaka Giichi denki*, I, pp. 422–425; Kawatani, *Tanaka Giichi den*, pp. 146–159; *Rikukaigun gunji nenkan*, 1937, pp. 551–554; "Teikoku zaigō gunjinkai no gaiyō," *Kaikōsha kiji*. April 1937, p. 90; *Teikoku zaigō gunjinkai gyōmu shishin*, p. 465; Byron K. Marshall, *Capitalism and Nationalism in Prewar Japan: The Ideology of the Business Elite, 1868–1941* (Stanford, 1967).

Takarabe Takeshi, on the other, the navy decided not to participate. Tanaka's *zaigō gunjinkai* began operations in 1910 without official navy participation although sailors were free to join if they chose. In 1914, Tanaka finally secured navy participation—why not join and exert a little influence since the organization existed anyway, navy officers reasoned. He assigned them one of the two assistant chairmen's posts, the first held by Vice Admiral Tomioka Sadayasu, an old acquaintance of Tanaka. Tanaka also gave the navy more than one-quarter of the headquarter's staff positions, and control of three (the Kure, Sasebo, and Yokosuka areas) of the seventy-four intermediate headquarters. Considering that sailors made up only about 2.5 percent of the membership, Tanaka gave the navy more than a fair share of the organization's control; nevertheless, he did it safely, for the reserve association remained army-dominated until 1945.[28]

The final problem Tanaka solved was the choice of a chairman (*kaichō*). Tanaka and the other planners wanted to select a man who shared their beliefs about the purpose and goals of the reserve association. After several years of intermittent deliberations on the subject—sporadic because Tanaka spent a year and a half in 1908–1909 outside the ministry commanding the Tokyo-based 3rd Infantry Regiment—they finally settled on Army Minister Terauchi himself. The beauty of this arrangement for Tanaka was that Terauchi held the job while at the same time serving as Army Minister from 1910 to 1911, Governor-General in Korea from 1910 to 1916, and Prime Minister in Tokyo from 1916 to 1918. Because these posts consumed most of the general's time, his trusted follower Tanaka dominated the organization from various subordinate positions.[29]

The unified reservist association came into being at the gala ceremony in Tokyo on November 3, 1910, described above; and by the end of the decade, despite problems—the use of improper fund raising techniques for a "spiritual organization," the inevitable involvement in local politics in many areas, and the participation of some members in the 1918 Rice Riots, to mention a few—the *zaigō gunjinkai* had established itself as an integral part of the national and local scene. The central headquarters supervised more than 13,000 branches and 2,300,000 men by 1918, and more than 14,000 branches and 2,900,000 men by 1936. When one considers that the army dominated the organization, that at least one branch existed in every community

28. *Sanjūnenshi*, pp. 33–36, 103–104; Inoue Kiyoshi, "Taishōki no seiji to gumbu" [Politics and the Military in the Taishō Period], in Inoue Kiyoshi, ed., *Taishōki no seiji to shakai* [Politics and Society in the Taishō Period] (Tokyo, 1969), p. 376.
29. *Sanjūnenshi*, pp. 34–35; *Tanaka Giichi denki*, I, p. 402.

in the country (over 250 in the city of Tokyo alone), that from 50 to 60 percent of the eligible men belonged, that half the members had never served in the military, and that the activities generally focused on community service, not military technique, it is apparent why the reserve association quickly made itself a potent force for educating civilians.[30]

---

30. To cite several examples of what national leaders considered improper fund raising, General Kameoka Bushin chastized branch chiefs at a Kumamoto gathering in September, 1911 for requiring local men not going on active duty to make contributions to the local branch. General Karasudani Akira told a similar gathering of leaders in Yamaguchi in March, 1912 that they should neither compete with local businessmen nor solicit gifts when raising money. Thereafter, the line between "solicited" and "voluntary" contributions must have been a fine one. *Senyū*, 13 (1911), pp. 56–59; 20 (1912), pp. 53–57. For warnings against political activity, see *Senyū*, 22 (1912), p. i., and 29 (1913), p. i. *Kokumin nenkan*, 1919 [1919 Citizens' Annual] (Tokyo, 1919), p. 170; "Teikoku zaigō gunjinkai no gaiyō," *Kaikōsha kiji*, April 1937, p. 80.

II

THE ARMY, YOUTH, AND WOMEN

1916 was the beginning of the era of national crisis in Japan. It is not an exaggeration to say that from 1919 until the time of the Manchurian Incident in 1931, Japan fell into the abyss of spiritual darkness. . . . Individualism, liberalism, and democratic thought flowed freely and the muddied waters of materialism, utilitarianism, and the worship of the almight yen (*kinkenshugi*) seeped in at every level. Socialism, communism and anarchistic thought spread like contagious diseases among students and young workers. Intellectually discriminating persons who thought of their country truthfully could not bear to see this.

Teikoku zaigō gunjinkai sanjūnenshi (Tokyo, 1944), p. 112

Three years ago [in 1921–1922], spitting at the Italian flag, cursing the army, and despising soldiers was advocated as progressive thought, and it was said to be all right to reduce the term of military service to six months. However, after Mussolini formed his cabinet, the spirit of the general populace made a basic change and today they no longer spit at the flag. . . . In 1921–1922, Italy had 643 labor disputes, but in 1925, only 154. Moreover, farm disputes fell in number from 46 to 2. These disputes were related to economic and political conditions, but most of them occurred because of dangerous ideas spread by socialists. Hence, as a result of the victory of fascism over socialism, disputes gradually disappeared and production became prosperous. We too must pay special attention to this point. . . . The main force in saving the Japanese people from this kind of national crisis is the army and the reservist association.

TANAKA GIICHI, quoted in Kawatani Yorio, *Tanaka Giichi den* (Tokyo, 1929), pp. 198–199

The fear of domestic unrest in the first quarter of the twentieth century had a tremendous impact on the thinking of Tanaka Giichi, Ugaki Kazushige, and other officers who followed in Yamagata's footsteps. Although these officers exaggerated the actual threats to national unity, Japanese society had in fact become more diverse and harder to control by the time World War I erupted in 1914. Universal education and wider university opportunities, expanding contacts with the outside world, urbanization, the increasing impersonality of the modernizing society, and industrialization unleashed forces that challenged Yamagata's dictum of "rich country and strong army." Most of the newly educated, imbued with the patriotic values of the *Imperial Rescript on Education,* enthusiastically followed the government's lead, but some did not. Even before 1910, a few intellectuals, inspired by foreign ideologies and conditions at home, had joined the miniscule Russo-Japanese War peace movement and the even tinier postwar socialist party, and had impelled Katsura Tarō's government to suppress them. It is not surprising that Tanaka and Ugaki cast a jaundiced eye on the larger antimilitary socialist and communist movements which coalesced after the successful October Revolution. At the same time as these winds from Europe fanned the radical blaze, labor disputes and rural antilandlord unrest added to the military leaders' sense of national disunity. Only 107 strikes occurred between 1903 and 1907. But as the industrial labor force and urban population increased, the frequency of strikes did also, to 497 in 1919, and 1202 in 1927. And the rural, antilandlord discontent of the same decade must have terrified Tanaka and Ugaki even more than labor and urban radical organizations since the generals modelled their ideal Japanese society on the "traditional" village. The rural unrest was most intense in those areas where the local elite abandoned paternalism for impersonal, modern contractual relationships with their tenants; and reservist planners felt compelled to build barriers to prevent further erosion of the traditional.[1]

---

1. Kishimoto Eitarō, *Nihon rōdō undōshi* [Japanese Labor Movement History] (Tokyo, 1950), p. 38; Ōkubo Toshiaki, *Nihon zenshi* [A Complete History of Japan], *Kindai* III [Modern Vol. 3] (Tokyo, 1964), pp. 218–234; Shiota Shōbē, *Shōwashi no shunkan* (Tokyo, 1966) I, pp. 78, 118, 122; Barbara Ann Waswo, *Landlords and*

Labor-farmer unrest, progressive party organization, and antimilitary feeling may have been moderate by European standards, but Yamagata's successors interpreted them as a major threat to the unity of Japanese society. Tanaka's speeches and articles, for example, contain many expressions of such fears. The following is one from a speech to reservist leaders in January, 1924:

> Today there are Japanese who think that mankind should know no national boundaries. They plead for a so-called internationalism and a world without national distinctions. They think war cannot occur again, and that we can limit or even ignore military preparedness. But while they talk of worldwide international cooperation, these Japanese also incite labor conflict and class struggles at home. Accordingly, they constantly create friction and antagonism among the people. Thus, people neglect their work. And tenant, antilandlord disputes are rife in agricultural areas. And patriotism is thought to be suitable only for old-fashioned bigots. These trends lead youths astray and some even dare the fiendishness of high treason. Last December's attempt on the life of the Crown Prince [The Toranomon Incident of December, 1923] originated from this kind of misguided subversive thought. . . . If we want to protect the national welfare, public order, and honor, we must destroy all of these 'isms' [internationalism, pacifism, socialism, etc.].[2]

At the same time that Tanaka feared these threats to Japanese national cohesion, the world's armies entered the era of total war (*sōryokusen*). Warfare became more sophisticated and called not only for the army's, but for the whole nation's participation. As early as the Napoleonic Wars, and especially after the American Civil War and Franco-Prussian War, Western observers had begun to see that the days of battles between rival kings, each with his own mercenary army, were over and that those of "national wars" had arrived. New technology leading to increased firepower and better transportation and communications, the tendency toward greater mass involvement in national affairs, the need to mobilize larger armies through conscription, and the necessity of industrial support for fighting machines compelled the populace to participate in military affairs. Tanaka and Ugaki realized this clearly after the outbreak of World War I. Tanaka believed, moreover, that national mobilization for cohesion had benefits even in defeat. He thought that revolution failed in postwar Germany because the German people respected, and had been trained to respect,

Social Change in Prewar Japan (Ann Arbor, 1970), pp. 198–199; Tanaka Giichi, *Taisho kōsho yori* (Tokyo, 1925), appendix, pp. 76–78.

2. "Akushisō o korobose" [Crush Subversive Thought], Kawatani Yorio, *Tanaka Giichi den* (Tokyo, 1929), pp. 201–202.

law and order. Japan too needed to be immunized against disunity.[3] Time and time again Tanaka stated that future wars (and peace) would demand total national mobilization, but never more clearly than in this speech to reservist officials in Tokyo in 1915:

> The outcome of future wars will not be determined by the strongest army, but by the strongest populace. A strong populace is one which has physical strength and spiritual health, one which is richly imbued with loyalty and patriotism, and one which respects cooperation, rules, and discipline. The populace which has this kind of education will not merely have a strong army, but will also be successful in conducting agricultural, manufacturing, commercial, and other industrial efforts. The reservists must achieve the reality of becoming good soldiers and good citizens and exert their influence (for these goals) in their home community.[4]

It was against this background of fear of increased disunity and belief in a greater need for national cohesion that Tanaka nurtured the reserve association, and that he and Ugaki looked for additional ways to crush opposition and create popular support for the military. They were not above suppression as one way of eliminating unorthodoxy and recreating unity; but this was only a temporary palliative. Real unity came through education.

TANAKA AND THE FORMATION OF A
NATIONAL YOUTH ASSOCIATION

With the rapid growth in the numbers of reservist local branches after 1910 and factory branches after 1914, Tanaka saw grow to fruition his military education network for physically fit twenty- to forty-year-old men (and to some extent for their neighbors, for whom reservists were to become models of civic propriety). Yet the army still did not have the means to influence all civilians. It is true that the school system trained all children, male and female, fit and unfit, in the ideals of Yamagata's *Imperial Rescript on Education* which were not unlike those of the soldier's ethos. But primary education was compulsory for only six years (although many students received an extra two years of schooling in upper elementary schools), and only 20 percent of the

---

3. Tanaka, "Osorubeki shisō no appaku" [The Frightening Ideological Pressure], *Senyū*, 93 (1918), pp. 9–12; Tanaka, "Otazune ni kotau" [Answering an Inquiry], *Senyū*, 92 (1918), p. 7; Ugaki Kazushige, *Ugaki Kazushige nikki* (Tokyo, 1968–1971), I, pp. 482–483, 519, 523; Fujiwara Akira, *Gunjishi* (Tokyo, 1961), pp. 134–138; Tanaka, *Taisho kōshoyori*, p. 45.

4. *Tanaka Giichi denki* (Tokyo, 1960), I, pp. 421–422.

graduates advanced to middle school. Formal education and nationalistic indoctrination ended for most at age fourteen or fifteen. Because of this five-year gap between the completion of primary school and entrance into the army or reserve association for the 60 to 70 percent of the male population that passed the conscription physical examination, Tanaka decided in 1915 to fill this educational lacuna by creating a unified, reservist-dominated, national youth association from the thousands of existing young men's groups. This centralized organization would recruit the unfit 30 to 40 percent as well.[5]

Organizing the unified national youth association was no easy task. Tanaka could centralize the reserve association with the backing of Yamagata and Terauchi alone, for the army had no problem justifying an organization of ex-servicemen (in the early years it played down the role of those who had not served). The same justification was not valid for unifying local youth groups, however, because the Education and Home Ministries had jurisdiction over youth education and regional organizations. The creation of a military-influenced youth association called for delicate negotiations between the army and these two ministries as well as an ability to deal with the Diet members and the newspapermen who might object. Tanaka showed himself capable of this kind of diplomacy.

When Tanaka returned from Europe in 1914 convinced not only of the need for reservist factory branches, but also for a centralized youth association oriented toward nationalistic and physical education, he contacted two civil bureaucrat acquaintances with similar ideas. These two men, Yamamoto Takinosuke, a long-time youth organizer and official, and Tadokoro Miharu, a division chief in the Education Ministry and reservist association adviser, also believed that a youth association could complement the educational system if it were used to propagate patriotic ideals and increase the health and physical conditioning of teenagers. These two men in turn acted as intermediaries between Tanaka and the appropriate cabinet ministers in the Ōkuma Shigenobu government of the time. These ministers, Home Minister Ōura Kanetake, and Education Minister Ichiki Kitokurō, both of whom were among Yamagata's closest civilian followers, agreed with Tanaka's ideas about youth groups. A fifth figure, Takada Sanae, joined the

---

5. Tokiomi Kaigo, *Japanese Education: Its Past and Present* (Tokyo, 1968), p. 89; Kumagai Tatsujirō, *Dainihon seinendanshi* [The History of the Greater Japan Youth Association] (Tokyo, 1942), pp. 113–114; Tanaka, "Seinendan no igi" [The Meaning of the Youth Association], *Tanaka chūjō kōenshū* (Tokyo, 1916), pp. 252, 256–257.

group in August, 1915, when Ōura was forced to resign because of allegations of election irregularities.[6]

A description of how Tanaka and these five civil bureaucrats joined forces is beyond the scope of this chapter, but Yamagata's shadow and Tanaka's skills as a "political general" must have influenced the development of the 1914–1915 plans. Even before his trip abroad, Tanaka had persuaded party politician Ōkuma, famed as an adversary of the army (rikugun girai), to speak to army and reservist gatherings about reservist association matters on at least six occasions. Tanaka may also have played a role in helping Ōkuma become Prime Minister and in winning from him the two divisions refused to the army in 1912. Finally, Tanaka persuaded Tadokoro, who soon became Vice Minister of Education, to serve as a zaigō gunjinkai adviser and frequent contributor to Comrades in Arms, the reservist monthly, and Ichiki to write in that magazine on youth group-reservist relations.[7] This civil-military cooperation resulted in the Home and Education Ministries' publication in September, 1915, of a joint order to establish a national youth group headquarters.

This government order and the explanatory letter from the Home and Education Vice Ministers which followed indicated that the founders conceived of the national youth association's local role as both similar and complementary to the reservists'. These bureaucrats and officers hoped that the seinendan, like the reservist branches, would popularize patriotic values and serve national goals through local acceptance and mutual cooperation with other community groups and leaders. The letter established four primary guidelines: (1) the youth association branch was to be both a work and community service organization, as it had been in the past, and an ideological and educa-

---

6. Matsumura Ken'ichi, "Shakai kyōiku ni okeru kokumin kyōka no tenkai" [The Development of National Enlightenment Through Social Education], in Waseda daigaku shakai kagaku kenkyujo, Nihon no fashizumu: keiseiki no kenkyū [Japanese Fascism: Studies in the Formative Period] (Tokyo, 1970), pp. 216–219; Oka Yoshitake, Yamagata Aritomo (Tokyo, 1958), p. 134; Roger F. Hackett, Yamagata Aritomo in the Rise of Modern Japan, 1838–1922 (Tokyo, 1971), pp. 146, 242, 256, 268, 279, 295–296; Kumagai, Seinendanshi, pp. 113–120; Tanaka Giichi denki, I, p. 608.

7. See Senyū, 9 (1911), pp. 1–2; 13 (1911), pp. 6–14; 16 (1912), pp. 1–10; 17 (1912), pp. 49–51; 20 (1912), pp. 2–10; 21 (1912), pp. 1, 90–91; 22 (1912), pp. 8–15; 29 (1913), pp. iii, 10–15 for Ōkuma speeches or reports of Ōkuma speeches to reservists; Teikoku zaigō gunjinkai sanjūnenshi (Tokyo, 1944), p. 77; Hosokawa Ryūgen, Tanaka Giichi (Tokyo, 1958), pp. 77–86; Tanaka Giichi denki, I, pp. 451–453; Tadokoro Miharu, "Kokumin no shūyō" [Training the People], Senyū, 27 (1913), pp. 6–15; Ichiki Kitokurō, "Zaigō gunjinkai to seinendan" [The Reservist Association and the Youth Group], Senyū, 96 (1918), pp. 7–9. Ichiki ironically was attacked as a "Minobe-ite" by radical reservists in 1935.

tional one; (2) it was to be organized with city, town, and village branches and hamlet subdivisions; (3) it was to seek the active support of village and school officials, the police, the reservists, and local religious leaders; and (4) it was to maintain a maximum age of twenty for membership.[8] Tanaka and the other founders viewed each of these four guidelines as crucial to attaining their goals.

According to the first guideline, Tanaka and his Education and Home Ministry colleagues forced the existing local groups to add three new functions: patriotic and ethical education, physical training, and military drill under reservist leadership. The patriotic and ethical education was easily acceptable to villagers because it was an extension of one of the main functions of the existing groups. Youth clubs (*wakamono-gumi, wakashū-ren*), dating back at least to the Tokugawa era, traditionally performed both labor tasks such as festival preparations, policing, and communal road and canal repairs, as well as moral education. Young men's groups in all of the seventeen, pre-1915 hamlets and hamlet clusters in Anjō, one of our case study communities, for example, carried out extensive labor and festival activities and enforced strict codes of ethical behavior. Such behavioral rules as those of the Yamazaki village (after 1906, part of Anjō) youth group, published in 1891, were reminiscent of parts of Tanaka's soldier's ethos.[9] They were as follows:

1. When one gambles in violation of the rules:
    a. if he lives in the hamlet or has his permanent address in the hamlet, he will be fined thirty sen.
    b. if he gambles where he lives, he will be fined fifty sen.
    c. anyone who reports gambling will be rewarded with ten sen.
2. All members will observe a ten o'clock curfew.
3. Bothering others by arguing and making excessive noise on the streets is strictly forbidden.
4. Taking a high position when entering or leaving, and lying around the house bothering others is strictly forbidden.
5. Trafficking with prostitutes, hanging around restaurants, or going to evil places (*aku basho*) is strictly forbidden.
6. Becoming infatuated with girls and maid servants and bothering them by saying or doing anything untoward is strictly forbidden.
7. Making uncalled for remarks when a bride (or adopted son-in-law) is moving to her husband's (or wife's) home is strictly forbidden.

---

8. Tanaka Giichi, *Shakaiteki kokumin kyōiku* [The Social Education of the Public] (Tokyo, 1915), p. 123; Kumagai, *Seinendanshi*, pp. 199–200.

9. *Anjō-machi seinendanshi* [A History of the Youth Association of Anjō Town] (Anjō, 1936), I, pp. 11–67.

8. Arguing or fighting during Shinto shrine festivals or when on sightseeing trips is forbidden and the transgressor will be sent home immediately.
9. Extraordinary behavior when going to or at the Buddhist temple is forbidden.
10. One must be careful to avoid damaging crops.
11. One must use the proper salutation when greeting others.
12. One must not spread rumors of events in Yamazaki to other hamlets.
13. One must honor superiors, show compassion to inferiors, revere his parents, maintain a harmonious family, be humane in dealing with other people, and always act with propriety.[10]

Local rules like these were aimed at maintaining the existing hamlet social hierarchy, at reinforcing such values as frugality and hard work, and at ensuring the conformity of all youths to community standards of behavior. Patriotic training actually helped the hamlet achieve these goals because it added the imperial and national sanction to community values. And, conversely, the members' commitment to community traditions, as we shall see in Chapter V, reinforced feelings of loyalty to the emperor and to the army. Even physical training and military drill helped hamlet leaders to strengthen the community's order; from 1915 on, Anjō reservists led youth group members in calisthenics and military drill on an average of one or two times a week at daybreak. As Tanaka himself pointed out, teenagers' participation in "early risers' clubs" helped to prevent frivolity in the evenings, kept the youths out of bars and restaurants, and forced them to save money —they were too tired after an hour and a half of early morning drill to cause trouble in the evening.[11] Tanaka's successful "character building" seinendan branches combined the new patriotic, athletic, and military training with the old ethical and work functions, and the result was mutually beneficial to both hamlet and national leadership.

The planners organized the youth association with its lowest official rural headquarters at the administrative village or town level, but the second guideline also allowed for the maintenance of hamlet subdivisions because the planners realized that such subunits were essential to educational success. Although after 1868, the amalgamation of Tokugawa hamlets into new larger administrative villages, migration to the cities, education, and military service began to break down particularistic local identity, hamlet allegiance remained important well into the postwar era. The 1915–1945 period under study here

---

10. *Anjō-machi seinendanshi*, I, pp. 60–62.
11. *Anjō-machi seinendanshi*, I, pp. 126–129; *Tanaka chūjō kōenshū*, p. 246.

was, as Satō Mamoru points out, a transitional one between the Tokugawa era when a farmer's whole world was his hamlet and the post-World War II epoch when land reform, the amalgamation of villages into larger communities, and out-migration destroyed local identity to a large extent. In 1850, a young man joined the *wakamono-gumi* out of loyalty to his family and hamlet; in 1935 he enrolled out of loyalty to family, hamlet, and nation; in 1970, he joined to fulfill his own individual needs. In transitional 1915, Tanaka probably felt compelled to maintain hamlet subunits to use the still important hamlet cohesiveness and sanctions against nonparticipation (i.e., against nonconformity) to ensure widespread enlistment and functional success, but at the same time to establish village and town level branches. In Anjō, for example, the *seinendan* was part of the national chain of command, had a town office headquarters and leadership, but also hamlet leaders. All of the members belonged to the hamlet subunits and performed most of their functions—military, physical training, and social as well as the older labor and religious ones there. By functioning in this way, the village or town youth branch benefited from hamlet cohesiveness, community office financing, and from government, school official, and reservist leadership and support.[12]

Tanaka, Ichiki, and Takada also urged youth group members to cooperate closely with leaders of other nationally centralized, but local organizations—the mayor, his community office subordinates, police (Home Ministry), school officials (Education Ministry), reservists (Army Ministry), and local Shinto and Buddhist priests. This clause of the national leaders' order caused no problems at all. It was natural and not new for the youth group to cooperate with the village office, which financed the youth group, with the school officials, who taught the members for six to eight years of their young lives, and with the local priests especially from Shinto shrines where most hamlet festivals took place. Cooperation with the *zaigō gunjinkai* presented no dilemma either. Reservists commanded respect because they were the community's fittest men in their prime work years and the leaders of other village organizations. Even if the reservists had not been charged with many youth group leadership roles, the hamlet's young men would have followed and respected these men. The new youth association regulations simply added three new types of activity—patriotic, athletic, and military—to the ones youths already carried out under

---

12. Satō Mamoru, *Kindai Nihon seinen shūdanshi kenkyū* [Studies in the History of Modern Japanese Youth Organization] (Tokyo, 1970), pp. 64–65, 539–540; *Anjō machi seinendanshi*, I, *passim*; *Anjō-shi seinendanshi* [A History of the Youth Association of Anjō City] II (Anjō, 1962), pp. 1–269.

the direction of these same elders. In Anjō, the reservist branch members drilled, led exercises, and taught the soldier's ethos to youth group members. In a different guise, reservists directed the young men in the volunteer fire department, road repairs, and other community services.[13] The two age groups added new functions after 1910–1915, but they did not develop new relationships.

The two ministers included in the youth association's regulations Tanaka's demand that the maximum age for youth group membership be twenty, and this turned out to be his only miscalculation. Tanaka insisted on this limit because he envisioned a system in which young men left the *seinendan* at the age when they became eligible for military service and reserve association membership. The former was to be a pipeline for the latter, and all males from the age of six to forty would receive patriotic and military training. The school system indoctrinated children from six to fourteen, the youth association teenagers from fourteen to twenty, and the army and reserve association from twenty to forty.[14]

Tanaka's insistence on an age limit of twenty ran counter to hamlet tradition and, for the ultimate success of the centralized youth association, was revised upward. This was because in the older *wakamonogumi*, which lacked national leadership, age requirements varied from hamlet to hamlet. Some considered a man a youth until he married or even until he assumed the family headship and required that he belong to the youth group well after he passed the age of thirty. Thus, although the Home and Education Ministry officials accepted Tanaka's proposal, some local leaders were recalcitrant. For the organization to perform as both a community service and a national educational one, some compromise had to be reached. In 1920, the central leadership raised the age limit to twenty-five, and in some communities eventually as high as forty-two.[15]

Several scholars, following the interpretation of Tazawa Yoshiharu,

13. *Anjō-machi seinendanshi*, I, pp. 124–138, 221–455; II, pp. 50–264; see also *Toyama-ken Nishi Tonami-gun Isurugi seinendanshi* [A History of the Toyama Prefecture Nishi Tonami County Isurugi Youth Association] (Kanazawa, 1937); *Toyama-ken Higashi Tonami-gun Higashi Nojiri-mura seinendanshi* [A History of the Toyama Prefecture Higashi Tonami County Higashi Nojiri Village Youth Association] (Kanazawa, 1935).

14. Kumagai, *Seinendanshi*, p. 116; *Tanaka Giichi denki*, I, pp. 615–619; Hori Shika, *Saishō to naru made Tanaka Giichi* (Tokyo, 1928), p. 133.

15. Kumagai, *Seinendanshi*, p. 116, 119–120; *Tanaka Giichi denki*, I, pp. 615, 620; Satō Mamoru, *Seinen shūdanshi kenkyū*, pp. 55, 226–228; Fukutake Tadashi, *Japanese Rural Society* (London and New York, 1967), pp. 103–104; *Asahi nenkan* [Asahi Yearbook], 1936, pp. 571–572. In 1936, 2 prefectures placed the age limit at forty-two, 19 at between thirty and forty, and 26 at twenty-five. The prefectures with the highest age limits tended to be the most agricultural ones.

Tanaka's more liberal rival in youth affairs, interpret the 1920 regulations as a move toward greater local autonomy and a defeat for Tanaka. Since local *seinendan* members from this time on were allowed to determine their own maximum age and to choose their own leaders, Tazawa and later scholars believe that 1920 marked the end of military influence over the youth association at least until the wartime years. Actually, the new age limit benefited the army and the reserve association. After 1920, men between the ages of twenty and twenty-five normally functioned in both the community's youth and reservist branch. Because they were the oldest and ablest of the youth branch members, reservists became leaders and exerted strong influence over local *seinendan* affairs. The Japanese scholars go astray by basing their interpretations on Tazawa's democratic intentions when he proposed the rules' changes, rather than on a study of the local level of the system where the new regulations had their actual impact.[16] We shall look at the relationship between local reservists and youth branch leaders in detail in Chapter IV.

Reservists influenced the two and one-half million member youth association even when they did not provide the organization's official leadership. Available evidence from local youth group and community histories, from reservist publications and Anjō documents, and from interviews and questionnaires, reveals that in the communities covered, youth branches conducted many functions in cooperation with and under the direction of the local reservist branch. The two organizations cooperated locally to perform such joint educational and service enterprises as military drill, patriotic ceremonies, disaster relief, public works, physical training, and athletic meets in Anjō, in its Hekikai County in general, in Isurugi Town and Higashi Nojiri Village in Toyama Prefecture, in Utsunomiya City just north of the capital, in Fuchū City and Tsubota Village in Tokyo Prefecture and throughout Nagano and Yamanashi Prefectures. Actually, every available local *seinendan* history except the one for Nagoya City refers frequently to reservist-youth group cooperation and to the leadership the former provided the latter. Even the Nagoya history indicates a strong army influence in that city's youth affairs. And Satō Mamoru, in his study of local youth organization in three widespread regions, specifically re-

16. In 1930, 99.6% of 53,210 youth association leaders were 20 years old or older. *Zenkoku seinendan kihon chōsa* [A Basic Survey of the Youth Association Nationwide] (Tokyo, 1934), p. 5. Matsumura, "Shakai kyōiku ni okeru kyōka no tenkai," *Nihon no fashizumu*, pp. 222–223; Tazawa Yoshiharu, *Seinendan no shimei* [The Mission of the Youth Association] (Tokyo, 1930), p. 308; Inoue Kiyoshi, "Taishōki no seiji to gumbu," in Inoue Kiyoshi, ed., *Taishōki no seiji to shakai* (Tokyo, 1969), p. 401; *Isurugi seinendanshi*, p. 67; *Higashi Nojiri-mura seinendanshi*, p. 74; *Anjō-machi seinendanshi*, I, pp. 190–215; II, pp. 35–49.

ports close reservist-youth cooperation in several of the communities he researched. He concludes that both organizations played important roles in educating young men in patriotic values.[17] We shall deal with local youth and reservist branch leadership, cooperation, and mutual community service and nationally oriented activities in Chapters IV and V. The evidence to be presented there indicates that the two organizations complemented each other in winning local acceptance for national, nationalistic, and military values and institutions.

THE NEED TO SUPPLEMENT
THE YOUTH ASSOCIATION

In spite of the youth association's success in helping the army spread its values to teenage Japanese males, in a little more than a decade the army established the parallel youth training center system. If the *seinendan* functioned so well for army purposes, the question we must raise is why did Tanaka and Ugaki, who became the prime mover of the army's system for civilian education after 1924, conclude so soon that they needed another organization? I think we can discern the answer fairly easily. They wanted to supplement the already existing youth branches with a related and complementary organization because they recognized a lack of nationwide uniformity in military education from branch to branch. These variations, while not large enough or extensive enough to threaten seriously the youth association's overall military endeavors, did impress Tanaka and Ugaki, officers obsessed with order and standardization. The problem arose from the inability of the army and the national reservist leaders to control securely enough the youth association's central headquarters and from their difficulties in obtaining and maintaining cooperation in a few local communities.

The first problem, the inability of the army to dictate to the nationally unified *seinendan,* resulted from civilian fear of excessive military influence. Many civilians in the Home and Education Ministries, but particularly in the press and the lower house of the Diet, believed Tanaka's goal was the militarization of Japanese youth. Their evidence was the twenty-year-old age limit which seemed to make the *seinendan* a reservist association auxiliary. Tanaka answered this criticism with the following statement to the press in 1915:

We have no intention of making youths into soldiers or giving them military preparatory training as in Russia or in France. The order clearly states that our goal is to make youths into healthy future citizens. According to the

17. See Chapter V, footnote one.

order . . . the *seinendan* is not a work organization, not a research organization, not an organization to aid in production, but an association for building character.[18]

Tanaka's statement did not confront squarely the issue raised by the civilian criticism because the training of soldiers which he mentioned and the militarization of youth which his critics feared were two related, but still different matters. Events proved that Tanaka had every intention of encouraging youth association military drill, not apparently with the short-range purpose of training recruits for the army, but rather to produce physically and spiritually fit citizens. Since Tanaka believed that good citizens are good soldiers, and good soldiers are good citizens, his long range youth association goal was the militarization of Japanese youth, that is of Japanese society. If by achieving this goal the army also gained pretrained recruits as a by-product, it was all well and good. But Tanaka's ideal youth association would have a broad, not a narrow goal; and, as his critics contended, it was a military goal.

Tanaka's disclaimers rightly fell on skeptical ears, and criticism continued after 1915. The two civilian ministers were questioned repeatedly during the next decade about the justification for Tanaka's twenty-year-old age limit and about his and the army's influence in youth association affairs.[19] This criticism undoubtedly helped motivate them to change the maximum age limit in 1920 but, as we have seen, neither criticism nor the regulation revisions ended the army's influence on the youth association.

To ameliorate the impact of the criticism over army influence on the youth association, the planners decided from the beginning to minimize the military's role in the central headquarters. When the Home and Education Ministers proclaimed the establishment of a national youth headquarters in 1915, they abandoned the original plan to have the Army Minister join. No soldier except Tanaka served on the organization's board of directors, and even he resigned and became an adviser in 1919. Tanaka was the only officer to serve in any official capacity until after the China War began in 1937.[20]

Although the Army Ministry had no official control over the *seinendan*'s central headquarters, this was an insufficient reason for Tanaka and Ugaki to think they needed a new, army-directed organization. Tanaka himself was able to exert military influence on the youth asso-

---

18. Kumagai, *Seinendanshi*, p. 116.
19. Kumagai, *Seinendanshi*, pp. 114–120, 219–223.
20. Kumagai, *Seinendanshi*, p. 114, Appendix VI, pp. 181–193; Hori, *Saishō to naru made Tanaka Giichi*, p. 133.

ciation at the highest levels, and he also knew that Takada, Ichiki, Yamamoto, Tadokoro and most of their colleagues and successors were committed to ideological values similar to his. He saw no need to bring the youth association under military supervision because his civilian colleagues had made the *seinendan* the character training organization he desired it to be.

Furthermore, the army could dominate the local youth branches without controlling the Tokyo headquarters. Taisho democracy, the liberal atmosphere which surrounded it, and the fear of militarism was primarily a condition of the cities. At the village level, this influence did not have the impact it had in Tokyo or Osaka. Thus, the youth branches after 1915, as before, operated under the leadership of the older members (although for the first five years they were not actually members because of the twenty-year-old age limit); most of them were simultaneously reservists, the army's rural representatives. Villagers did not perceive these reservists, approximately two-thirds of the 20 to 40-year-old age group in the community, to be militarists infiltrating the local *seinendan*. They saw them rather as the healthiest men in the community, men in their prime, asserting their leadership over their natural followers, the local teenagers.

Tanaka recognized the rural opportunity the army had because villagers accepted *zaigō gunjinkai* branches as integral parts of their communities. Therefore, between 1914 and 1925, he devoted himself to educating reservists about youth leadership so that they would utilize this potential and lead teenagers in the "right" direction. He ground out numerous articles in the issues of *Comrades in Arms* and presented frequent speeches which were then published in his collected writings on the subject of reservist youth guidance. Tanaka also wrote an important pamphlet on the subject, *The Social Education of the Public* (*Shakaiteki kokumin kyōiku*), which, according to the youth association's official historian, Kumagai Tatsujirō, reached a circulation of 700,000 copies, including one to every reservist branch and elementary school in the country. In all of these articles and pamphlets, Tanaka urged reservist and local school and civil officials to cooperate in the essential enterprise of strengthening young people's characters through rigorous patriotic, military, physical, moral, and vocational training. The evidence to be presented in Chapter V indicates that Tanaka's efforts at indoctrination without central control by the military worked well in the communities studied.[21]

---

21. See Matsumura, "Shakai kyōiku ni okeru kokumin kyōka no tenkai," *Nihon no fashizumu*, pp. 209–219, for a discussion of Tanaka and Yamamoto's views on the functions of the youth association. Kumagai, *Seinendanshi*, p. 114; Tanaka,

There were, nevertheless, minor exceptions to this pattern of success which may have influenced Ugaki and Tanaka to build a new organization. The 1915 youth association organizers met scattered and temporary "traditional" resistance to their centralization efforts, resistance which was overcome, but which led to a lack of total uniformity of practice nationwide. Several Japanese scholars report cases, for example, of villages in which each household sent only one son to the pre-1915 *wakamono-gumi*. This presented problems in centralization because the ministers' orders required that all young males between the ages of thirteen or fourteen and twenty join the *seinendan*. The Oikata hamlet in Akita Prefecture met this problem by maintaining two youth organizations, one to perform "national," and one to conduct "local" functions. This in turn jeopardized the use of local practices to spread military ideals since the new imposed organization remained a bureaucratic one without profiting from the benefits of hamlet cohesion. Luckily for the national leaders' success, the two Oikata groups gradually merged and helped fulfill the central officials' goal.[22] Although we have no idea whether or not this type of local problem was widespread, and although this one seems to have been shortlived, it and others like it may have provided an incentive to the military's formation of a more tightly controlled and standardized supplementary young men's organization.

Tanaka and Ugaki seem also to have searched for a way to supplement youth association military education because of radical activity which prevented the army and the reservist association from dominating certain branches. In a few areas in the nation, "proletarian" leaders seized control of local youth association organs. A carefully documented case of this was in Shimo-ina County in southern Nagano Prefecture. Here in the 1920s the local youth association leaders, many of whom were Communist Party members, successfully withdrew the county organization from the national and prefectural organization and fought to a draw local government and reservist efforts to create a conservative, rival youth association. They even blocked the development of the county's youth training centers for a few years after 1926 by refusing to allow their *seinendan* members to attend. The movement collapsed in the early Showa period largely because in 1928 the Tanaka government jailed hundreds of Communist Party

Shakaiteki kokumin kyōiku especially pp. 119–127; *Tanaka chūjō kōenshū*, pp. 170–182, 197–230, 236–264; *Senyū*, 90 (1917), pp. 6–7. The 43 issues of *Imperial Youth*, 1916–1923, housed in the library of the Japan Youth Hall (*Nihon seinenkan*) include 25 articles and advertisements for four books by Tanaka.

22. Satō Mamoru, *Seinen shūdanshi kenkyū*, p. 55.

members, and in doing so decimated the Shimo-ina radical leadership. The increased parochialism and chauvinism of the early 1930s destroyed the radical movement's remaining popular support. It is difficult to determine the national incidence of radical youth activity in rural Japan during the 1920s—Hirayama Kazuhiko, a student of the Shimo-ina case and sympathetic to the radical movement, thinks this southern Nagano situation was a rare example. Nevertheless, Tanaka, a staunch anti-Communist with nostalgic memories of his student years in imperial Russia, and Ugaki must have been impressed.[23] Shimo-ina County presented, from the military's point of view, a chaotic and unacceptable youth association situation. It provided an incentive for the establishment of a more highly controlled youth training system in 1926 to supplement the officers' earlier attempts to create patriotism, military popularity, and national unity out of hamlet particularism.

TANAKA, UGAKI AND THE
YOUTH TRAINING CENTERS

General Ugaki, Tanaka's successor as Army Minister in 1924, was the officer most involved in the creation of the youth training center system. Ugaki, who served as the army's cabinet representative when the Education Ministry issued the order in 1926, established centers as part of his "readjustment of the army" (gumbi seiri). Under strong public and political pressure for disarmament, the minister eliminated four army divisions, but he used the funds saved to mechanize the army and to add to the national mobilization structure. The keys to this addition were the youth training centers and the assignment of active duty officers to middle schools as military instructors.

Ugaki, echoing Yamagata and Tanaka, wrote that he believed military drill for teenagers was vital for producing better individual citizens, for bringing young men into intimate contact with the army, and for fulfilling his desire of unifying the entire society as a disciplined national power under the emperor. He stated that only the army, by training soldiers, reservists, youths, and women, could produce citizens who worked cooperatively to increase Japan's wealth and military strength. The army could do this because it served the whole nation,

---

23. Hirayama Kazuhiko, "Chihō seinen undō no tenkai" [The Development of the Regional Youth Movement], in Furushima Toshio et. al., Meiji Taishō kyōdoshi kenkyūhō [Research Methods in Meiji and Taishō Local History] (Tokyo, 1970), pp. 248–250; Nagano-ken seinen hattatsushi [A History of the Development of Nagano Prefecture Youth] (Nagano, 1935), pp. 156–163, 250–251.

not special interests as the political parties did, and it "touched" most of the populace, not just a few members as the navy did. Ugaki considered the establishment of youth centers to be one of his most important contributions to Japan.[24]

Without question, Tanaka's intellectual influence, support, and patronage made Ugaki's training centers possible. Although General Ugaki did not credit anyone else with helping him establish the youth drill system and although he was extremely critical of Tanaka in his famous diary, Ugaki clearly worked in the Yamagata-Tanaka tradition of building national unity, and he rose to high military position, including even that of Army Minister, because of Tanaka's very real support.[25]

Tanaka was willing to patronize Ugaki, a non-Choshu officer, because they shared similar views on national mobilization. To both, a strong army depended on modern armaments, rational organization, and strict discipline founded on a solid basis of national popular support, unity, and wealth. Tanaka's influence and role in creating the youth training centers must not be overlooked.

One Japanese scholar has pointed out that the fundamental idea that supported the need for the centers, the necessity for educating young men in national and military values, was essentially Tanaka's. Ugaki believed in the same ideas and spoke of them with as much intensity as the Choshu general, but Ugaki was a Tanaka follower and absorbed the ideas from his mentor. Moreover, shortly after Tanaka became president of the *Seiyūkai* opposition party, he took the unprecedented political step of having his party publicly urge the Katō Kōmei cabinet to adopt Ugaki's December, 1925 proposal for military training centers for youths. It was the Katō government which promulgated the order establishing the centers in 1926. At the high-water mark of "Taisho democracy," the leadership of both major political parties supported the creation of one of the army's major institutions in its efforts to militarize Japanese society.[26]

---

24. *Ugaki nikki*, I, pp. 482–483, 497–498, 519–521, 523, 528, 547–550; Yabe Teiji, *Konoe Fumimaro* (Tokyo, 1952), I, p. 301. The novelist, Takeda Taijun, in a series of essays on politicians' writing styles, points out sarcastically that "to touch" (*sesshoku suru*) was clearly a euphemism for "to manage" (*shihai suru*) or "to mobilize" (*dōin suru*). *Seijika no bunshō* [The Writings of Politicians] (Tokyo, 1960), p. 6.

25. See Matsushita Yoshio, *Nihon no gumbatsuzō* [A Portrait of the Japanese Military Clique] (Tokyo, 1969), pp. 221–222, for a discussion of Tanaka's crucial role in making Ugaki Army Minister in 1924. *Tanaka Giichi denki*, II, pp. 329–336.

26. Kubo Yoshizō, *Nihon fashizumu kyōiku seisakushi* [A History of the Educational Policies of Japanese Fascism] (Tokyo, 1969), pp. 113–114; *Tanaka Giichi denki*, II, p. 398.

General Ugaki received help in establishing youth training centers from his colleague, Education Minister Okada Ryōhei, in the two Katō and Wakatsuki Cabinets in 1924–1926, as well as from Tanaka and the two major political parties. The centers, after all, came under the jurisdiction of the Education, not the Army, Ministry, and could not exist without Okada's approval. Ugaki and Okada, a youth association adviser along with Tanaka, had first cooperated in early 1925 when the two men assigned army officers to middle schools as drill instructors. The plan not only rescued the army from the necessity of retiring the officers displaced by the elimination of four divisions, but also required the ministry to recruit more to fill all of the educational needs. It also brought the 20 percent of the teenage population which went into secondary education under military influence. Okada backed Ugaki's plan because the Education Minister believed systematic military drill helped build physically and morally strong, patriotic citizens. Later in the year, Ugaki and Okada presented the second part of their military socialization plan for teenagers. On December 18, they presented the youth training center proposal to the second Katō Cabinet's Educational Deliberations Committee. This committee quickly accepted the proposal and within months the Diet, dominated by Katō's government party and Tanaka Giichi's opposition party, passed the necessary budget bill to fund the centers. In July, 1926, Ugaki's and Okada's centers, made possible by Army, Education Ministry, and political party cooperation, were in operation.[27]

According to the April 20, 1926 order establishing the centers, and several subsequent Education and Army Ministry orders, local communities were required to set up and finance four year schools for the 80 percent of the Japanese male youths who did not continue with higher education after completing compulsory education. These young people between the ages of fifteen and twenty, the majority of whom simultaneously held jobs or labored on their families' farms, received eight hundred hours of education, including four hundred of military drill and one hundred of ethical education, over a period of four years in the new centers. Although the Education Ministry alone had official jurisdiction over the youth training centers, the army's influence was inescapable. Reservists directed the 400 hours of drill, provided 40,000 of the 110,000 teachers, and the army's regimental area commanders had the duty to inspect annually the state of the student's military proficiency. From 1926 on, the army worked through both organizations. It used the centers for military drill and patriotic training and the youth association branches for broader military, physical,

---

27. Kubo, *Nihon fashizumu kyōiku seisakushi,* pp. 117, 121–123.

and patriotic training, to maintain army-community ties, and thus to recruit students for the youth training centers. In some communities, the youth association relinquished its drill responsibilities to the new centers, although in others, Anjō for example, young men drilled in both.[28]

Several Japanese historians have written that the centers met immediate and widespread opposition in 1926. These scholars, however, support their contention with only two examples of opposition: that of a Tokyo newspaper, expressed in an editorial, which tells us nothing about rural acceptance of youth centers, and that of the Japan Peasants' Association. This association, it must be admitted, was the most important of the prewar, antilandlord organizations, but one must remember that all of the farmers' unions, at their peak membership, enrolled only 6 percent of the agricultural families in the nation. Moreover, the Japan Peasants' Association splintered before 1926 into four separate organizations, only two of which by any stretch of the imagination could be considered "proletarian." Thus when one of the authors states that the union opposed the centers because they were classless and broke down class distinctions by giving military drill to the rural "proletariat" as well as to the more affluent people, we can surmise that his reference did not point to all four parts of the union. The reference was rather to its radical wing, representing at most 2 percent of the rural population. The army's ability to recruit students for its centers and members for its other organizations depended on the farmers' perceptions of themselves as members of a corporative and cohesive vertical hamlet, not as part of a horizontal social class. A prewar Japanese peasant union that based its chances of success on farmers' class consciousness was doomed never to recruit a large membership.[29]

Reports in the *Asahi shimbun*, Tokyo's leading newspaper, and enrollment figures also belie these scholars' claims. The newspaper published a series of articles between July, 1926 and July, 1927 which reported continued success for Ugaki's training centers, and when they opened their doors in 1926, the centers enrolled the significant

28. Okabe Tomio, ed., *Dainihon kyōikushi* [The History of Education in Greater Japan] (Tokyo, 1939), pp. 1237–1242; Ishikawa Ken, ed., *Kindai Nihon kyōiku seidō shiryō* [Materials on the Modern Japanese Educational System] (Tokyo, 1956), III, pp. 553–555; Mombushō, *Gakusei hachijūnenshi* [The Eighty Year History of the Educational System] (Tokyo, 1954), pp. 290, 348–350; *Anjō-machi seinendanshi*, I, pp. 453–454.

29. Kubo, *Nihon fashizumu kyōiku seisakushi*, pp. 123–125; Ōtsuka Shigakkai, *Shimpan kyōdoshi jiten* (Tokyo, 1969), p. 454; Ronald P. Dore, *Land Reform in Japan* (London, 1959), pp. 75–80; Tokinoya Katsu, ed., *Nihon kindaishi jiten* (Tokyo, 1960), p. 141.

number of 800,000 male teenagers. The number grew steadily thereafter. By 1934, 915,000, or over one-third of the nation's young men
in the appropriate age bracket—about 40 percent of those who were
eligible (students who entered middle school did not enroll in youth
training centers)—studied in the 15,000 centers. The percentages
ranged from less than 10 percent in Tokyo, to over 50 percent in
highly agricultural Yamagata Prefecture.[30] The basic reason for the
difference in urban and rural matriculation is clear and has been
mentioned several times before in discussing the army's other local
organizations. Hamlet cohesion and emphasis on conformity resulted
in high enrollment and attendance rates. Although the Education
Ministry organized the training centers by "artificial" school districts
and not by "natural" hamlets, this did not lessen the impact of
community pressure. The students usually belonged simultaneously
to the *seinendan* with its hamlet subdivisions, and received drill instruction from neighborhood reservists. The pressures from their
youth association peers and reservist elders were potent in the case of
the centers as well as in that of the other organizations. The young villagers' commitment to their hamlet enforced participation in a curriculum which emphasized military drill and nationalistic ideals. This
is another example of local particularism which helped the army
mold national villagers. The number of students would have been
even higher if the curriculum had not duplicated youth association
functions in some communities and if many youths had not studied
concurrently in similar but partly competitive vocational schools. The
latter problem was solved in 1935, as we shall see, by the merger of
the centers and vocational schools into militaristic youth schools.

YOUTH SCHOOLS AND THE EXTENSION OF MILITARY DRILL FOR TEENAGERS

The year 1935 saw a major expansion of the prewar military socialization system for male Japanese; in that year, the youth training centers
merged with the nationwide system of supplementary technical schools
(*jitsugyō hoshū gakkō*) and became the basis of a broader network of
military indoctrination. In 1893–94, the government created a series
of vocational schools at different educational levels to give secondary
and higher education to many of the primary and middle school

---

30. See Table 11 in Chapter Three. The *Asahi shimbun* articles not only reported the centers' success, but welcomed it as well. See especially July 2, 1926, p. 1;
July 4, p. 6; July 8, p. 2; August 14, p. 3; October 5, p. 4; October 20, p. 3; July 9,
1927, p. 7; July 10, p. 7.

graduates who did not go on to study in colleges and universities. The system included three types of practical schools: higher technical schools for middle school graduates which turned out such skilled technicians as doctors, veterinarians, and agronomists; technical schools in which elementary school graduates studied full time for two to five years, depending on their educational background; and supplementary technical schools in which graduates of compulsory elementary education studied part-time while they held jobs or worked on their families' farms. The students in the last type of vocational schools, which had by far the largest enrollment—in 1927, the higher schools educated 21,000, the technical schools 250,000, and the supplementary schools almost one million students—studied ethics, Japanese language, arithmetic, and the type of technical education appropriate to the school's geographical area. About 75 percent of the 7,000 schools specialized in agriculture, and only about 400 in commerce and industrial technology. In other words, a very high percentage of the schools was located in rural areas. It was the supplementary schools which overlapped and competed with the youth training centers. By 1935, the schools played important roles in the educational life of their communities and had become the focus of intense civic pride. The author of the history of the town of Nambu, just west of Kofu, for example, bragged that the Mutsuzawa Village (one of the villages amalgamated into Nambu after the war) Vocational School was of such high quality that it was as good as a second-rate middle school. Because of their local prestige, large enrollment, competition, and wide distribution in rural Japan, it is easy to understand why the army cast a covetous eye on the schools.[31]

The merger had an important benefit for the army; it allowed the military to increase its indoctrination network considerably. In 1935, 915,000 students studied in the youth training centers, but another 944,000 males and 470,000 females enrolled in the supplementary technical schools. Although a half million male students attended both types of schools concurrently, another half million did not. Thus the army concluded that if the two systems merged, it could reach 50 percent more young men as well as a large number of girls. The Education Ministry also probably favored the amalgamation as a means of avoiding the extra expense of maintaining two school systems, each with overlapping functions and students.

In 1935, therefore, the Army and the Education Ministries created

---

31. *Shimpan kyōdoshi jiten,* p. 253; *Gakusei hachijūnenshi,* p. 348; *Nambu-chōshi* [The History of Nambu Town] (Kofu, 1964), pp. 639–641; See also *Kawai-mura kyōdoshi* [The Local History of Kawai Village] (Morioka, 1962), I, 1092–1095.

youth schools, and enrollment increased immediately to almost two million students, including 500,000 young women. The schools continued, as the centers had, to give military, patriotic, and ethical training, but added more extensive academic and vocational education than before. From 1926 until 1936, center students spent half of their two hundred hours of education per year in drill training; after 1935, drill consumed only 70 to 90 of 210 annual school hours. Girls did not receive military drill. Instead they undertook 30 hours of physical education and 40 hours of "housewife" training, mostly sewing.[32]

After the merger, well over 50 percent of the nation's teenage males participated in the youth schools and received military drill training. In this case, as in that of all the army's educational organizations, more rural and fewer urban youths enrolled. In a number of agricultural prefectures, the power of the hamlet insured that 75 to 80 percent of the eligibles matriculated. The army, with its rural foundations secure, began to search for ways to expand city enrollment, particularly when surveys showed that youth school graduates achieved better results both on the conscription examination and on active duty. In wartime 1939, therefore, the Army and the Education Ministry made attendance compulsory. Their aim was to enforce attendance with each new class and achieve full enrollment by 1943. By that year, three million boys and girls, almost 80 percent of Japan's sixteen- to twenty-year-olds, participated in the youth schools. The other 20 percent were either young men on active duty in the military or teenagers (mostly urban?) who somehow still managed to evade enrollment. The youth school students provided a large part of the labor in Japan's factories in the closing two years of the war.[33]

THE NATIONAL DEFENSE WOMEN'S ASSOCIATION

Women were the last group the army attempted to educate in military values. Before the "crisis" decade of the 1930s, officers made only two sporadic efforts to reach women. One was through the army's influence on the existing women's groups, particularly the Patriotic Women's Association (aikoku fujinkai); the other was through the reservist association's publication of a magazine for women, Our Family (Wagaie).[34] Tanaka, Ugaki, and their associates had seen no

32. Gakusei hachijūnenshi, pp. 289–291, 348–351; Kindai Nihon kyōiku seidō shiryō, III, pp. 554–557; Gonda Morinosuke, Nihon kyōiku tōkei [Japanese Educational Statistics] (Tokyo, 1938), p. 213.

33. Shimpan kyōdoshi jiten, pp. 310–311.

34. A typical example of Our Family is the November, 1935 edition. The cover featured a picture of a mother in formal black kimono with two children visiting

need to recruit women because, given the family-oriented and male-dominated nature of Japanese society, organizing men automatically involved organizing women. Even before the 1930s, women aided reservists and youth group members in many of their community services and other activities. When hamlet reservists, for example, helped the families of men on active duty farm, the reservists' women joined in. If the aid included rice transplanting, a female duty, mothers and wives did the work. Hamlet women were unofficially part of the army's local system before they became defense women.

The army first decided to organize women officially after the events of the early 1930s led to increased foreign pressure against Japanese emigration, development of military armaments, and expansionist policies. In the "crisis" era of the 1930s, Japanese military men felt that their nation needed to strengthen its internal unity in an increasingly hostile international milieu and to prepare for total national mobilization in case of what they believed was almost inevitable war. This atmosphere led to the creation of the Greater Japan National Defense Women's Association in 1932 and to its expansion to gigantic proportions by the end of the decade.[35]

The original founders of the defense women's association were Osaka women, most of whom were army wives, and military police officers. This regional beginning led army authorities to boast later that the organization had grass roots origins in the patriotism of the rank and file of Japanese women. To the extent that a group of officers' wives and the kempeitai commander represented grass roots, they were right. The Tokyo authorities, including the Army Minister of the day, Araki Sadao, showed immediate interest, and by 1938 the famed "white apron" organization grew to nationwide dimensions with al-

Yasukuni Shrine, the shrine dedicated to Japan's war dead, on the day of a childrens' festival (shichi-go-san). The issue contained articles on the imperial family, on educating natives in Japanese territories, on brave Ethiopian women fighting next to their men for their country, on the mother of Oishi Yoshio, the hero of the 47 Ronin, on Basho, a seventeenth-century poet, on heroines of the Meiji Restoration and Russo–Japanese War, on recipes, on growing bean sprouts, and on diaper covers. There were also pictures of Atsuta Shrine, the location of one of the three imperial regalia, of defense women helping fire victims, of girls receiving rifle training, and of reservist and defense women's association leaders and a Shintō priest at the time of a local ceremony to commemorate the fourth anniversary of the Manchurian Incident. Advertisements included those for life insurance, a midwifery school, defense bonds, perfume, seals, patent medicine, and a book on Taiwan. In other words, the contents included a combination of patriotic, military, romantic and practical material.

35. The major source of information on the defense womens' association is the Dainihon kokubō fujinkai jūnenshi [The Ten Year History of the Greater Japan National Defense Women's Association] (Tokyo, 1943). In 1938, the organization enrolled 7,929,684 members (p. 159).

most eight million members. By the time war broke out in China in 1937, the army controlled a women's organization which had branches in every city, town, and village in the nation.[36]

The army dominated the new women's association to a much greater degree than it did the youth association and schools, and it shared only minimal influence with the Home, Education, and even Navy Ministries. The army alone created the defense women's group, and in its bylaws gave to the Army and Navy Ministers "supervisory leadership" (*kantoku shidō*) over the organization, but to the two civil ministers only "leadership" (*shidō*). Moreover, an active duty army major or lieutenant general always served as the general manager (*sōmu buchō*), the person who actually directed the *fujinkai;* six of the nine bureaucratic advisors to the new organization were drawn from the two military ministries so that officers could outvote civilians six to three; and the organization located its headquarters from 1932 until 1936 within the Army Ministry itself. Finally, the top positions, which were actually held by women, reflected the army's domination. The chairwoman of the organization was the wife of a prominent general, Mutō Akira, and the list of the names of women who served as vice chairmen, directors, advisors, and councillors reads like a roster of the army's Showa leadership—Suzuki, Minami, Araki, Hayashi, Sugiyama, Hata, Tōjō, etc. Only a few famous navy names such as Yonai and Nagano and civilian names such as Tokutomi and Kiyoura punctuate the list.[37] The army controlled the *kokubō fujinkai* throughout its history and shared some of its power only with the navy.

The army's dominance was even stronger at the intermediate and local than at the central level. The army asserted its power by structuring the organization according to the format of the reserve association and establishing defense women's headquarters at divisional, regimental, administrative community, and hamlet levels. At the division and regimental levels, active duty officers supervised and directed women's association affairs. Their wives, or the wives of prefectural governors or locally prestigious families—the wives of former feudal ruling families, like the Hosokawa in Kumamoto and the Tsugaru in Hirosaki—held the titular posts, but real power lay in the military headquarters. This structure bypassed the Home and Education Ministries, and the navy could claim authority only in the areas of their Yokosuka, Sasebo, and Kure bases, where they already held responsibility for *zaigō gunjinkai* affairs.[38]

36. *Kokubō fujinkai jūnenshi*, pp. 26, 159, 236, 285.

37. *Kokubō fujinkai jūnenshi*, pp. 12, 109, 114, 265–266, 322–323, 619–623.

38. *Kokubō fujinkai jūnenshi*, pp. 109–114, 265, 630–635.

At the lowest levels, even in the navy districts, army influence was absolute. This was because the reservist branches, the army's local appendages, dominated their communities' women's associations. Not only did the *kokubō fujinkai* structure exactly parallel that of the reservists, but, more important, the local *zaigō gunjinkai* units, under army direction, took the initiative in enlisting the women in their communities into the new organization and in providing guidance and leadership for women's activities. Jointly sponsored lectures, patriotic ceremonies, funerals for the war dead, aid to active duty families, and reservist-directed rifle training, drill, and maneuvers were carried out all over the country between 1932 and 1945. Reservists even led women in the famed "bamboo spear" units, organized to prepare for the American invasion of Japan in the closing year of the Pacific War. In a sense, the National Defense Women's Association became the women's arm of the *zaigō gunjinkai* and thus, at the local level, responded to the same kind of army control as the reservists.[39]

This spectacular army-reservist success in organizing women also led to the major obstacle to the new organization's development. The preexisting national women's organization, the Patriotic Women's Association, resented the new organization's competition and tried, albeit unsuccessfully, to block its development. The reasons for the resistance and for the failure to halt the army's efforts call for a short description of the older organization and its inability to sink roots into the rural hamlet.

The Patriotic Women's Association dated back to 1901, when a group of socially prestigious women with the support of a field marshal from Satsuma and the Speaker of the House of Peers, who was also the scion of the most illustrious princely house in Japan, established the organization primarily to conduct war relief for soldiers. The army praised it highly for its efforts to comfort soldiers in the 1904–1905 Russo-Japanese War. The association's leaders from its inception envisaged it as a primarily national, not a local organization, tended to recruit members from the well-to-do—one had to pay substantial dues to join—and made no effort to set up local branches. It gained the reputation of being "an upper class women's club," never built a solid local base, and thus did not carry out systematic organi-

39. *Kokubō fujinkai jūnenshi,* pp. 26, 288–289, 345–346, 429, 448, 454–455, 492–498, 541; *Tokushima nichinichi shimpō* [The Tokushima Daily News] included thirty-two articles between February 15 and July 8, 1935 which revealed reservist-defense women's cooperation. See especially February 15, p. 3; February 19, p. 2; March 3, p. 2; March 11, p. 1; March 26, p. 2; April 27, p. 2.

zational and educational activities on the hamlet level. The Patriotic Women's Association, under Home Ministry patronage, began to organize local branches and carry out policies to win rural support only after it first felt threatened by the army's group.[40]

By late 1937, the *aikoku fujinkai* had grown to almost three million members, but its membership was still only a little more than one-third its rivals. The Patriotic Women's Association, despite its prestigious history, Home Ministry support, and post-1931 efforts, could not successfully compete with the new organization because it lacked the local advantages of its rival. Home Ministry patronage guaranteed the patriotic women the assistance of prefectural and even of community governmental officials—the wife of the chief executive at each level usually served as *aikoku fujinkai* leader for that jurisdiction—but this local backing was strictly bureaucratic. The defense women's organization, on the other hand, had its own preexisting parallel structure on which to build. It maintained subdivisions like the *zaigō gunjinkai* at the hamlet level, and most potential members were the mothers, wives, and daughters of reservists and youth branch members. Family and community pressure enforced enrollment. It is no wonder that the membership grew to eight million in five years.[41]

The army-dominated organization also performed a much wider range of activities than the older, "upper class" group, despite *aikoku fujinkai* claims to the contrary. The defense women's association branches, usually in conjunction with community youth and reservists, provided labor for the families of men on active duty, helped prepare and perform the funerals of war dead, sponsored lectures and movies to disseminate military ideas, conducted all manner of savings, frugality, and antiluxury campaigns, helped at the army's annual draft examination and inspection of youths and reservists, sent off and greeted soldiers to and from the barracks, and performed war relief. Even the war relief efforts of the new organization differed from those of the old. When the Patriotic Women's Association members raised money from their dues to buy and send newspapers, cigarettes, and comfort packages to soldiers at the front, they did so on an imper-

40. *Kindaishi jiten*, p. 4; *Shimpan kyōdoshi jiten*, p. 1; Shimonaka Yasaburō, ed., *Yokusan kokumin undōshi* [The History of the National Imperial Rule Movement] (Tokyo, 1954), p. 1058; *Aikoku fujinkai yonjūnenshi* [The Forty Year History of the Patriotic Women's Association] (Tokyo, 1941), I, 478–484, 506–537; II, 67. Several interview respondents expressed the same feeling as three of the published sources, that the Patriotic Women's Association was an elitist organization.

41. *Aikoku fujinkai yonjūnenshi*, I, pp. 506–537, 830; *Kokubō fujinkai jūnenshi*, p. 159.

sonal level because of their lack of a local base. When the defense women performed the same function, they did it for men from their own communities. Thus, they could include pictures, letters, and other personal items. Even in the area of the older group's greatest success, the new group outperformed them. The army easily countered the *aikoku fujinkai*'s claim that its efforts were duplicated by the new organization; officers said that the military's association carried out a much wider range of activities. The older group's recognition of this and its efforts to compete after 1937 came too late.[42]

The final reason for the army association's triumph was the most damaging to the older group's efforts at competition—the army successfully claimed its organization had a "spiritual" mission which made it both superior and more Japanese than its rival. To paraphrase Colonel Nakamura Akihito, Army Ministry officer responsible for Defense Women's Association affairs, the older group's leaders completely misunderstood the true situation if they thought the purposes of the two organizations overlapped at all. The National Defense Women's Association, he wrote, aimed not only at fulfilling its activities—better run funerals, greater savings for investment in national projects, etc., it also aimed at spreading and deepening among women a belief in the uniquely Japanese "way of women," and in Japanese military values like "familism," the soldier's ethos, and the concepts of "good citizens are good soldiers" and "all the citizens are soldiers." A woman, by joining the army-dominated women's club, he concluded, fulfilled her military obligation as a citizen, served as a "home front soldier," and performed a spiritual mission for her people. How could a "materialistic" organization like the Patriotic Women's Association, with its better educated and more cosmopolitan membership, counter this kind of attack in the crisis and "spiritualistic" atmosphere of Japan in the 1930s? [43]

CONCLUSION

Between 1890 and 1935, the Choshu clique's leaders and their successors built a machine to mobilize the rural populace for total war in the face of growing threats to Japan's national unity. These army officers established four nationally centralized organizations with local village and hamlet branches and subdivisions for teenagers, adult men, and

---

42. *Aikoku fujinkai yonjūnenshi*, I, pp. 481, 831–832; *Kokubō fujinkai jūnenshi*, pp. 287–289, 345–346, 543–544.
43. *Aikoku fujinkai yonjūnenshi*, I, p. 830; *Kokubō fujinkai jūnenshi*, pp. 542–547.

women. The purpose of these groups—the reservist, youth and defense women's associations, and the youth schools—was to use the members' commitment to their agricultural hamlet and its values to mold patriotic "national villagers" who supported the army and its "rural" and military ideals. By 1935, the four organizations were in full operation and enrolled eleven to twelve million people.

III

THE ARMY, THE HAMLET, AND THE VILLAGE: The Structure and Membership of the Organizations

The Japanese sociologist, Suzuki Eitarō, wrote that although such bureaucratically controlled, centralized organizations as the school and police systems and youth and reservist associations helped develop a sense of national consciousness, they also gradually destroyed traditional hamlet identity among Japanese villagers. This occurred, he believed, because the government imposed the systems and associations from above; they, therefore, had no connections with the "natural village." [1] John Embree in his study of Suyemura stated that national not local everyday needs kept these organizations together and functioning. "If the government and school should cease to encourage them, they would die a natural death." [2] In the case of the youth, women's and reservist organizations, I am compelled to question the views of both of these eminent scholars. Military leaders established a judicious balance between local hamlet and village custom and national goals and interests in order to make their organizations an integral part of rural Japan and to popularize military, national, and nationalistic practices and values. The army's ideals reinforced local organizations and identity, and the latter in turn strengthened villagers' belief in the former.

The purpose of this chapter and the two that follow is to discuss the army's utilization of hamlet, village, and town structure and

---

1. Suzuki Eitarō, *Nihon nōson shakaigaku genri* [Principles of Japanese Rural Sociology] (Tokyo, 1940), pp. 361–362.
2. John Embree, *Suyemura: A Japanese Village* (Chicago, 1964), p. 170.

membership recruitment techniques, traditional local leadership, and a combination of nationally and locally oriented activities. The discussion will also include an analysis of the relative degree of success that the army leaders achieved in their efforts at indoctrination in national values through local institutions. It will be shown that in rural areas where a majority of the inhabitants supported themselves through agriculture, the reservist branch, youth association and school, and women's club had greater success than in cities. The only exceptions to the predominance of agrarian patterns of success were in those factories in which both the army and the company used the family and rural community models for factory organization.

In order to elucidate one aspect of how and why the military achieved rural and factory success, in this chapter I will treat the organizations' structure and membership. In the first part of the chapter, I will begin by tracing the military and its Home and Education Ministry collaborators' separate channels to rural Japan—that is, their Tokyo-local "chains of command." Then I shall turn to the exactly parallel ordering of the military's organizations with those of the rural community, even below the level of formal government and organizational command structure, and illustrate this point by introducing three case study communities. I shall make a similar comparison for the elementary schools and police to show how and why they differed from the army's organizations, and for cities to show how and why they differed from farm towns and villages. In the second part of the chapter, I will discuss the army system's membership and its significance by analyzing the degree to which an area was urban or rural, the percentage of the local labor force engaged in agriculture, and the extent to which qualified people joined the organizations under study. This analysis of the relationship of membership to the non-urban and agricultural nature of communities will lead to conclusions, based on questionnaires and interviews as well as published and documentary evidence, about why rural people joined more often than urban people and the effects of this membership pattern on army success. The chapter will also include a short discussion of factory branch membership, mostly urban, which provided the one exception to the pattern of greater rural and agricultural area success.

THE TOKYO-LOCAL CHAIN OF COMMAND

The army was able to direct the reservists and to influence the two youth and one women's civilian organizations locally through reservist leadership, and from above through the authority of its own sub-

Tokyo intermediate headquarters. Both the army leaders of the four organizations and their civilian colleagues established chains of command originating in Tokyo and descending to the county level, the highest "grass roots" headquarters, in order to impose some central control over the local scene. The two merged at the county-based headquarters, the highest level at which nonbureaucratic, local members or supporters of the organizations controlled their own activities.

The Home and Education Ministries' chain of command ran through local government. They maintained their highest regional headquarters at the highest level of local government, the prefecture. The Home Minister appointed the chief officials of each of the forty-seven prefectures, and these men and most of their subordinates were, in the twentieth century, career civil servants. The governor and his staff had overall local jurisdiction for the youth organizations and cooperated with the army in directing the defense women.[3]

The reservists who fell officially under army supervision, and the defense women and youths in some aspects of their activities, received parallel supervision from the military's divisional and regimental area commanders. The army divided the nation for military matters, after its 1925 reorganization, into fourteen division and fifty-seven regimental areas. None of the former and only twenty-five of the latter coincided exactly with prefectural boundaries, probably because of the military's desire to show its independence of civil government. For example, the Toyohashi regimental district, which had jurisdiction over one of our case study communities, Anjō, included parts of both Aichi and Shizuoka Prefectures. The Kofu district, into which fell Ōkamada-Futagawa and Katsunuma, the Yamanashi case study localities, regulated military matters in both Yamanashi and Kanagawa (Yokohama) Prefectures. Each regimental and divisional area was commanded by an active duty colonel and major general, respectively; through these two levels the Army Ministry and the General Staff in Tokyo asserted their official influence over the local, rural community.[4]

At Yamagata's behest, the government established counties (gun) below these forty-seven prefectures and fifty-seven (seventy-four before 1925) regimental areas. It was at this level that both the civil and military hierarchies came in contact with local leadership. Home Minister Yamagata, with his military belief in a tight chain of com-

---

3. Kumagai Tatsujirō, *Dainihon seinendanshi* (Tokyo, 1942), pp. 172–173, Appendix Five, pp. 166, 169; *Dainihon kokubō fujinkai jūnenshi* (Tokyo, 1943), pp. 266–267.

4. "Teikoku zaigō gunjinkai no gaiyō," *Kaikōsha kiji*, April 1937, p. 90; *Senyū*, 15 (1912), pp. i–ii; *Senyū*, 27 (1913), pp. i–ii; Naikaku kambō kirokuka, *Genkō hōrei shūran* [Collection of Existing Statutes and Laws] (Tokyo, 1927), Vol. II, Chapter 13, pp. 13–14, *Rikukaigun gunji nenkan*, 1938, pp. 190–195.

mand, urged this level on the other 1885–1889 local government planners; his self-government system included fifteen or twenty counties per prefecture—eighteen in Aichi and nine in Yamanashi, for example—between prefectural and town or village government.[5] This level seemed superfluous to many subsequent Home Ministry officials since all of the nation's nonurban land was simultaneously incorporated into towns and villages, and county officials performed few functions that other local officials could not. And yet, although the government officially abolished counties in 1926, shortly after the field marshal's death, these units continued to play a role in the structure of the army's organizations and in the popular mind at least until 1945.[6]

The reservist, youth, and defense women's associations all had county headquarters, and at this level actual members rather than government officials served as leaders. Since the town and village branch chiefs from the three organizations often chose their own county leaders, as we shall see in Chapter IV, this headquarters was the apex of a "grass roots" pyramid which had its base at the hamlet. Both the reservist and the youth associations continued to use the county headquarters after 1926. The women's group also created a county level of command even though it did not exist before the *gun* were abolished. The Education Ministry's youth training centers had no official county level headquarters because of the requirement that they parallel the elementary school system which had none, but they drew almost half of their teachers and many of their members from the local reserve and youth association branches which did have county headquarters. It was at this county level that the two "bureaucratic" chains of command from above merged and were linked to the "grass roots" pyramid from below.[7]

THE NATURE OF THE COOPERATIVE HAMLET

The army and the two civilian ministries maintained their separate vertical control mechanisms over the four organizations, but it was at the hamlet and village where the real socialization took place. The hamlet or *buraku* is the basic Japanese agricultural unit except for

5. *Zenkoku shichōsonjimei daikan* [A Guide to the Nation's City, Town, Village, and Hamlet Names] (Tokyo, 1951), pp. 130–135, 250–259.

6. Roger F. Hackett, *Yamagata Aritomo in the Rise of Modern Japan, 1838–1922* (Cambridge, 1971), p. 113; Kurt Steiner, *Local Government in Japan* (Stanford, 1965), pp. 48–49; Steiner points out that counties continued to be used as electoral districts after 1926. According to Richard Sims, the major political parties also continued to maintain county headquarters.

7. *Kokubō fujinkai jūnenshi*, p. 267; *Rikukaigun gunji nenkan*, 1938, pp. 507–511; Hugh L. Keenleyside and A. F. Thomas, *History of Japanese Education and Present Educational System* (Tokyo, 1937), p. 128.

the family or *ie* and has a long history dating back into deep antiquity. The hamlet is a cluster of houses, surrounded by its fields, where the residents work together to maintain the local irrigation system and roads, to use the common timber and grass lands, and to transplant and harvest their rice. The nature of these functions demands cooperation since, for example, very few farmers can build and maintain their own private irrigation system. After centuries of living together, Japanese farmers have developed communities in which each member depends on the others to help carry out functions essential to his agricultural livelihood.

Cooperation has its costs for the villager. Residents consider internal hamlet unity and harmony essential and demand conformity by all members to community standards. Nonconformity and nonparticipation in hamlet functions—i.e., individualism which threatens unity—leads to punishment. The collective community uses a wide variety of sanctions to enforce this conformity; these range from timely gossip to ostracism (*mura-hachibu*), a punishment which bars a family from receiving its neighbors' aid, and which if continued for a long time, can lead to its economic ruin. The hamlet also provides the narrow focus of its members' loyalty. Before the establishment of a modern, centralized government in 1868, a farmer's world was his hamlet, and his primary commitment was to the hamlet collectivity and its leaders. Although rural Japanese became increasingly nationalistic in the twentieth century, their hamlet identity remained strong well into the post-World War II period.[8]

When the Meiji government leaders came to power in the mid-nineteenth century, one of their first acts was to amalgamate the hamlets into a higher level of official local government, the village or *mura*. The Home Ministry's efforts at creating new and larger administrative organs experienced a number of vicissitudes and finally led to the formation of about 12,000 *mura* from the 76,000 Tokugawa era hamlets. It was not by accident that civil government officials called the new villages *mura*. They wanted to destroy the residents' hamlet consciousness and build larger loyalties, and *mura* was the term that cultivators used to describe their hamlets. (The official term for a hamlet, *buraku*, is a modern one and is still not in common use among Japanese farmers). It was at the new village level that all of the official governmental administrative organs were located. The village, not the hamlet, had a mayor, a village office and bureaucracy, a school, an

---

8. Robert Smith, "The Japanese Rural Community: Norms, Sanctions, and Ostracism," in Jack M. Potter et al., eds., *Peasant Society: A Reader* (Boston, 1967), pp. 246–255; Fukutake Tadashi, *Japanese Rural Society* (London and New York, 1967), pp. 81–95.

officially elected assembly, a formally established agricultural cooperative, and even the official local headquarters of the organizations under
study here.

In spite of the government's repeated efforts to merge hamlets into
larger administrative jurisdictions, and in spite of mass education,
military service and national news media, hamlet consciousness did not
lose its potency. In fact, in the name of orderly government, each of
the modern villages contained subdivisions which coincided exactly
with the former hamlets. As late as 1960, the boundaries of 76 percent
of these town and village subdivisions were the same as those of the
older hamlets, and the other one-quarter were formed either from
small clusters of them or by further subdivision.[9] The hamlet-district
and the family remained the center of most meaningful rural activity;
its members lived and cultivated together, elected representatives to
the village assembly, and maintained their separate farm cooperatives.
The army and civilian ministries with which it cooperated enhanced
their chances of success by employing the structure of rural community
when they created their reservist, youth, and women's organizations.
They established branches in the village, but subbranch units in its
hamlet divisions. It was in the hamlet that the members of the four
organizations performed their primary functions, and it was hamlet
cohesion and its sanctions which guaranteed 100 percent membership
of eligibles.

THREE CASE STUDY COMMUNITIES: ANJŌ, ŌKAMADA-FUTAGAWA, AND KATSUNUMA

Anjō, Ōkamada-Futagawa, and Katsunuma, the communities from
which most of our local evidence was gleaned, provide examples of
how the army used village-town structure for its own purposes and
also represent the kinds of communities in which the army worked.
The three locales are similar in that they were all predominately agricultural in the prewar epoch, but provide the necessary contrasts to
give us insights into the flexible nature of the army's efforts to reach
rural Japan. Each varied from the other in size, population, social and
economic structure, prosperity, extent of industrialization and com-
mercialization, and in the nature of its modern growth and development; and each had a slightly different pattern of army-hamlet articu-
lation and degree of success.

Anjō. Anjō remained from its formation in 1906 into the postwar era

---

9. Kurt Steiner, "Popular Political Participation and Political Development in
Japan: The Rural Level," in Robert E. Ward, ed., *Political Development in Modern
Japan* (Princeton, 1968), p. 236; Fukutake, *Japanese Rural Society*, pp. 81, 88–89.

a predominantly agricultural town and thus a fertile area for military-reservist organization. Anjō's inhabitants increased in number from 15,000 in 1906, to 23,000 in 1930, to 30,000 at the war's end, but in 1930, 55.5 percent of Anjō's population still supported itself by farming. Located in a small agricultural plain about fifteen miles southeast of the major industrial city of Nagoya, a plain watered by the Yahagi River and a large Meiji period irrigation system (*Meiji yōsui*), Anjō was in 1930 the major agricultural center of eastern Aichi Prefecture and the seat of Hekikai County. In Tokugawa times, the county had been a marginal agricultural area specializing in cotton cultivation for local mills. But the new irrigation system which allowed for wet rice cultivation (over 6000 hectares of uncultivated or dry field land were quickly converted to paddies), the development of new crops, local initiative, and government favor turned the area in the present century into the agriculturally prosperous "Japan Denmark" in which landlord exploitation and tenant unrest were relatively uncommon. In 1930, Anjō's population ranked sixth in Aichi, but since it alone did not have an urban history as a Tokugawa era castle, commercial or industrial town, but was an amalgamation of nineteen separate farm hamlets, Anjō remained uniquely an agricultural community. It was the only one of the six to be called a town rather than a city.

The mature Anjō of the 1930s included nineteen subdivisions. Sixteen of these coincided exactly with cooperative hamlets, one merged three traditionally related *buraku* into one district, and the other two centered on the areas nearest the Tokaido mainline railroad station built in Anjō in 1891.

Three of the army's four groups—the reservists, youth, and national defense women's associations—enhanced their chances of success because they followed this pattern exactly. They established both town-level headquarters located in the Anjō town hall, and hamlet subunits. Each of the three had nineteen subdivisions, the sixteen separate hamlets, the one merger of three small but associated hamlets, and the two new commercial communities. The three organizations performed most of their functions at this subtown hamlet level. Only the youth training centers, which the Education Ministry organized along the lines of the existing schools, differed. The town maintained five centers, one attached to each of its elementary schools, but even in this case attendance depended on hamlet solidarity and on pressure applied through the youth association branch's subunits.[10]

_____

10. Inagaki Koreasa, "Anjō-shiiku ni okeru jinkō kōsatsu" [An Analysis of Population in the Anjō City Area], *Anjō-shi kenkyū hōkoku* [A Report of Anjō City Re-

Ōkamada-Futagawa. Ōkamada and Futagawa, two small farming villages of about 1450 and 950 inhabitants respectively, were amalgamated for administrative purposes because of their size. They are located in the heart of Yamanashi Prefecture's agricultural basin about ninety miles west of Tokyo and are situated on the west bank of the Ara and Fuefuki Rivers where the two join just south of Kofu. Ōkamada and Futagawa occupy a small part of an agricultural region which until the railroad was built there at the turn of the century maintained an independent tradition and dialect from the nearby, but difficult to reach national capital. The inhabitants of these two Yamanashi villages depended even more on agriculture for their livelihood than the Anjōites. In 1930, 87.3 percent of their work force farmed. Farmers in the two villages raised a variety of dry field crops, particularly mulberry trees and thus silk cocoons, and only secondarily cultivated rice. (Only one-third of the local fields were paddies.) These Yamanashi villages differed from Anjō in another way; more of their inhabitants were tenants. Three-quarters of the Ōkamada-Futagawa farmers were full or part time tenants, and over two-thirds of the land was not owned by its cultivators. In Anjō, tenants farmed only 40 percent of the town's agricultural land.

Ōkamada-Futagawa, much smaller in area and population than Anjō, contained eleven *buraku,* but only five village subdivisions. There were two hamlets in Futagawa and they each became separate village subdistricts. The eight Ōkamada hamlets, on the other hand, because of their small area and size, merged into three subdistricts. Thus, after 1889, Ōkamada-Futagawa contained five subordinate divisions—one made up of four hamlets, one of three, one of two, and the two Futagawa districts of one each. Until 1938, when the government reorganized the community into eleven hamlet-sized districts, the military organizations mirrored the villages' structure, and operated through both hamlet and multi-hamlet districts. The reservist, youth, and defense women's association branches each contained five subunits, and the town maintained one youth (and elementary) school. Although Ōkamada is an exception to the rule of a one hamlet-one subdistrict organization, the nature of the military's local operations did not change. Because of Ōkamada's compactness, the organizations

---

search], 3 (1968), pp. 56–58; Naikaku tōkeikyoku, *Kokusei chōsa hōkoku: Shōwa gōnen* [The National Census Report for 1930] (Tokyo, 1933), Part IV, Aichi Prefecture Volume, pp. 4, 56; *Aichi-ken nōchishi* [A History of Agricultural Land in Aichi Prefecture] (Nagoya, 1957), I, pp. 312, 559–560; *Nōchi kaikaku temmatsu gaiyō* [A Summary of the Circumstances of Land Reform] (Tokyo, 1951), pp. 648–649; *Anjō-shi seinendanshi* (Anjō, 1962), II, p. 34.

used the traditional, cooperative "natural village" structure to reinforce their larger goals.[11]

Katsunuma. The third community, Katsunuma, in 1930 a small town of 2,550 people, is located to the east of Kofu in the hills overlooking the Yamanashi basin. As in Anjō and Ōkamada-Futagawa, Katsunuma's citizens specialized in agriculture—in 1930, 61.5 percent of its working force farmed. Unlike the other two communities, however, almost all of Katsunuma's farmers specialized in a single crop, one almost unique in Japan to their small region. Katsunuma lay in the heart of Japan's main grape growing and wine producing area. Of the twenty-seven farmers in my sample of thirty-four ex-reservists there, twenty-five raised grapes; the other two specialized in mulberry and silk cocoon production. The Katsunuma economy depended even more on tenant farming than did Ōkamada-Futagawa. In 1928, tenants cultivated fully 94.2 percent of the town's land. The area's tenant, antilandlord movement was active and strong.

Katsunuma was originally founded as a town in 1903 from five Meiji era villages, themselves consolidations of twelve Edo period communities. Thus, the amalgamated town in the 1930s included twelve subdistricts—the twelve cooperative hamlets. Moreover, all of the nine independent prewar villages, which the postwar national government merged into today's Katsunuma, had hamlet subdivisions as well. Hishiyama included six *buraku,* and Todoriki five, for example. All of the military's organizations except the youth training centers, here as elsewhere, maintained village level headquarters, and also hamlet subunits where they performed most of their duties. Thus the Katsunuma, Hishiyama, and Todoriki branches each had its own town or village headquarters, and twelve, six and five hamlet subunits respectively.[12] The army in all of these agricultural communities (and dozens of others, as local histories and questionnaires demonstrate) employed the traditional cooperative hamlet along with the administrative village as its basic unit for organizing local reservists, youths, and women.

---

11. *Kokusei chōsa hōkoku,* 1930, Vol. IV, Yamanashi Prefecture Volume, pp. 4, 66; *Ōkamada-Futagawa kōhō* [Public Report on Ōkamada and Futagawa], 46. An introduction to a report on Ōkamada-Futagawa social structure and landlord-tenant relations by Ariga Kizaemon and four other scholars shown to the author by one of the participants, Morioka Kiyomi, indicates a long series of antilandlord disputes in Ōkamada-Futagawa continuing until 1938 and beginning again with the postwar land reform.

12. *Kokusei chōsa hōkoku,* 1930, Part IV, Yamanashi Prefecture Volume, pp. 4, 62; *Katsunuma-chōshi* [The History of Katsunuma Town] (Kofu, 1962), pp. 12–13, 229. Interviews with the Deputy Mayor of Katsunuma and two former reservist branch chiefs; information from 35 Katsunuma questionnaire respondents. Not all

ANJŌ AS AN AGRICULTURAL TOWN

The comparability of the structural information from Anjō on the one hand, and Ōkamada-Futagawa and Katsunuma on the other, requires some justification in the face of what appear to be striking differences in population and in the nature of the communities. In the one case, Anjō was in 1930 a town of 23,000 inhabitants divided into 19 subdivisions; in the others, Ōkamada and Futagawa were villages with a combined population of 2,400 people in 11 hamlets, and Katsunuma contained over 2,500 residents in 12 hamlets. In 1930, each of Anjō's 21 subdivisions contained an average of over 1,000 people, on the surface too many to serve as the army's local cohesive group. Moreover, Anjō's population grew at a much more rapid rate than the other communities, an indication that it was losing its agricultural nature. The Anjō population grew by 26 percent between 1906 and 1920, and by 42 percent between 1920 and 1940. The number of Ōkamada-Futagawa inhabitants, on the other hand, increased by only 3.4 percent in the latter twenty years. The same was true within Hekikai County; Anjō's population increased more rapidly than any other community except highly industrialized Kariya. (See Tables 1, 2, and 3.) If, as I contend,

Table 1

ANJŌ POPULATION
GROWTH, 1906–1940 [a]

1906	14,739	
1920	18,520	0.0%
1930	22,965	24.0%
1935	24,206	30.7%
1940	26,355	42.3%

[a] Inagaki, "Anjō-shiiku ni okeru jinkō kōsatsu," p. 57; *Kokusei chōsa hōkoku*, 1920, Part II, Aichi Prefecture Volume, p. 4; 1930, Part IV, Aichi Prefecture Volume, p. 4; 1935, Part II, Aichi Prefecture Volume, p. 4; 1950, Part VII, Aichi Prefecture Volume, p. 28.

Table 2

ŌKAMADA-FUTAGAWA
POPULATION GROWTH,
1920–1940 [a]

1920	2,324	0.0%
1930	2,390	2.9%
1935	2,435	4.8%
1940	2,404	3.4%

[a] *Kokusei chōsa hōkoku*, 1920, Part II, Yamanashi Prefecture Volume, p. 4; 1930, Part IV, Yamanashi Prefecture Volume, p. 4; 1935, Part II, Yamanashi Prefecture Volume, p. 4; 1950, Part VII, Yamanashi Prefecture Volume, p. 32.

of the Katsunuma interview and questionnaire respondents had been members of Katsunuma's reservist branch. Some lived and served in the other nine villages which make up Katsunuma today.

the army achieved its greatest success at winning support for its values and goals in areas where it worked through compact, cooperative agricultural hamlets, how did it triumph in Anjō?

Anjō's usefulness to the army persisted throughout the modern period because it remained a primarily agricultural town of Anjō-ites in spite of its rapid growth. Anjō's population development began from a basis of comparatively large but sparsely populated hamlets and was spurred on at least partly by agricultural prosperity. Even when industrial production and commerce captured an increasingly larger share of the Anjō economy, and nonagricultural workers occupied a more important place in the work force in the 1920s and 1930s, the changes were grafted on to the agricultural foundations. Anjō remained a town predominantly made up of the native born, that is, those most likely to be involved in a primary industry like agriculture.

When the story of Anjō's modern history began in the early Meiji period, the constituent hamlets were larger than those in other areas of Japan because much of the land in the area was either uncultivated or not planted with paddy field rice, a crop that gives a high yield per acre and supports a dense population. If we compare Anjō's Hekikai County with Ōkamada-Futagawa's Naka-Koma County, we can see the contrast sharply. In 1950, 27 of 32 Naka-Koma villages were smaller than any village in Hekikai County. Ōkamada-Futagawa had an area of only 5.52 square kilometers for 11 hamlets; Anjō's area was seven times larger, but Anjō was made up of 19 constituent subdivisions (16 hamlets, one cluster of 3 hamlets, and 2 new downtown

Table 3

POPULATION GROWTH OF ANJŌ IN COMPARISON TO
SURROUNDING COMMUNITIES, 1920–1935 [a]

Community	1920	1935	Percentage of Increase
Hekikai County	140,831	175,482	24.6
Anjō Town	18,520	24,206	30.7
Kariya Town	8,648	19,980	131.0
Takaoka Village	9,398	10,543	12.1
Asahi Village	5,591	5,956	6.5

[a] *Kokusei chōsa hōkoku*, 1920, Part II, Aichi Prefecture Volume, p. 4; 1935, Part II, Aichi Prefecture Volume, p. 4.

Table 4

NUMBER OF MEMBERS AND PERCENTAGE OF WORK FORCE
IN AGRICULTURE IN ANJŌ AND SURROUNDING
COMMUNITIES, 1920, 1930, 1950 [a]

Community	1920		1930		1950	
Hekikai County	46,538	65.8%	48,034	58.6%	48,765	58.7%
Anjō Town	6,102	62.4%	6,508	55.6%	7,728	45.9%
Kariya Town	2,175	50.6%	2,001	27.8%	2,165	16.1%
Takaoka Village	4,599	90.5%	4,763	86.7%	6,134	73.3%
Asahi Village	1,816	62.6%	1,991	66.8%	(Amalgamated into Hekinan City, October 1, 1947)	

[a] *Kokusei chōsa hōkoku,* 1920, Part II, Aichi Prefecture Volume, p. 34; 1930, Part IV, Aichi Prefecture Volume, pp. 38, 56; 1950, Part VII, Aichi Prefecture Volume, p. 154.

districts). In other words, the average Anjō hamlet was three or four times larger than its Ōkamada-Futagawa counterpart, and it had considerably more room for expanding its agricultural work force.[13]

Anjō's agricultural work force was able to grow rapidly in the twentieth century, although at a slower rate than the population of the community as a whole. It grew by almost 27 percent between 1920 and 1950, faster than Ōkamada-Futagawa's total population growth (see Tables 4 and 5). The reason for this growth in agricultural work force must be attributed to the government's extensive irrigation projects, which allowed for land reclamation and rice cultivation, and because it also situated important agricultural stations and schools in the town. Since the irrigation system, stations and schools predated 1920, it seems safe to assume that the number of farmers in Anjō grew dramatically before 1920. Anjō developed from being a sparsely populated, marginal agricultural area in the 1870s to being the agricultural center of eastern Aichi in the 1930s. Even in 1946, more than half of Anjō's population still farmed part time.[14]

13. *Kokusei chōsa hōkoku,* 1950, Part VII, Aichi Prefecture Volume, pp. 31–32; Yamanashi Prefecture Volume, p. 34.

14. *Aichi-ken nōchishi,* I, p. 312; *Aichi-ken tōkeisho* [Aichi Prefecture Statistical Handbook], 1946, pp. 86–87. The amount of paddy land under cultivation in Hekikai County expanded from 4,900 acres in 1877 to 31,850 acres in 1909.

Table 5
PERCENTAGE OF INCREASE IN NUMBER OF MEMBERS OF WORK
FORCE IN AGRICULTURE IN ANJŌ AND SURROUNDING
COMMUNITIES, 1920–1930, 1920–1950 [a]

Community	1920–1930	1920–1950
Hekikai County	3.2%	4.7%
Anjō Town	6.7%	26.6%
Kariya Town	−8.0%	−0.4%
Takaoka Village	3.6%	33.3%
Asahi Village	9.6%	no data

[a] *Kokusei chōsa hōkoku*, 1920, Part II, Aichi Prefecture Volume, p. 34; 1930, Part IV, Aichi Prefecture Volume, pp. 38, 56; 1950, Part VII, Aichi Prefecture Volume, p. 154.

Table 6
NUMBER AND PERCENTAGE OF POPULATION BORN IN
TOWN OR VILLAGE OF RESIDENCE IN ANJŌ AND
SURROUNDING COMMUNITIES, 1930 [a]

Community	Total Population	Number born in Community	Percentage
Anjō Town	22,965	14,591	63.5
Kariya Town	14,779	7,128	48.2
Takaoka Village	10,093	7,593	75.2
Asahi Village	5,878	4,377	74.5

[a] *Kokusei chōsa hōkoku*, 1920, Part II, Aichi Prefecture Volume, p. 34; 1930, Part IV, Aichi Prefecture Volume, pp. 38, 56; 1950, Part VII, Aichi Prefecture Volume, p. 154.

Anjō also maintained a solid agricultural core in its population at the same time as the percentage of community members not involved in agriculture grew steadily in the prewar epoch. The town in the 1930s might best be labelled a dual "agricultural and industrial-residential" community. Population density statistics for each Anjō subdivision for 1960 to 1965 indicate that the town's population density can be viewed as a series of concentric circles, with the most densely populated areas near the national railway's station, the next most densely populated areas surrounding them, and the areas of sparsest population at the extremities. The only exception to this rule is one area of moderately dense population in the north near the Nagoya Electric Railway's Shin-Anjō (Imamura) Station. The reason for this pattern of population growth in Anjō is two-fold: both the most important industrial and commercial enterprises and the railroad station are located in the central districts. These areas support practically no agriculture since, as we have seen, they were uninhabited when the government built the station there in 1891. The circle surrounding these two districts is made up of a series of Tokugawa era villages that increased in population as residential areas because of their proximity both to Anjō's factories and to her transportation facilities. The outside ring of hamlets remained relatively sparsely populated because of the inconvenience to factory and transportation. Thus the two inner, nonhamlet districts have practically no agricultural work force; the secondary ring has a combination of farmers and industrial workers; and the outer group has more farmers than laborers. There is no reason to believe that this 1960–1965 pattern did not hold true in the 1930s, when there was probably a much higher percentage of farmers outside the two downtown districts.[15] Because of this pattern of population growth in Anjō, the nonagricultural population per hamlet increased after 1891 in comparison to Ōkamada-Futagawa. At the same time, the army still found a significant 55 percent—and if one excluded the two Meijis and counted only the former hamlets, two-thirds—of the population that farmed. These Anjō agriculturalists provided as fertile a field for army indoctrination as farmers did elsewhere, in Ōkamada-Futagawa, for example (it was in downtown Kita and Minami Meiji that both of Anjō's factory branches were located).

Anjō also continued to be primarily a town of "Anjō-ites" until after World War II. The 1930 census reveals that almost two-thirds of its population had been born there, a very high percentage for a community whose population had grown as rapidly as Anjō's. (See Table 6). Since the least mobile parts of the population are most likely to support themselves through primary occupations—in this noncoastal town's case, agriculture—it is fair to conclude that an inordinately high percentage of these Anjō "home towners" farmed. It is my contention that the army had its greatest indoctrination success among farmers whose families had long histories of residence in the same community. Since all "villagers" did "vounteer" for all voluntary organizations for which they were eligible, Anjō's hamlets provided the army with a solid foundation for socialization.

---

15. Inagaki, "Anjō-shiiku ni okeru jinkō kōsatsu," p. 61.

THE FAILURE OF THE SCHOOLS AND POLICE
TO USE THE HAMLET

It is striking that the military used the hamlet in Anjō, Ōkamada-Futagawa, Katsunuma and elsewhere as the basis for its local arms, but that no other national group did so, unless it worked through the army's organizations. Professor Suzuki's belief that a wide gap existed between national organizations and local communities is valid for other centralized organizations, but not for the army's. The normal division of the nonmilitary local organizations was between those related to the inhabitants' everyday lives, and the nationally centralized ones. The former operated at the cooperative hamlet or even subhamlet level, the latter did not.

The nationally centralized schools, for example, drew on students from the entire administrative village (mura), and used nonhamlet members as teachers (leaders). Even when a town such as Anjō maintained more than one elementary school, the districts were much larger than a single hamlet area. Anjō had nineteen subdivisions, but only five elementary schools. The teachers served in a national bureaucracy, frequently came from other communities to teach in the village and, even if they were employed in their own village, by necessity taught students from other hamlets. Although local teachers often scorned the local "rustics" and strived to make them more cosmopolitan, there is no reason to believe that educational authorities intentionally ignored hamlet structure. One could argue that it would have been financially disastrous to organize schools by hamlet since none had enough students to fill a whole school. Whatever the reason—teacher disregard for local customs, the teacher's role as an outsider, the realities of financing schools, or the educational goal of creating broader national loyalties—it is clear that the school system did not use local community structure and leadership and did not perform community service activities to the extent that the reservists', women's, and youth associations did.[16]

John Embree observed that the national organizations under study depended on the schools. It is true that the educational system complemented the army's organizations in performing patriotic education. Ethics courses and nationalistic content in other subjects held an important place in the schools' curriculum. There is no question but that most rural Japanese considered education to be desirable and sent

---

16. Steiner, *Local Government in Japan*, p. 50; Ronald S. Anderson, *Japan: Three Epochs of Modern Education* (Washington, D.C., 1959), pp. 73–78; Embree, *Suyemura*, pp. 65–68, 165; Suzuki, *Nihon nōson shakaigaku genri*, pp. 361–363.

their children to the schools, and thus to their indoctrination network, even though the schools did not operate like the army's organizations at the hamlet level. Moreover, the schools were not entirely isolated from the traditional community. They fit themselves into the pattern of hamlet life through cooperation with the reservist, women's and youth associations, and particularly by the joint elementary school-reservist efforts at running the youth training centers and youth schools (which will be discussed in detail in Chapters IV and V). It would be ludicrous to say that the school system depended for its continued existence on its cooperation with the army's hamlet-based organizations; but it is also incorrect to say that the national organizations existed only because of the support of the schools and local government. The army's local organizations utilized the basic units of rural Japan much more thoroughly than the schools did, and by doing so carved out a position independent of the schools.[17]

The local police system is a second example of a nationwide hierarchy established without official village or hamlet organization. The policeman was a national, not a local representative, responsible only to central authority, and he did not necessarily have roots in the area where he served. Even when a local native functioned as policeman, his jurisdiction always included many hamlets and even a number of administrative villages; he had to perform his duties in hamlets other than his own. There are even reported cases of policemen visiting a village as infrequently as once a week and hamlets only when crimes were committed, as in the case of Suyemura. In other words, the policeman was even less an integral part of the hamlet (and village) scene than the local school principal and his teachers. As John Embree wrote, "For the most part the *mura* can get along pretty well without a prefectural policeman." [18]

Policemen were not needed in hamlets and villages because local internal cohesion and social sanctions maintained order and obviated the need for close surveillance and because the youth and reservist branches undertook many local policing functions. Unless a hamlet as a whole caused unrest, as they did occasionally when they rose against landlords, the police had little fear that villagers would commit crimes in their own villages. Even the danger of outsiders causing trouble was lessened considerably because of reservist and youth group police and disaster relief duties. Local youth and town and village histories and the activities section of *Comrades in Arms* are replete with examples of young men's and reservists' branches functioning in police roles,

17. Embree, *Suyemura*, p. 170.
18. Embree, *Suyemura*, p. 171; Steiner, *Local Government in Japan*, p. 50.

particularly in times of crisis. While we shall discuss this activity of the army's organizations in detail in Chapter V, one example of how a hamlet and its reservists suppressed a violent uprising in one community will illustrate both why the police were not compelled to act frequently at the local level and why the army's organizations were more a part of the local scene than the policemen were.

In Tsubota Village (a one-hamlet village) on the island of Miyake, a hundred or more transient sea-weed diving girls from Cheju Island went on strike for higher wages in the summer of 1937. The mayor made every effort to settle the dispute (undoubtedly not to the benefit of the Korean women), and quickly became the target of the women's wrath. He escaped his interview with them only after they had attacked him and torn off his clothes. The mayor, on his return to the village office, immediately consulted with the *zaigō gunjinkai* branch chief (it was he who reported the incident to the author) concerning the use of reservists to suppress the disturbance. The chief responded that he thought reservist intervention would be inappropriate (soldiers attacking women?) and recommended the fire department, of which he was also head, to do the job. The mayor approved and the fire department intervened and ended the dispute by deporting the diving girls. What is striking about this incident is that in Tsubota reservists had as one of their official duties fighting fires. Thus the men who put down the disturbance were the village's reservists led by their branch chief, but wearing different "hats." In other words, in Tsubota, as elsewhere, the reserve branch was so tightly integrated into the local scene that it was essentially an age-group organization for men between the ages of twenty and forty. The police did not need to station officers in the village or hamlet because the village and hamlet, through the men who served in the army's organizations, maintained local order for the police. Both the schools and the police benefitted from hamlet cohesiveness without maintaining any official headquarters in the hamlet. They would have been less able to use the *buraku* if the army had not organized reservists, young men, and later women.

THE ARMY AND THE CITY: A COMPARISON
WITH RURAL JAPAN

The army's local organizations had less success in using the structure of urban society than they did with its rural counterpart. The major reason for this difference was the larger area and population of city subdivisions, the army's failure to utilize all of the available structural organs, and the looser internal integration of urban society. Tokyo,

Osaka, Nagoya, Kyoto, Yokohama, and Kobe, the six largest cities were divided into wards (*ku*) with a population of about two hundred thousand people each as compared to twenty thousand for even the largest agricultural communities like Anjō.[19] (These wards in turn were further subdivided into precincts [*machi, chō,* etc.]). Until the mid-1930s, each Tokyo ward contained only one reserve association branch; thus, each branch contained too many members to be effective. At the same time this large enrollment was not evidence that a high percentage of eligibles belonged. The average Tokyo branch had over 5,000 men, but only 15 to 20 percent of the 20–40-year-olds in the area. (See Tables 7 and 8). These immense branches were divided, like their rural counterparts, into subunits. They were not organized, however, one subunit per precinct, but rather one per three-to-fifteen precincts each. Tokyo's Shiba Ward branch, for example, enrolled 8,600 members, but they functioned in only six subdistricts (plus one factory and one naval detachment). More men served in each subunit than in most rural branches, and, since each drew on men from at least ten precincts and thus a wide geographic area, the basic unit of urban reservist organization did not reach the city's "asphalt roots." If the reserve association's leaders had further subdivided the *han* (the subbranch reservist unit) into one precinct-sized unit, they would have brought the organization to the basic urban subdivision. From 1933 to 1936, the leadership partly rectified its error by making each of these multi-precinct subunits into a separate branch, but the new branches contained no subdistricts at all, and each still enrolled more members than most rural branches.[20]

Smaller cities had similar problems. Although they contained no wards, they generally were made up of precincts. The organizations did not exploit the geographic possibilities of this urban structure any more than in large cities. Ichinomiya, a textile manufacturing city near Nagoya with more than 100 precincts, for example, contained six reservist branches, two in factories and four geographically based. The latter four branches were set up by dividing the city into four equal parts, with no more consideration for existing city organization than in

---

19. See the census volumes (*Kokusei chōsa hōkoku*) for 1920, 1925, 1930, and 1935. Population data are broken down into ward subtotals for the six largest cities. The statistics are presented on a community-wide basis for villages, towns, and other cities.

20. *Shiba-kushi* [The History of Shiba Ward] (Tokyo, 1938), pp. 922–924. See also *Hongō-kushi* [The History of Hongō Ward] (Tokyo, 1937), p. 977; *Kyōbashi-kushi* [The History of Kyōbashi Ward] (Tokyo, 1942), II, p. 916; *Nihombashi-kushi* [The History of Nihombashi Ward] (Tokyo, 1937), II, p. 902; *Azabu-kushi* [The History of Azabu Ward] (Tokyo, 1941), p. 716; etc.

Tokyo. Each branch had multi-precinct subdivisions but, as we shall see later, was not organized closely enough to the city's basic neighborhoods to be as effective as the company- and plant-centered factory branches. The Ichinomiya circumstances were mirrored in other small and medium-sized industrial cities like Ōtsu, Ashikaga, Fukui, and Matsumoto.[21]

Although the large membership of urban branches, the absence of small subdivisions, and the army's mistakes may have hindered its success at using the city's structure for socialization purposes, the major drawback sprung from the nature of urban society itself. The needs for harmony and cooperation did not exist in city neighborhoods to the extent that they did in the country, and this made urban areas harder to use. In villages, where almost everyone in the community made his living the same way, at the same place, and by using the same irrigation system, farmers had to work together or they failed. In cities, where neighborhoods were largely residential and most people commuted elsewhere to work, cooperation became less important. The rural cohesiveness, moreover, was reinforced because most local families had lived in the hamlet for generations or even centuries. Conversely, because of Japan's rapid modern urbanization, most city dwellers were newcomers to their communities who had not developed the same network of interrelationships that their rural brethren had.[22]

The occupational similarity, the proximity of residence and farm, the need for reciprocal help, as well as the family-centered nature of Japanese agriculture allowed rural reservists to carry out a number of community-oriented activities. Farmer-reservists could win prestige by assisting in rice transplanting for a local family with a son-farmhand on active duty. It is hard to imagine an urban branch sending its members to aid a neighborhood soldier's father when he worked in an office at Mitsui Trading Company, or on the assembly line at Toyota

---

21. *Ichinomiya-shishi* [The History of Ichinomiya City] (Ichinomiya, 1939), II, pp. 910–913; *Matsumoto-shishi* [The History of Matsumoto City] (Matsumoto, 1933), II, pp. 365–368; *Fukui-shishi* [The History of Fukui City] (Fukui, 1941), II, pp. 234–236; *Shin Ōtsu-shishi* [The New History of Ōtsu City] (Ōtsu, 1962), I, 262–263; *Ashikaga-shishi* [The History of Ashikaga City] (Ashikaga, 1928–1929), II, pp. 1079–1080.

22. In 1930, 71.3 percent of the inhabitants of Ōkamada-Futagawa, and 58.1 percent of those of Katsunuma had been born in their communities. This compared with 41.1 percent for Ichinomiya City, and 31.8 percent and 41.2 percent for Tokyo's Hongō and Shiba Wards, respectively. The reader must remember that the Hongō and Shiba Ward figures represent that percentage of the ward's residents born in all of Tokyo, not in the wards themselves alone. *Kokusei chōsa hōkoku*, 1930, Part IV, Yamanashi Prefecture Volume, pp. 29–31; Aichi Prefecture Volume, p. 36; Tokyo Volume, p. 33.

Motors. And even more important, the cohesiveness and interrelation-ships of a rural hamlet enforced complete participation on all eligible people in all of the army's organizations. The greater freedom of urban life allowed potential members more frequent opportunities to decide for themselves whether or not they wanted to serve, and thus often not to serve.

The urban neighborhoods that may have differed from this pattern were the older shopkeeper or small-scale industrial neighborhoods where cohesiveness was important, although certainly less so than in rural communities. Data on these neighborhoods is difficult to isolate for study, however, because most membership and census data is presented on a ward or city-wide level. Thus, I cannot determine whether or not more men served in the reserve association, for example, in older Tokyo than in newer, "bedroom," neighborhoods. One can imagine that people living in even these traditional urban neighbor-hoods must have felt the unsettling effects of steady migration from the country, of alternate employment opportunities leading to the separation of residence and place of work and to the demise of family enterprise, and of new, imported ideas and values, more quickly and pervasively than even the residents of Anjō's agricultural hamlets. The impact of the army and its organizations on urban Japan is a subject that requires future investigation.

RURAL AND URBAN MEMBERSHIP COMPARED

To understand this rural-urban dichotomy more clearly, it is crucial to study the membership of the organization as well as the structure. Membership figures show that farmers joined much more often than urbanites. An explanation of why this was so will reinforce the thesis that the army used traditional rural values and institutions to build itself a rural basis of support and to popularize military and national-istic values.

Reservist Membership

Table 7 compares reservist membership for seventy-eight communities throughout Japan over a nineteen-year period with census data for 20–39-year-old males from the 1920, 1925, 1930, and 1935 Japanese national censuses. Since twenty to forty were the age limits of re-servist eligibility, one can gain a clear idea of how many men in this age bracket belonged. There are two qualifications, however. One percent of those in the age group served on active military duty for two years and did not join the zaigō gunjinkai until they returned home from the barracks at age twenty-two; the other 20–22-year-old men who passed the draft physical but had not been drafted could join immediately. This one percent on active duty must be added to those who served in the military socialization system during these two decades. And even more significant is the fact that, since only about 60 to 70 percent of the 20-year-olds passed the annual conscription physical examination, the 28 percent Japan-wide reserve association membership figure means that 45 to 50 percent of the eligibles (adjusting for the one percent on active duty) joined the *zaigō gunjinkai* each year and the 57 percent village figure means that almost everyone joined. Other evidence supports this conclusion. In Anjō, 91 percent of the men with reservist obligations enrolled in the *zaigō gunjinkai*

Table 7

PERCENTAGE OF 20–39-YEAR-OLD MEN ENROLLED IN THE
RESERVIST ASSOCIATION COMPARED TO PERCENTAGE OF
LABOR FORCE IN AGRICULTURE, 1921–1939 [a]

	Percentage of labor force in agriculture (1930 census)	Percentage of 20–39-year-old men enrolled in Reservist Association
15 Villages, 1921–1939	77	57
20 Counties, 1921–1939	71	45
Anjō Town, 1927	56	38 (42) [b]
Anjō Town, 1939	56	42
24 Towns, 1921–1939	40	34
9 Cities (shi), 1921–1939	7	23
10 Wards, (ku), 1921–1939	0.5	19
National, 1931	48	28
National, 1936	48	28

[a] The data in Table 7 are drawn from the following communities: Asahi, Meiji, Miwa, Mutsumi, Takaoka, and Tsukude Villages in Aichi, Fujita, Shiozaki, and Yutaka Villages in Yamanashi, Nirahama Village in Gumma, Kami-Katagiri Village in Nagano, Nojiri Village in Toyama, Tawashi Village in Gifu, Miyoshi Village in Okayama, and Tonga Village in Hiroshima; Higashi-Kasugai, Nishi-Kamo, Yana, Hazu, and Hekikai Counties in Aichi, Kita-Koma, Naka-Koma, and Kita-Tsuru Counties in Yamanashi, Gumma County in Gumma, Hamana County in Shizuoka, Kasai County in Hyōgo Asaguchi, Atetsu and Tsukubo Counties in Okayama, Numaguma County in Hiroshima, Hino County in Tottori, Yatsuka County in Shimane, Ogi County in Saga, and Aso and Kamoto Counties in Kumamoto; Anjō, Asai, Isshiki, Iwatsu, Kariya, Koromo, Nishio and Ono Towns in Aichi, Katsunuma and Uenohara Towns in Yamanashi, Mizusawa Town in Iwate, Ōmama Town in Gumma, Kaibara Town in Hyōgo, Kawachi, Konkō, Niimi, Takashima, Tsurashima and Yori

in 1918.[23] The data show clearly that the less urban and the more agricultural a community was, the higher the percentage of local men who belonged to the reservist association. Villagers led in the percentage of participation; counties which usually included one or two towns as well as villages followed; towns and cities came next; and Tokyo wards (and in our sample, one Nagoya ward), by far the least agricultural, came last.

One important reason more rural men joined was that more were eligible. The *zaigō gunjinkai* was the only organization under study here which maintained an entrance requirement other than age or sex; one had to pass the army's conscription physical examination to be eligible for membership. Three to ten percent more rural than urban 20-year-olds met this requirement. Rural branches had a larger number

---

Towns in Okayama, Kakemachi Town in Hiroshima, Nogata Town in Fukuoka, and Kutami, Ueki and Yumaka Towns in Kumamoto; Hakodate, Ashikaga, Matsumoto, Fuchū, Shizuoka, Fukui, Ichinomiya, Okayama and Kurashiki Cities; Arakawa, Azabu, Edogawa, Hongō, Koishikawa, Kyōbashi, Nihombashi, Shiba and Shitaya Wards in Tokyo, and Naka Ward in Nagoya.

The percentage of membership fell slightly in each category of community in the 1930s compared to the 1920s. This is probably attributable to the declining percentage of eligibles—that is, of those who actually passed the physical examination and thus could join the reservist association.

b The 1927 Anjō figures, taken from the records of that town's geographically-based reservist branch, do not include figures for factory branches. According to the 1939 data, drawn from county-wide records, four percent of Anjō's reservists were organized into two textile factory branches. The figure in parentheses in Table 7 thus represents the percentage of Anjō reservists for 1927 if the same percentage of reservists served in factory branches in 1927 as in 1939.

The factory branch figures present another problem which must be discussed: it is unlikely that all of the factory worker-reservists actually resided in the same community in which they worked. If they commuted to and from another city, town, or village, they were listed as residents of one place in the census data, and as reservists in another in the membership figures. This is particularly a problem in discussing an industrial city such as Anjō's neighbor, Kariya. The geographical Kariya reservist branch in 1939 enrolled 622 members, 28 percent of that city's 20–39-year-olds. Eight hundred sixty-one reservists served in Kariya factory branches. If all of these men lived in Kariya, fully 68 percent of its 20–39-year-old men were reservists. Since that high a percentage of men was not eligible for membership (because the draft examination passage rate was under 68 percent), we cannot possibly reach this conclusion. But we do know that industrial Kariya drew more workers from surrounding communities than it provided them. We can thus surmise that a good percentage of the Kariya factory reservists lived elsewhere. Conversely, Anjō, one of Kariya's bedrooms, probably had 1 to 2 percent more reservists than the 1927 and 1939 figures revealed. If this analysis is correct for Anjō and Kariya, and I believe it is, membership percentages for other cities and wards, all of which include factory branch statistics, may be even slightly lower, and that for some towns and villages slightly higher.

23. *Zaigō gunjin meibo* [Register of All Anjō Reservists], 1918; *Anjō-chōshi* [The History of Anjō Town] (Anjō, 1919), pp. 123–124.

of eligible men to draw on and thus enlisted a higher percentage of 20–40-year-olds as members.

The men eligible for active duty and the *zaigō gunjinkai* were selected on the basis of a series of tests, the most important of which was a physical examination. The government required that all male Japanese be examined unless they had previously enlisted in the army or navy, or had received a temporary educational deferment. All 20-year-old men were under obligation to report on certain days each spring for this test of their eligibility to serve. Army doctors came to the community, and assisted by local reservists and after 1932, defense women, ranked the examinees in five categories: A(*kō*), B-1(*otsu-ichi*), B-2(*otsu-ni*), C(*hei*), and D(*tei*). Those in the first three groups qualified for service (although only about one-quarter of them actually served before 1937); those in the C category qualified for emergency service; and those in the D category were ineligible for any military participation whatsoever.[24]

Only those who passed with grades of A, B-1, or B-2, that is, those qualified to serve in the army, were eligible to serve in the reserve association as well. These three categories in the 1920s comprised about 72 or 73 percent of all examinees, the C group about 20 percent, and the failing group about 7 to 8 percent; in the 1930s, only a little over 60 percent passed with A and B grades, about 30 percent with C, and 10 percent failed completely.[25]

As Table 8 indicates, 3.4 percent more youths from the seven most agricultural prefectures in 1925, 3.6 percent more in 1930, and 3.0 percent more in 1935 passed the conscription examination than their peers in the seven least agricultural ones. The percentage of 20-year-olds who passed the examination from seven rural-urban and seven urban-rural prefectures falls between the two extremes in these years. It would seem that this evidence does not support the 3 to 10 percent rural-urban differential mentioned above; but, as the labor force figures demonstrate, this is because much of the population of even the highly urban prefectures lived outside the cities. Fully one-quarter of their work force still made its living in agriculture. Thus we must look at strictly urban figures. There are available data for four Tokyo wards in which less than one percent of the work force was in agriculture. These data indicate that only 56.6 percent of the examinees passed in the years from 1926 to 1935—56.8 percent in Nihombashi

---

24. *Rikukaigun gunji nenkan*, 1937, p. 330.
25. *Rikugunshō tōkei nenkan* [The Army Ministry Statistical Yearbook], 1925, pp. 10–11; 1932, pp. 10–11; 1935, pp. 10–11.

Table 8

PERCENTAGE OF DRAFT EXAMINATION A AND B CATEGORY
EXAMINEES COMPARED TO PERCENTAGE OF LABOR
FORCE IN AGRICULTURE BY PREFECTURES [a]

	Percentage of labor force in agriculture, 1930	Percentage of A and B examinees		
		1925	1930	1935
7 most urban prefectures: Tokyo, Kanagawa, Kyoto, Fukuoka, Hyōgo, Aichi, Osaka	29.2	69.7	60.0	59.8
7 urban-rural prefectures: Nagasaki, Nara, Hiroshima, Yamaguchi, Ishikawa, Shizuoka, Fukui	50.2	71.9	60.8	61.4
7 rural-urban prefectures: Kumamoto, Saitama, Tochigi, Yamanashi, Shiga, Miyagi, Tokushima	60.6	71.7	62.1	62.2
7 most rural prefectures, excluding Okinawa: Kagoshima, Ibaragi, Iwate, Shimane, Akita, Tottori, Fukushima	67.8	73.1	63.6	62.8

[a] *Rikugunshō tōkei nenkan,* 1925, pp. 10–11; 1930, pp. 10–11; 1935, pp. 10–11. Okinawa maintained a larger percentage of its work force in agriculture than any other prefecture, but ranked consistently near the bottom in the draft physical examination success. It has been excluded from consideration here, however, because it has been integrated into Japan proper only in modern times, and because it had a small population and marginal economy. It presents too many variables for adequate comparison with the prefectures of the four main islands. Karafuto, another late addition which was also included in the sources from which this data was drawn, has also been excluded.

Ward, 56.8 percent in Shiba Ward, 58.7 percent in Kyōbashi Ward, and 54.2 percent in Hongō Ward.[26] When we compare these figures with the national average of 63.4 percent and with the seven most rural prefectures' average of 66.9 percent over the same period, we find that the difference between the almost completely nonagricultural wards and the nation as a whole and the rural areas is 6.8 percent and 10.3 percent, respectively. Thus one may conclude that rural youths tended to be healthier and to pass the draft physical examination more often than their urban counterparts and that the degree of difference fell between 3 and 10 percent. Part of the advantage reservist leaders had in recruiting members in agricultural compared to urban communities was that they had more eligibles from which to draw. But the greater number of eligibles does not explain why the reservist, young men's and young women's associations all recruited many more rural than urban members. Before discussing other reasons for the army's and all of the organization's rural success, therefore, let us look at rural-urban membership data for the youth association, youth training centers-schools, and women's organization, which mirrored the *zaigō gunjinkai*'s pattern of greater rural success in recruiting members.

YOUTH ASSOCIATION MEMBERSHIP

Table 9 indicates that, as in the case of the reservists' organization, more eligible young men in rural than in urban Japan joined the Greater Japan Youth Association. Since the organization had no entrance requirement other than age and sex, all males between the ages of twelve to sixteen and twenty-five to forty-two were eligible. In 1935, 2,704,248 young men, about 40 percent of all eligibles, belonged.[27] In both 1930 and 1935, and as other evidence shows, in every year between 1930 and 1941, urban prefectures enrolled the lowest percent of eligibles, and the branches in major cities within these prefectures achieved even less success in attracting young men. (See Table 10). Only the Osaka organization of those in the four largest cities attracted more than 17 percent of its city's youth, and even in that case the city fell 7 percent behind the rest of the prefecture. The youth association from the most rural prefecture, Kagoshima, apparently enlisted all of its young men in the youth association. Even highly agricultural Chiba, although maintaining a relatively low

---

26. *Nihombashi-kushi*, II, pp. 896–897; *Shiba-kushi*, pp. 900–901, 904; *Kyōbashi-kushi*, II, pp. 904–905; *Hongō-kushi*, pp. 966–972.

27. Kumagai, *Seinendanshi*, Appendix III, p. 64; Hugh Borton, *Japan Since 1931: Its Political and Social Development* (New York, 1940), p. 34.

Table 9

YOUTH ASSOCIATION MEMBERSHIP [a]

Prefecture	Age limits	Percentage of labor force in agriculture	Percentage of age-group eligibles who became members	
		1930	1930	1935
Nationwide				39.71
5 urban prefectures:				
Tokyo	15–25	6.5	12.7	17.2
Osaka	12–25	10.5	23.5	30.4
Kyoto	15–25	26.1	26.5	26.1
Fukuoka	14–25	33.3	22.7	23.7
Aichi	14–25	36.6	28.8	24.2
5 rural and urban prefectures:				
Yamaguchi	14–25	51.0	37.4	37.5
Toyama	13–25	55.2	70.9	70.4
Okayama	15–25	58.5	58.6	55.6
Shiga	14–25	60.3	46.9	46.2
Yamanashi	13–25	60.6	40.8	38.3
5 rural prefectures:				
Kumamoto	13–25	61.7	40.3	40.8
Aomori	15–25	61.8	44.4	57.6
Chiba	14–25	62.7	33.5	32.8
Yamagata	13–25	63.6	43.4	39.0
Kagoshima	16–25	71.2	67.5	103.7

[a] Kumagai, *Seinendanshi*, Appendix III, pp. 61–64. These fifteen prefectures were chosen because of the comparability of data. In these the maximum age for eligibility of membership was twenty-five years. Other prefectures, especially more rural ones, might have yielded more fruitful comparisons, but were not chosen because most had widely ranging upper-age limits. Variations in age limits at the bottom of the membership scale appear in our sample, but do not skew the results significantly since most, if not all, teenagers who planned to join did so as soon as they became eligible. At the top, however, especially in those prefectures with very high maximum age limits (35 to 42 years old in some cases), many men left the youth association before reaching the required resignation age. Thus accurate comparisons with census data are impossible.

Kagoshima Prefecture, needless to say, did not have a 1935 membership of over 100 per cent of the eligibles. Since the census includes only the following relevant age categories: 15–19, 20, 21–24, the 16–24-year figure for that prefecture had to be reached on the basis of an arbitrary decision that one-fifth of the 15–19-year-olds in Kagoshima were 15. This, as well as the slightly different reporting periods for the two types of data, probably accounts for the high percentage.

75

Table 10

YOUTH ASSOCIATION MEMBERSHIP IN THE NATION'S FOUR MAJOR
CITIES AND THEIR PREFECTURES, 1936 [a]

Prefecture	City	Prefectural percentage of membership	City percentage of membership	Prefecture exclusive of city percentage of membership
Tokyo	Tokyo	17.2	15.6	51.8
Osaka	Osaka	32.7	31.1	38.6
Kyoto	Kyoto	26.1	15.3	—
Aichi	Nagoya	24.2	16.9	—

[a] Kumagai, *Seinendanshi*, Appendix III, pp. 61–64.

membership percentage, attracted proportionately more youths to the *seinendan* than any of the five urban prefectures.

Two directly comparable examples, one from Akita and the other from Gumma Prefectures, reinforce the data of Tables 9 and 10. In 1930, three-quarters of the youths in Akita Prefecture, itself two-thirds agricultural, belonged to the *seinendan*. The internal composition of that three-quarters reflects a clear urban-rural split. In Semboku County, even more agricultural than the prefecture as a whole, 80 percent of the eligibles belonged; in Akita City, where practically no farming took place, 5.5 percent joined. In 1936, 62 percent of the youths in Gumma's Yamada County, almost half agricultural, belonged; 91 percent of the young men in the county's Nirakawa Village, three-quarters agricultural, joined, but only 17.3 percent in nearby Ōmama Town, one-fifth agricultural, did so.[28] In other words, the evidence clearly shows that a much higher percentage of the nation's farm as compared to urban teenagers belonged to the 2,700,000 member youth association in the 1930s.

YOUTH TRAINING CENTER–YOUTH SCHOOL MEMBERSHIP

There are several points that we must make about the Youth Training Center and Youth School data presented below in Table 11. The figures indicate the percentage of students compared to all 15–19-year-old males, not students compared to boys eligible to attend. Fifteen

---

28. *Akita-kenshi* [The History of Akita Prefecture] (Tokyo, 1965), VI, p. 854; *Yamada-gunshi* [The History of Yamada County] (Maebashi, 1939), pp. 62–63, 673–679.

percent of the nation's 15–19-year-old males studied in middle schools and received their military training there; thus the table's percentages must be adjusted upward accordingly. When almost 80 percent of Yamagata Prefecture's teenage males enrolled in youth schools, for example, this indicated that over 90 percent of those eligible to attend did so.

Table 11 shows that youth training centers-youth schools also recruited a higher percentage of eligibles in rural than in urban areas. Tokyo and Osaka Prefectures, the least agricultural, had by far the lowest percentage of teenagers attending the schools both in 1930 and 1935, and the other three highly urban areas followed closely behind. Conversely, Shiga, Chiba, and Yamagata Prefectures, among the most agricultural, had the highest. Only Kagoshima, the prefecture in our sample with the highest percentage of its work force in farming, had a moderately lower (still over half) proportion of its male youths in the military drill training schools.

Finally, many young men participated in the youth schools and at the same time belonged to their local *seinendan* branch. In Akita's Yokobori Village, for example, 184 of the 211 teenage youth association members also attended the youth schools, and the other 27 were exempted only because they had matriculated in middle and high schools. John Embree reports a similar phenomenon for Suyemura; and even in Kagoshima Prefecture, with its puzzling low youth school enrollment percentage, at least half of the male teenagers must have belonged to both groups.[29]

We cannot leave this discussion of training center–youth school membership without mentioning its rapid growth, especially after 1935. In 1926–1927, the new centers enrolled 900,000 students, or 20 to 30 percent of the eligibles. Rural areas, of course, drew as high as 35 to 45 percent (when adjusted upward 15 percent), but in Tokyo and Osaka, local authorities established few centers and recruited very few students except in centers attached to factories. In 1935, after the Education Ministry and army combined the centers and parallel vocational schools to form youth schools, enrollment rose sharply from slightly under one million to over two million, including 470,000 girls. Attendance continued to increase after 1935; in 1940, under the impact of wartime mobilization, 2.6 million studied in youth schools, and by 1943, after the government made participation compulsory,

---

29. John Embree, *Suyemura*, pp. 168–169; *Akita-ken sōgō kyōdo kenkyū* [Akita Prefecture Collective Local Research] (Akita, 1966), pp. 868–869. In Yokobori, moreover, 77 of the 107 youth branch members who were over 20 years old simultaneously belonged to the reservist branch.

Table 11
YOUTH TRAINING CENTER–YOUTH SCHOOL ENROLLMENT [a]

Prefecture	Percent of labor force in agriculture, 1930	Percent of student enrollment to 15–19-Year-old eligibles		
		1930 (15–19 males)	1935 (Male and Female)	1935 (Male)
5 Urban Prefectures				
Tokyo	6.5	4.3	6.1	9.7
Osaka	10.5	12.0	9.9	15.8
Kyoto	26.1	15.2	16.0	25.5
Fukuoka	33.3	20.2	20.8	33.3
Aichi	36.6	22.5	21.9	35.0
5 Rural and Urban Prefectures:				
Yamaguchi	51.0	23.9	31.9	51.1
Toyama	55.2	31.2	29.8	47.7
Okayama	58.5	27.0	32.3	51.7
Shiga	60.3	32.3	46.5	74.4
Yamanashi	60.6	31.8	44.2	70.7
5 Rural Prefectures:				
Kumamoto	61.7	35.1	42.0	69.2
Aomori	61.8	35.8	40.6	64.9
Chiba	62.7	26.9	46.0	73.5
Yamagata	63.6	42.7	49.9	79.8
Kagoshima	71.2	30.0	32.9	52.7

a Mombushō, *Sōtei kyōiku chōsa gaikyō* [The General Report of a Survey of Pre-Induction Training for Recruits] (Tokyo, 1931), *passim; Nihon teikoku tōkei nenkan* [The Statistical Yearbook of the Japanese Empire], 51 (1932), p. 264; 57 (1938), p. 304. Before the youth training center–vocational school merger in 1935, only young men attended the training centers. After the merger, girls also attended. As of October 1, 1935, males accounted for 80.1 percent of the students, females 19.9 per cent. The table's premerger 1930 figures show the percentage of center students among 15–19-year-old males, and the first 1935 figure, the percentage of students among all 15–19 year olds. Since prefectural data for student enrollment by sex are not available, figures in the last column represent an approximation of the actual male enrollment percentages based on the national 80.1–19.9 percent division.

over 3 million enrolled. These students became a major source of late wartime factory labor. Most large, post-1937 increases in attendance occurred in urban areas. Already, before the China Incident, village pressures and cohesion had guided most rural youth into the schools, as Table 11 indicates. After 1937, intense army and government pressure and then law coerced all but the most recalcitrant urban youths to follow suit.[30]

NATIONAL DEFENSE WOMEN'S ASSOCIATION MEMBERSHIP

Since the National Defense Women's Association did not reach maturity until 1936 and developed at varying rates of speed in different parts of the country before that, rural-urban comparisons in the first few years of its growth are not conclusive. National membership in December, 1935 was only one and a half million. By 1938 it had grown to eight million, and by 1941, nine and a half million; but under the compulsion of wartime mobilization, urban women joined as often as their rural counterpart. In other words, the defense women's association differed from all of the other organizations because it and it alone was truly a wartime creation.[31] Therefore, it developed solid urban and rural bases almost simultaneously.

Some evidence suggests that the women's organization grew more rapidly and more solidly in rural rather than urban areas. The one available set of comparative statistics reveals that agrarian communities in at least one area developed more quickly than industrial and commercial sectors. In Gumma's Yamada County, introduced above, one-quarter of the women belonged in 1938. This broke down to about one-third in the county's agricultural villages like Nirakawa, but only one-tenth in the more highly industrial and commercial Ōmama Town.[32] Moreover, the Tokushima City daily newspaper reports that when the authorities founded the defense women's association in that area in 1935, the rural branches were founded first and became active more quickly. The content of the articles reveals that it was recruitment drives by reservists and the fact that wives of reservist branch officials became defense women's association leaders which led to this development. One cannot escape the conclusion that it was community cohesiveness that allowed reservists to have greater success at organizing village rather than town and city women.[33]

---

30. Ōtsuka shigakkai, *Shimpan kyōdoshi jiten* (Tokyo, 1969), pp. 310–311; Anderson, *Japan: Three Epochs of Modern Education*, pp. 40–41; Ishikawa Ken, ed., *Kindai Nihon kyōiku seidō shiryō* (Tokyo, 1956), III, p. 351.

31. *Kokubō fujinkai jūnenshi*, pp. 739–744. 33. See Chapter Two, footnote 41.
32. *Yamada-gunshi*, pp. 792–794.

Although National Defense Women's Association urban branches recruited members as successfully as rural branches, the organization still did not play as important a role in city life. The nature of the rural community allowed the new women's group to become an active part of the hamlet quickly, and hence to help the army spread its values; the urban community differed. John Embree wrote of what he called the "Women's Patriotic Association"—the name he uses indictates the *aikoku fujinkai,* but the activities he describes are those of the defense women—that it was difficult to distinguish between a woman as a hamlet member and a woman as an association member.[34] My questionnaire and interview returns reinforce this view. All of the most frequently mentioned defense women's activities—the consolation of men on active duty, rice transplanting and harvest aid to the families of soldiers, and local community service—as well as most of the less important ones, had as much if not more value to the community than to the army directly. Most had been carried out long before the army established the defense women's association. Village women, for example, had long prepared going-away banquets for departing servicemen. They continued to do so after 1931–1937, but then they did so in the name of "national defense," not just as one of their normal hamlet duties. We shall discuss defense women's association duties in more detail in Chapter V. Suffice it to say at this juncture that the new organization added the army's seal of approval and a few new duties to activities which rural Japanese women had performed for decades. The defense women's association made informal village women's organizations into official branches of a national association.

In many areas of urban Japan before the 1930s, on the other hand, no precinct level women's organizations existed at all; if they did exist, not every local woman joined, and the precincts were considerably larger than rural hamlets. When the older Patriotic Women's Association was formed at the turn of the century, it was primarily an urban organization; but it was not organized by neighborhoods and precincts, and its membership was comparatively small. In Kurashiki and Ichinomiya Cities in 1936, for example, the "upper class" Patriotic Women's Association branches enlisted only half as many members as the newer rival, and they were organized city wide and not divided into precinct subunits.[35] Moreover, except in the

---

34. Embree, *Suyemura,* p. 167.

35. *Kyōdo nenkan* [The Local Yearbook] (Okayama, 1937), p. 127; *Ichinomiya-shishi,* p. 934. In rural Nirakawa in Yamada County the older organization had only 33 members to 520 for the army's group. *Yamada-gunshi,* pp. 782–783; 790–791.

older city neighborhoods, there were few independent urban women's groups. Most modern city neighborhoods lacked the internal cohesion demanded by agriculture, and thus did not have a need for local women's groups to symbolize and carry out activities demanded by that cohesion. Even where women's clubs existed, the sanctions to compel membership were weaker; the collective membership of a Tokyo precinct did not hold the coercive power over the wife of our hypothetical Mitsui Trading Company employee (see above) that hamlet residents had over a fellow farmer's wife. Thus, the National Defense Women's Association organizers found few preexisting women's groups to build on in urban Japan and, when they found them, the preestablished groups were not as easily used as their rural counterparts. The army leaders enrolled two million urban women in their socialization system in 1941, almost as high a percentage of eligibles as among their rural sisters, but because they found either a weak or no preexisting base, the military had less success at indoctrinating urban than rural women.

HAMLET COHESION, SOCIAL PRESSURE, AND MEMBERSHIP

Just as the army, even during the 1937–1945 war effort, had more success at mobilizing rural than urban women, so all of its organizations had more members before 1937, plus greater local acceptance both before and during the war, in nonurban than urban areas. By patterning its organizations after the internal divisions of the village and hamlet and by using local recruiting techniques, the army enrolled most qualified people into all the various rural branches. In urban areas, the military did not often organize its groups along existing community lines, but even when it did, the precinct or neighborhood membership as a whole did not have the power to coerce each individual to join the groups in the same way the hamlet did.

Questionnaires and interviews with former members show clearly that the army used hamlet cohesiveness and social order to recruit members for the older reservist association. To begin with, its branches tended to mirror the social order of the hamlet and village. Of the thirty-one Anjō farmers who responded to the questionnaire, eleven were small-scale landlord-cultivators, twelve were owner-farmers, and eight were tenant-farmers of between one-quarter and five acres. The largest landholder in the sample, and the only one to meet Ronald Dore's definition of a landlord—someone who owned at least five *chō*, 12¼ acres of land—was the only ex-branch chief respondent. The second largest landowner, just below Dore's minimum standard, served as assistant chief.[36] Moreover, the four other former assistant branch chiefs who answered the questionnaire were either small-scale landlord-cultivators, or owner-farmers; conversely, none of the eight tenant farmers rose to the Anjō branch's top two positions. In other words, the reservists' answers concerning prewar land ownership and branch position suggest that the local reserve branch was an organization of owner- and tenant-farmers led by small scale landlord-cultivators. Only the landlords with the largest holdings, many of whom resided outside of the village, tended not to become directly involved in the day-to-day operations of the organization; but even they, as we shall see in the next chapter, helped support it financially. The Anjō evidence suggests that the reserve association's membership there reflected the town's social hierarchy, with only the very top stratum missing and even that top stratum patronized the Anjō reservist branch.[37]

The questionnaires and interviews also reveal that members joined the *zaigō gunjinkai* out of hamlet-village custom. When asked, "For which of the following reasons did you join the reservist association? a) because of personal interest, b) because of social pressure, against your will, c) because it was a citizen's natural duty, d) other," 90.9 percent—149 of the 164 respondents—answered because it was a citizen's natural duty. Only two stated that they were forced to join, three that they enrolled because of personal interest, while ten answered "other." In their reaction to what kind of "natural duty" obliged them to join, most made no distinction between local and national duty. Comments like the following were most common: "joining was the natural (*tōzen*) action for a discharged soldier in our village"; "I joined without really knowing why"; "I had a social obligation to join" (*shakaiteki gimu*); "all citizens are soldiers"; "everybody joined"; "it was my military duty to join"; "the military affairs clerk in the village office automatically signed up all eligible people"; "I joined although I felt no pressure or military obligation to do so." In fact, the answers and comments reveal that most of the 164 rural respondents believed there was no alternative to joining, even though before 1939 they faced no legal obligation to do so. The interview respondents' answers were similar. All fourteen former reservists, when asked "What happened to local men who chose not to join the *zaigō*

---

36. Ronald P. Dore, *Land Reform in Japan* (London, 1959), p. 29.

37. Maruyama Masao, *Nihon no shisō* [Japanese Thought] (Tokyo, 1961), pp. 45–46, and many others have discussed the concept of *kyōdōtai*, the idea that all hamlet organizations mirror the social stratification of the community as a whole.

gunjinkai?", looked at the interviewer with disbelief and answered, "Everyone always joined." "Everyone always joined" and for that matter enrolled in all hamlet organizations essential to local harmony for which they were eligible because of a long-standing hamlet tradition that emphasized unity, cooperation, and conformity at the expense of individual values. In other words, hamlet pressure for social conformity required that all eligible villagers enter the reservists and the other three of the army's local branches. Rural residents considered the local branches of what were actually centrally created and imposed organizations to be the hamlet's and to be essential to local harmony, evidence of the army's local acceptance.

The residents of the collective hamlet not only joined all hamlet organizations for which they were eligible, but they demanded that all other community members join as well. Anyone who did not join an organization proclaimed that he as an individual stood outside the collective hamlet membership. He had to be forced back into line. The sanctions against individualism, as we have seen, ranged from ridicule and gossip to the ultimate, but logical, punishment for a person who claimed nonmembership in the group: ostracism. I know of no instance in which these sanctions needed to be imposed on those eligible for the army's organizations, although one of the fourteen interview respondents, when asked the question, "What happened to a local man who chose not to join the *zaigō gunjinkai?"*, answered frankly, "ostracism." He felt that the ultimate hamlet sanction *could* be applied to any eligible person not joining the reserve association. This response suggests that in his community the reserve association was such an important part of hamlet and village life that the inhabitants would use their strongest weapon to enforce membership; but it does not mean that ostracism needed to be imposed. The other thirteen respondents did not answer "ostracism," because everyone joined. There was no need to talk of sanctions.[38]

The army so skillfully interfused its organizations into the existing village-hamlet structure that by the time the China War began in 1937, virtually all eligible villagers belonged to the reservist, youth, and women's branches. They had become hamlet organizations. Thus the military had made "an official out of an unofficial system," ensured almost universal rural membership in its organizations, and built itself an acquiescent basis for militarism in Japanese farm communities. As Horibe Senjin wrote in the Home Ministry journal, *Shimin,* in 1936, the reservist, defense women's, and two youth associations,

38. Smith, "The Japanese Rural Community: Norms, Sanctions, and Ostracism," pp. 250–251.

along with the agricultural cooperative and the elementary schools, had become the essential community institutions of rural Japan.[39] This does not necessarily prove that villagers were imbued with patriotic and military values, however. A rural Japanese reservist, or youth, or woman could serve the army as he did the community out of a fear that if he did not his family would be punished. But I believe that this was only half the story. By 1937, the Japanese farmer had become a patriotic "national villager" as well. We shall turn to a discussion of this subject when we analyze the organizations' activities in Chapter V.

FACTORY BRANCHES: THE URBAN VILLAGE

Our statistics indicate that most eligibles joined all of the organizations in cohesive rural Japan, but that very few men and women enrolled in the more fluid urban society. Factory branches, however, were urban successes. Tanaka realized even before World War I that the establishment of *zaigō gunjinkai* factory branches had tremendous possibilities for the army; by the late 1930s, factory managers in conjunction with army officers had also established youth schools and even *seinendan* for young workers, and branches of the National Defense Women's Association for wives and female employees. Both the army leaders and the paternalistic company managers benefitted from this mutual cooperation.

There is evidence, especially for the *zaigō gunjinkai*, to suggest successful industrial branch organization. A very large proportion of the male work force fell into the age group of reservist eligibility. Thus it is not surprising that by 1937 the reserve association maintained 567 factory branches with fifty to one hundred thousand members, mostly in the major industrial areas around Tokyo, Osaka, Nagoya, and northern Kyushu.[40] The partial listing of reservist plants published in the hostile magazine, *Reconstruction (Kaizō)*, in July, 1932, reads like a roster of the elite of Japan's modern factories: Ishikawajima Shipyard, Tōyō Cotton, Mitsubishi Kobe Electric Plant, Kanebo Silk, Sumitomo Electric, Osaka Electric (scene of a 1924 strike suppressed with reservist assistance), Kobe Steel, etc. One can add to these branches in the nation's major department stores: Tokyo Matsuzakaya, Osaka Takashimaya, Kyoto Daimaru, Nagoya Matsuzakaya, etc., and various government sponsored installations: Shiga Prefec-

---

39. Horibe Senjin, "Yūryō chōson o miru" [Viewing Superior Towns and Villages], *Shimin* [Good Citizen], XXXI (1936), p. 87.

40. *Rikukaigun gunji nenkan*, 1937, pp. 551–554.

tural Office, Osaka Arsenal, and the National Railroad's Ōmiya yards. Apparently, most of the nation's major plants, stores, and offices maintained *zaigō gunjinkai* branches.[41] The predominantly rural Hekikai County consolidated reserve branch maintained five reservist factory branches: two Toyota Automobile plants and one Toyota textile machinery plant in or near Kariya, and two textile mills in Anjō. Altogether, 8.6 percent of the county's, and 58.1 percent of industrial Kariya's reservists served in factory branches. This pattern repeated itself throughout the industrial areas of Japan and among Japanese workers in Korea, Manchuria, and the Chinese treaty ports in the 1930s.[42]

A prime example of successful reservist industrial organization is that of the Kaijima Daishibaura Company, a mining enterprise in Fukuoka's Kurate County. This company, founded by Kaijima Tasuke in the late nineteenth century, employed 16 percent of the county's total labor force. Kaijima established a reserve association branch for his mines in 1915, the first year that factory branches were sanctioned. By 1919, the company sponsored four branches, one at each major mine, organized into Kaijima Daishibaura's own consolidated branch. The first chief of the company reservists after 1919 was none other than the president's son, reserve Lieutenant Kaijima Teiji, who had previously headed the county's reserve association. In 1928, the company employed 8,700 persons, of whom 6,000 were males; in 1934, its reservist branches enrolled 1,436 members. Thus, about one-quarter of the male employees of the company belonged. When one considers the number of workers under twenty, and the 65 percent rate of success for the county's physical examination eligibles, he can see that the Kaijima Company's branches recruited a high percentage of their potential members. In fact, all but 758 of Kurate County's 8,075 eligibles belonged to the *zaigō gunjinkai*. Thus, even if all 758 worked for the Kaijima Company, which is very unlikely, two-thirds of the potential members in the company still belonged.

The Kaijima family, like industrial entrepreneurs nationwide, did not stop at organizing reservists. It also created youth training centers for teenage workers. Here 541 youths under *zaigō gunjinkai* leadership learned, according to the company's public relations brochure, "to cultivate their minds and bodies and to respect the values and customs

41. Seta Kaku, "Zaigō gunjindan no gensei" [The Present Status of Reservist Groups], *Kaizō* [Reconstruction], July 1932, pp. 95–97; *Shin Ōtsu-shishi*, I, p. 263.
42. Hekikai County reservist consolidated branch report on national and prefectural government financial aid to branches, dated April 15, 1939, in Anjō documents, Volume XI, *Yosan kessansho tsuzuri* [A Notebook of Proposed and Completed Budgets]; *Rikukaigun gunji nenkan*, 1937, pp. 551–554.

of the mines." The youths learned cultivation and respect through reservist-led close-order drill, physical training, and ethical and patriotic lessons, needless to say.[43]

What was true at Kaijima Daishibaura's mines was true in many other industrial areas as well. Higashi Ward in Osaka in 1939 supported 17,647 youth school students; 41.4 percent of them studied in company or government enterprise sponsored factory schools. In 1929, Shitaya-ku in Tokyo maintained only three youth training centers; one was for the young male workers in Asakusa's Matsuzakaya Department Store. Companies organized four of the nineteen youth schools in Nagoya's Naka Ward, and two of seven in Tokyo's Shiba Ward.[44] Companies established their own National Defense Women's Association branches as well. We know, for example, that the Osaka Arsenal reported 6,083, and Osaka's Mitsukoshi Department Store, 600 members in 1940.[45] Unfortunately, few local histories were written during the wartime years, and postwar versions tend to ignore organizations like the National Defense Women's Association because they no longer exist; thus we cannot determine accurately how extensive was the cooperation of companies and the army in organizing women. Given the military leader's desire to establish geographically based women's branches exactly parallel to reservist ones, however, one can infer that wherever the army built a *zaigō gunjinkai* factory branch, they founded a National Defense Women's Association branch.

Military-company cooperation in establishing branches of the army's organizations in the nation's factories benefitted both the soldiers and the managers. The factory people wanted an organization of workers to help reinforce order, increase productivity, and eliminate labor unrest in their plants. The Kaijima directors viewed military drill for youth in this way, as we have seen, and there are a number of reports of factory managers using their *zaigō gunjinkai* branches to slow labor organization and to break strikes.[46] The army officers also revered order and productivity and opposed labor activism and subversive ideologies. But more important, they saw factory branches as their urban foothold for building support for the military.

43. *Fukuoka-ken Kurate-gunshi* [The History of Kurate County in Fukuoka Prefecture] (Fukuoka, 1934), pp. 1029, 1208, 1326–1327.
44. *Higashi-kushi* [The History of Higashi Ward] (Osaka, 1940), pp. 584–589; *Shitaya-kushi* [The History of Shitaya Ward] (Tokyo, 1935), I, pp. 924–925; *Nagoya Naka-kushi* [The History of Nagoya Naka Ward] (Kyoto, 1944), pp. 262–266; *Shiba-kushi*, p. 747.
45. *Higashi-kushi*, pp. 674–675.
46. Shinobu Seizaburō *Taishō demokurashishi* [A History of Taishō Democracy] (Tokyo, 1954–1959), I, pp. 401, 551; *Higashi-kushi*, p. 1000.

One other mutually held belief reinforced army-company coopera-tion. Just as officers introduced paternalism and rural values in their soldier's ethos after the Russo-Japanese War, company owners and managers began to use the same values at the same time to control their employees. Both believed paternalism and a social organization akin to the cohesive and cooperative family and hamlet an effective way to strengthen internal organization and discipline. The officer and the manager offered security, social welfare facilities, and total involvement in his life to the soldier and worker; in return, the sub-ordinates gave obedience, loyalty, and hard work to the army and company. The Kaijima company, for example, ensured permanent employment, built schools and hospitals, and helped the survivors of those killed in mining accidents (while the reserve branch, financed by the company, did the same for the survivors of those killed on active duty).[47] All they demanded of the employee in return was his total obedience. The army organization's branches and their familistic soldier's ethos served to strengthen this lord-vassal reciprocal relation-ship within the company. At the same time, the paternalism and its concomitant obedience and hierarchical cohesiveness practically en-sured the army that at least in factory branches it would have solid urban membership. When peer group pressure did not force a young worker to join, management pressure did. The factory became the urban counterpart of the hamlet.

CONCLUSION

Satō Mamoru has written that the reasons for rural young men enlist-ing in youth organizations in the past one hundred years should be viewed in terms of a continuous development from hamlet cohesive-ness to individual motivation. Rural youth groups developed from nineteenth century independent hamlet groups in which members participated because of their internal *buraku* "sympathetic communi-cation" to post–World War II groups in which members enrolled be-cause of a personal interest in individual self-improvement. What provided the transition between the two periods and attitudes was a half century during which youths participated in centralized *seinendan* activities out of both the earlier hamlet "emotional unity" and a com-mitment, spawned and developed through the organization, to na-tional goals.[48] It was this transition that the army both used and helped to create through all four of its organizations. Rather than

47. *Kurate-gunshi,* pp. 1029, 1588.
48. Satō Mamoru, *Kindai Nihon seinen shūdanshi,* pp. 537–541.

attempt to destroy local hamlet-consciousness and build a new centralized Japan based on individual commitment to national goals, a venture that certainly would have ended in failure, the army utilized local cohesiveness and "sympathetic communication" for its own purposes. Although we shall not discuss the growth of villagers' commitment to national goals until Chapter V, we can at least conclude here that the branches of the army's associations became integral parts of their communities to a much greater degree than other centralized and bureaucratically directed organizations. The rural reservist, youth, and women's branches organized themselves exactly parallel to their communities, and thus used the hamlet's "sympathetic communication" and "emotional unity" to ensure that a high percentage of eligibles enrolled. In city neighborhoods, where communication tended to be unsympathetic and emotional unity was nil, very few people joined. Stated the other way around, high nonurban (and factory) branch membership percentages were one reflection of the army's success at building a rural (and urban village) basis of support for itself.

IV

THE LOCAL LEADERSHIP AND
FINANCING OF THE ORGANIZATIONS

The success of military officers in creating rural acceptance of the army depended on their branches' use of existing rural institutions and customs in the selection of leaders and in financing, as well as in the recruitment of members. The army-dominated reservists' and other organizations placed their greatest emphasis on local, not military, criteria in selecting leaders. Reservist leaders tended to be chosen from the hamlet and the village wealthy and well-educated elite; the village and town-wide positions rotated from hamlet to hamlet to maintain local harmony; and men with histories of service to the local community invariably became leaders. Military criteria such as rank and a successful active duty career seldom outweighed the necessity of choosing branch chiefs with high status, extensive landholdings, or a record of activism. Even when the martial criteria were applied, they had a direct relationship to hamlet-village values. In selecting leaders, both young men's organizations relied on local-military criteria similar to those of the *zaigō gunjinkai*. *Seinendan* branches generally chose their officials from among reservists, and especially from among men who were reservist leaders of the future. The youth training centers–youth schools' drill instructors were always outstanding ex-servicemen who served in the reservist branch. The defense women's association's community officials were appointed on the basis of local qualities alone. The chief and her key subordinates were almost always the wives of powerful local leaders like the mayor, a landlord, or the reservist branch chief. But the real if unofficial leadership for the women's branch, and for that matter, for both youth groups (when reservists did not provide the official leadership) was provided by the reservist branch's members. The *zaigō gunjinkai* was an organization for the rural community's fittest 20–40-year-old men, and these men were the natural subvillage office leaders for women and teenagers. Official and unofficial reservist direction, therefore, integrated the army's system in each rural village and town in Japan.

In financing, the organizations' most successful branches depended on village government allocations or elite contributions. Where little or no such support was forthcoming, the army found comparatively less acceptance. Branches with local government-elite funding tended to be more successful because this type of support indicated that the branches had become community organizations. Branches which were compelled to support themselves through other means, such as the collection of dues, were less completely integrated into the local village-hamlet structure and thus less fully accepted. In other words, in rural Japan the army's organizations were most effective in communities where they received the backing of the informal and formal government of the village and its constituent hamlets.

THE HAMLET, THE VILLAGE, AND THE RESERVIST ASSOCIATION'S LEADERSHIP

Article Twenty of the bylaws of the reservist association, published at the time of its establishment in 1910, stated the following provisions for the choice of branch officials:

The branches will have a chairman and assistant chairman, a few directors, councillors, and secretaries. The councillors will be elected by all members of the branch, and the branch councillors in turn will elect the chairman, assistant chairman, secretaries, and directors. However, in the case of the chairman and assistant chairman, the election must be reported to the national headquarters through the district (regimental area) headquarters. The president (*sōsai*) will officially appoint them on the advice of the elders (*kairō*).[1]

Anjō provides an example of how this branch chief selection system functioned. The Anjō reserve association branch had from June, 1931 on thirty-two member-officials: one branch chief, two assistant chiefs, three directors, two secretaries, five division chiefs at the school district level, and nineteen squad leaders at the hamlet or hamlet-cluster level.[2]

---

1. Section V, Article 20, Bylaws of the reservist association in *Senyū*, 1 (1910), pp. 56–61.

2. Anjō documents, Volume V, *Yakuin meibo* [A Register of Officials]. The branch also had seven honorary member-advisers listed in the register: the mayor, military affairs' clerk, and the five elementary school principals.

The regular branch officials, beginning at the hamlet subunit level, were all chosen by election. The members in each of the nineteen subunits elected their local squad leaders (*kumichō*), who became the Anjō branch's equivalent of the bylaw's councillors. Since these branch-town subdivisions were organized into larger divisions coinciding with the town's five elementary school districts, the reserve association branch, like most other Anjō organizations, set up a second set of subbranch headquarters there. The four or five squad leader-councillors in each of these districts in turn chose their school district group chief (*hanchō*). All twenty-four of these officials, along with the five directors and secretaries whom they elected, chose the chief and his two assistants. The top three officials also participated in the process when their position was not the one being filled. In other words, each holder of the top three posts was selected by the remaining thirty-one of the Anjō branch's cadre (*kambu*).

In spite of repeated changes in regulations, branch members or their representatives in Anjō and elsewhere continued to choose their own leaders from 1910 until 1945. They did so even after December, 1938, when Tokyo abolished the local selection of branch chiefs in favor of direct appointment by the central headquarters. Theoretically, Tokyo appointed chiefs on the advice of the district-regimental area commander, but in practice the active duty officers accepted the local branches' recommendations. According to the 14 interviewed reservists and 95 percent of the questionnaire respondents (158 of 166 answers), all of whom joined or still served the organization after 1938, members or branch cadre chose the chief and assistant chief.[3]

Local reservists were allowed to choose their leaders because it was the army's intent to have the branches become integral parts of the local scene in which hamlet and village organizations selected their own leaders. If the army had imposed leadership from above, *zaigō gunjinkai* branches could not have been accepted as local groups. Branch chiefs did not command their subordinates, army-like, but guided them as other hamlet-village leaders did in other organizations, by consultation and the building of consensus. All 14 interviews and 95 percent of the questionnaire respondents (157 of 165 answers) stated that their branch chiefs (and in the case of the 21 branch chief respondents, they themselves) made decisions through consultation with the

---

3. Question number 35 of the questionnaire reads as follows:
"How was the branch chief chosen?
a. elected by the general membership;
b. chosen by the branch officials;
c. appointed by the consolidated branch chief;
d. other."
Not one respondent answered "c".

branch cadre, and even occasionally with the members in general.[4] Because they led by winning the cooperation of the members rather than by command, leaders had to have the respect of the members. A chief chosen by his fellow villagers was more likely to win this respect and receive cooperation than one imposed from above.

The army's goal was to win local cooperation "naturally" from below for the achievement of its national military goals above. It is not surprising, therefore, that the criteria used by branch officials when they gathered to select their chief emphasized hamlet-village needs primarily and military needs only secondarily. One can decipher from evidence six interrelated criteria.[5] Only two—military career success, and rank and education—placed a premium on military ability. The other four—the crucial community status and landholdings; wealth and availability; community activism; and hamlet balance—each weighed local virtues and values more heavily. Even the two "military" criteria were evidence of a man's local position and ability. Military career success indicated that a villager was physically and morally strong and committed to his community. High military rank and its concomitant education often reflected local elite social status.

It does not necessarily follow that the most successful branch chief excelled equally in all six criteria. If one were to evaluate a chief on a comparative scale for each criterion, he would find that the leader received higher scores in some criteria than in others. The chief's ability to lead successfully would then be judged on the basis of an overall aggregate score, not on the results on any one criteria. Several of the leaders in our sample are examples of men who totally failed to meet one or two criteria but compensated for this by excelling in

---

4. The wording of question number 36 was as follows:
"How did the branch chief lead (*tōsotsu*) your branch?"

a. he commanded (*meirei shita*) the branch as in the army;

b. he directed (*shirei shita*) the branch after consultation with other branch officials;

c. he managed (*un'ei shita*) the branch with the help (*sewa*) of the general membership."

5. The criteria were selected largely on the basis of the qualities for branch leadership most frequently mentioned by the interview respondents. The questionnaires were also useful. Question number 1 asked about the respondent's educational background, number 2 about his occupation, number 4 his landholdings, number 5 his official position in the community, number 13 his rank, and number 40 his branch leadership position. Question number 32 requested information about the rank of the respondent's branch chief, and number 34 about the respondent's perception of his branch chief's occupation. One hundred fifty respondents answered question number 34. Of the 194 answers (there were many multiple answers), 130 or 67 percent stated that their branch chief was a landlord or owner-farmer. Other answers included village official (16), school teacher (7), priest (5), and tenant-farmer (1).

others. One chief had never served on active duty and therefore had neither military rank nor success, but he came from a wealthy, land owning family of high social status, and had had a career of community activism. Another chief of high military rank, education, active duty success, elite community status, landholdings, and great wealth, became branch chief at age 22 before he had had the opportunity to serve his community. In the one case, local criteria outweighed military history. In the other, membership in the community's most elite family obviated the need to prove reliability through activism.

MILITARY CAREER SUCCESS

One would expect the men selecting branch chiefs and other top reservist officials to choose men who had had outstanding military careers. But the selectors did so not only because they wanted the best soldiers in command of a quasi-military organization, but also because they believed that "good soldiers" had proven themselves to be the local men most interested in community service. By falling into line and working hard on active duty, these soldiers proved that they would do likewise back home. One early Taisho observer of rural Japan noted, "I heard talk in this village and in others of the influence of the local army reservists' society. 'Young men on returning from their army service are always influential.' " [6] He wrote about soldiers in general, not necessarily good soldiers. Villagers in prewar Japan respected soldiers when they returned home from the barracks. Servicemen had two intensely disciplined and physical years to mold and test the strength of their character; they left home as boys and returned men. Those among them who excelled, were good soldiers, came home men among men, were men who were, as several nonreservist villagers said, "all there" (*shikkari shita*).

Rural Japanese also believed a successful active duty career indicated a man's commitment to his community. One characteristic of the cooperative hamlet, Robert Smith points out, is that it, like an individual, can lose face.[7] Understanding this, the army successfully promoted the idea that an outstanding recruit brought honor not only to himself, but also to his family and community. The good soldier helped Japan, hamlet, and family; the bad one endangered the nation's defenses and the honor of his village and parents. Thus the army and

---

6. J. W. Robertson Scott, *The Foundations of Japan* (London, 1922), p. 133.

7. Robert Smith, "The Japanese Rural Community: Norms, Sanctions, and Ostracism," in Jack M. Potter et al., eds., *Peasant Society: A Reader* (Boston, 1967), p. 248.

the village leaders forced recalcitrant recruits into line by letters and visits from home, often from the branch chief, and by the threat of sanctions, even ostracism, against his family. Fourteen interview respondents representing six different villages and towns recalled no recalcitrance or radicalism on the part of recruits from their communities. The soldier who came home after a successful two-year stint in the army so honored his village that often its leaders rewarded him for his military attainments.[8] Such a soldier could be trusted as a future community leader. His army career brought credit to the town or village and showed him to be a person willing to accept discipline, to forego personal desires, and to conform for the good of those three closely related organizations: the army, the community, and the family. The outstanding soldier had proven his commitment to his community by his army success, and became a prime candidate for village and town offices, including that of reservist branch leadership.

Seventeen of our twenty-one branch chiefs had outstanding military careers, one had never served on active duty, one provided inadequate information by which to judge, and two had only normal success at the barracks. We can identify active duty success by each soldier's rank at the time of discharge. Of our sample, six men were reserve lieutenants and fifteen were enlisted men. Reserve officers received commissions by joining a program for which all middle school or higher graduates were eligible. Since only a small percentage of secondary education graduates volunteered, those who enlisted must have represented that part of the more highly educated population most interested in the military, and, therefore, more likely to become outstanding soldiers. Moreover, all six of our volunteers became officers. The volunteers served as sergeants during their year on active duty (they provided one major source of noncommissioned officers for the Japanese army), and received their commissions as reserve lieutenants when they returned home (with no possibility of a regular military career even after recall). This is significant because only the outstanding upper segment of these volunteers became officers: the rest remained reserve sergeants.[9]

---

8. *Kariya-chōshi* [The History of Kariya Town] (Kariya, 1932), p. 168.

9. Fujiwara Akira, *Gunjishi* (Tokyo, 1961), p. 146; Matsushita Yoshio, *Nihon gunjishi jitsuwa* [True Stories of Japanese Military History] (Tokyo, 1966), p. 330. In 1928, the one-year volunteer system was replaced by a slightly different program, the "cadre candidate system" (*kambu kōhosei seidō*). Fujiwara reports that the new program was no more successful at winning over the educated class (*chishiki kaikyū*) than its predecessor. The total number of volunteers in all categories, however, rose from 7,000 applications and 4,000 accepted per year between 1918 and 1929, to 26,000 applications and 14,000 accepted in 1935. The number of reserve officer applications and trainees probably increased also.

Military success among conscripted soldiers also can be judged by rank. Youth training center graduates sometimes received a five- or six-month reduction in their term of service, but most men served two years. Draftees who remained second class privates (*nitōhei*) when they returned home were considered failures, those who became first class privates (*ittōhei*) were adequate, and those promoted to superior privates (*jōtōhei*) or lance corporals (*heichō*) were outstanding. Ten of our thirteen enlisted men branch chiefs left the army as superior privates, one actually became a lance corporal, and two remained first-class privates. (One of the latter served only one and a half years on active duty, a half year short of the period usually required for promotion to superior private). When one compares our sample with all recruits, he can see that our branch chiefs had more outstanding military records than most. Less than one-third of all Anjō draftees became superior privates or lance corporals.[10] It was the successful who most clearly proved their loyalty to their community and thus were selected to perform various community tasks when they returned home. Almost all of our branch chiefs were successful.

RANK AND EDUCATION

More than half of the branch chiefs in the early 1930s were not officers, but reservist national leaders preferred that local community members select officers as their branch officials both for military and community-oriented reasons. Nagaoka Gaishi and Tanaka requested in 1911 and 1918, respectively, that local reservists choose their top leaders from men of high military rank and local status. If a reserve officer lived in the community, he was the obvious choice for local chief. Tanaka wrote that "since reservists are soldiers as well as citizens, it is good to select men of high military rank as branch officials." [11]

Officers were usually the hamlet and village's natural leaders because they tended to receive better educations and have higher local status than enlisted men. If they became branch chiefs they enhanced the army's chances of successful integration into the local scene. It was in this context that Tanaka continued the article quoted above by stating that "in many cases officers who have high local status and authority are chosen as branch chiefs, and the Tokyo headquarters considers this desirable." [12] Members of the local elite became officers through

10. *Anjō-chōshi* (Anjō, 1919), p. 112; *Anjō-machi seinendanshi* (Anjō, 1936), I, pp. 385–386.

11. Tanaka, "Tokuni kōryo o yōsuru jūyō mondai," *Senyū*, 96 (1918), pp. 12–13.

12. Tanaka, "Tokuni kōryo o yōsuru jūyō mondai," *Senyū*, 96 (1918), p. 13.

the "one-year volunteer system" before 1928, and the "cadre candidate system" thereafter, for training reserve officers. According to these programs, all graduates of middle or higher schools could enlist in the army, serve one year on active duty, and return home as reserve second lieutenants. The goal of the programs was twofold. First, the army wanted to produce a large pool of reserve officers who, when recalled in time of emergency, would supplement the career officers who had graduated from the military academy at Ichigaya; and second, the programs provided a large number of officers to help militarize their local communities.[13]

The one-year volunteer officers belonged to community families of high status—they needed at least a middle school education to enter the program. Before 1945 and the postwar educational reforms, very few Japanese received more than an elementary or a youth school education. Less than 20 percent of the nation's young people went on to middle school or higher even in the 1930s when secondary education attained its largest prewar enrollments. Although the Meiji reforms opened the educational system to people of every status, in Japan as elsewhere the well-to-do tended to receive more and higher education. The combination of educated parents (most nonelite rural Japanese before the end of the nineteenth century were illiterate), wealth, free time for study, etc., produced an educated class which tended to reproduce itself generation after generation. The best educated, the wealthiest, and the most prestigious in each rural community tended to belong to the same families.[14]

In our sample, there is a correlation between rank, education, and elite status on the one hand, and service as branch chief on the other. Nine or 5.1 percent of the interview and questionnaire respondents were officers. (See Table 12) Six of these nine reserve officers served as branch chiefs, one as an assistant chief, and two as lower level branch officials. Twenty-one men or 11.9 percent of our sample graduated from middle school or higher. (See Table 13.) Seven of the twenty-one held the post of branch chief. When we look at our eight top elite-branch chiefs, we find that five of them were both officers and graduates of middle or higher school.

In spite of Tanaka's desire that branch chiefs be officers, Colonel Matsumura Shōin, the Army Ministry staff officer responsible for reservist affairs in 1933, reported that a little over half of the top

---

13. Fujiwara, *Gunjishi*, p. 55.
14. Herbert Passin, *Society and Education in Japan* (New York, 1965), pp. 117–122.

Table 12
MILITARY RANK OF QUESTIONNAIRE-INTERVIEW RESPONDENTS [a]

Rank	All respondents		Branch chief respondents	
Officer	9	5.1%	6	28.6%
Non-commissioned officer	14	7.9%	2	9.5%
Enlisted man	135	76.3%	12	57.1%
No active service	16	9.0%	1	4.8%
No answer	3	1.7%	0	0.0%
Total	177	100.0%	21	100.0%

[a] The sample includes 173 questionnaire respondents, and four interview respondents not included in the questionnaire sample.

Table 13
EDUCATION LEVEL OF QUESTIONNAIRE-INTERVIEW RESPONDENTS [a]

Educational level	All respondents		Branch chief respondents	
Middle school or higher	21	11.9%	7	33.3%
Vocational school	19	10.7%	1	4.8%
Youth center/school	89	50.3%	8	38.1%
Higher elementary school	41	23.2%	5	23.8%
Compulsory education	6	3.4%	0	0.0%
No answer	1	0.6%	0	0.0%
Total	177	100.0%	21	100.0%

[a] The sample for Table 13 is the same as for Table 12.

reservist branch leaders in that year were not officers.[15] The reason is that there were not enough reserve officers available to fill all of the leadership posts, especially in rural areas. In 1931, the *zaigō gunjinkai*

15. Matsumura Shōin, "Teikoku zaigō gunjinkai kiyaku kaisei ni tsuite," *Kaikōsha kiji*, April 1933, p. 135.

Table 14

MILITARY RANK OF RESERVIST ASSOCIATION MEMBERS, 1931 [a]

Rank	Army		Navy		Total	
	Number	Percentage	Number	Percentage	Number	Percentage
Officers	50,040	1.9	3,016	4.6	53,056	2.0
Non-commissioned officers	63,783	2.5	16,655	25.6	80,438	3.1
Ex-servicemen enlisted men	1,217,532	47.4	43,109	66.1	1,260,641	47.9
No active service	1,236,607	48.2	2,397	3.7	1,239,004	47.1
Total	2,567,962	100.0	65,177	100.0	2,633,139	100.0

a Matsumura Shōin, "Teikoku zaigō gunjinkai kiyaku kaisei ni tsuite," *Kaikōsha kiji*, April 1933, p. 130.

enrolled only 53,056 officers, 2 percent of the membership. (See Table
14.) When one excludes those officers who served in consolidated
branch and higher headquarters, at most 50,000 men remained to head
14,000 branches. Unfortunately for Nagaoka's and Tanaka's hopes,
the distribution of these officers was not equal throughout the nation.
Only 1 percent of the members in the sample of eight regular and
consolidated rural branches presented in Table 15 came from officer's
ranks; conversely, over 4.5 percent of the urban members in five areas
recorded in the table were lieutenants or higher. In agricultural Anjō
in 1927, only 9 of 1,029 members were officers. Shimajiri County in
Okinawa in 1935 reported 9 of 23 branches with no officers. The

Table 15

PERCENTAGE OF OFFICERS AMONG MEMBERS, RURAL AND URBAN RESERVIST
BRANCHES AND CONSOLIDATED BRANCHES [a]

Community	Year	Officers	Members	Percentage
Ichinomiya City, Aichi	1936	45	1,691	2.7
Ashikaga City, Tochigi	1927	3	1,643	0.2
Hongō Ward, Tokyo	1934	438	5,432	8.1
Shitaya Ward, Tokyo	1929	135	4,862	2.8
Matsumoto City, Nagano	1928	40	1,225	3.3
Total		661	14,853	4.5
Asaguchi County, Okayama	1922	52	5,347	1.0
Kasai County, Hyōgo	1928	27	2,409	1.7
Shimajiri County, Okinawa	1935	22	6,544	0.3
Gumma County, Gumma	1930	97	7,296	1.3
Hamana County, Shizuoka	1925	145	11,051	1.3
Naka-Kubiki County, Niigata	1916	96	11,362	0.8
Kaibara Town, Hyōgo	1922	6	230	2.6
Anjō Town, Aichi	1927	9	1,029	0.9
Nojiri Village, Toyama	1927	4	142	2.7
Total		458	45,410	1.0

[a] The data was culled from the local histories of the communities listed in the
chart and from the Anjō documents. See especially *Hongō-kushi*, p. 977; *Shimajiri-
gunshi* [The History of Shimajiri County] (Naha, 1937), pp. 116–119; Anjō membership as of April 20, 1927, "Shōwa gannendō bunkai jōkyō hōkoku" [A Report of
Branch Conditions for 1926] in Anjō documents, Volume X, *Jigyō yotei oyobi
jisshihyō tsuzuri* [A Notebook of Planned and Completed Activities].

Tokyo Hongō Ward branch before it was divided into a dozen or so branches, in 1936, on the other hand, had 438 officers, and 30 to 35 per branch even after that. Hongō had no difficulty finding an officer with all of the qualifications to be branch chief, but many rural branches did not have officers as branch chiefs because none lived in the village.

The findings presented in Table 16 reinforce the conclusion that urban branches enrolled many more officers than rural branches. Not only was the percentage of officers among members more than three times higher in city than in village branches, but the total number of officers was seven times larger. Table 17 reveals the village dilemma even more starkly. Twenty-six and five-tenths percent of the branches in this category had no officers at all, and 48.5 percent more enlisted only one or two. Conversely, all of the forty-four city, town, and factory branches had at least one officer, and only eleven contained two or less. Proportionately fewer officers lived in farm than in urban communities.

More officers lived in cities than in towns, and in towns than in villages, because a higher percentage of urban than rural youths matriculated in middle schools and because urban areas provided more job opportunities for those who graduated, whether or not they originally lived in the city. The best-educated villagers migrated to the cities, and particularly to Tokyo, to work in companies and government offices and left their less well-educated brothers and fellow villagers to till the soil (and collect the rents). Even among our elite branch chiefs, we find a middle school graduate-reserve officer (and poet) who became chief only after illness forced him to give up his job in Tokyo and and return to his village. But enlisted men often functioned as branch chiefs even when officers belonged to their branch because the lieutenants for a variety of reasons lacked some of the other qualifications to serve. It is to these other criteria that we must turn next.

COMMUNITY STATUS AND LANDHOLDING

High community status, often but not always related to military rank and education, was an important prerequisite for holding the post of branch chief. As we have seen, Tanaka emphasized the importance of choosing men of high social position in the village because he felt that important local leaders could better win the cooperation of the members. People naturally followed their traditional leaders, and

Table 16

NUMBER OF OFFICERS AND MEMBERS PER BRANCH AND PERCENTAGE OF
OFFICERS TO TOTAL MEMBERS IN VILLAGE, FACTORY, TOWN, AND CITY
BRANCHES LISTED IN THE MODEL BRANCH HISTORY FOR 1926 [a]

Type of community	Number of branches	Number of officers	Average number per branch	Number of members	Average number per branch	Percentage of officers among members
City branches	8	110	13.8	3,746	468	2.9
Town branches	31	165	5.3	12,394	400	1.3
Factory branches	5	22	4.4	2,046	409	1.1
Village branches	196	363	1.9	40,671	207	0.9
Total	240	655	2.7	58,857	241	1.1
No data	42	—	—	—	—	—

[a] Murata Kikugorō, ed., *Teikoku zaigō gunjinkai mohan bunkaishi* (Kawagoe, 1927), passim.

Table 17

NUMBER OF OFFICERS PER BRANCH BY CATEGORY AMONG BRANCHES LISTED IN THE MODEL BRANCH HISTORY FOR 1926 [a]

Type of community	Total branches	Number of branches with no officers	Percentage of branches with no officers	Number of branches with 1–2 officers	Percentage of branches with 1–2 officers	Number of branches with 3 or more officers	Percentage of branches with 3 or more officers
City branches	8	0	0.0	1	12.5	7	87.5
Town branches	31	0	0.0	8	25.8	23	74.2
Factory branches	5	0	0.0	2	40.0	3	60.0
Village branches	196	52	26.5	95	48.5	49	25.0

[a] Murata, *Mohan bunkaishi*, passim.

Tanaka thought that by making them reservist leaders and utilizing the existing village social order the army would benefit.

Our evidence shows that villagers followed Tanaka's guidelines. Of the twenty-one branch chiefs in the interview-questionnaire sample, five were landlords or their sons, one was a landlord-village official who became mayor shortly after resigning as branch chief, and two belonged to families that owned prosperous businesses. Four others were small landlords or businessmen, five owner-farmers, and four were owner-tenant farmers. Sixteen of these twenty-one were farmers, and 75 percent of the sixteen were owner-cultivators or landlords, as compared to the overall figure for all the nation's farmers of 31.2 percent in 1941. All sixteen owned some land and cultivated it, whereas 27.7 percent of the nation's cultivators were full-time tenants and did not own any land at all. Even the four tenant-branch chiefs cultivated more of their own than rented land. All sixteen were farmer-branch chiefs in the more prosperous upper half of the nation's rural society. (See Table 18.) When one realizes that all of these branch chiefs were under forty years of age and most had not yet succeeded their fathers as family heads, and in some cases were the younger sons of powerful landlords, the data is compelling. Since these men had not yet taken charge of their families' affairs, many did not yet have large landholdings to report; if they had, their elite status would have been easier to detect. Although only eight of the twenty-one can be said to belong to the very top layer, the elite within the elite, all except one or two were from the group which Fukutake Tadashi identifies as a community's "prominent stratum" (omodachi sō). These were the people in a village: landlords, absentee landlords' local representatives

Table 18

SAMPLE BRANCH CHIEF AND NATIONAL
OWNERSHIP STATUS COMPARED [a]

	Branch chief	National (1946)
Owner-farmer/landlord	75%	32.8%
Owner-tenant	25%	19.8%
Tenant-owner	0%	18.6%
Tenant	0%	28.7%

[a] Fukutake Tadashi, *Japanese Rural Society* (London and New York, 1967), p. 18; interviews and questionnaires.

(*sahai*), owner-farmers, and occasionally even tenant farmers who dominated the local scene. The powerful absentee landlords not only turned over management of their tenants, but often other important local jobs as well to these men, the next most prestigious community leaders.[16]

WEALTH AND AVAILABILITY

Two important prerequisites for a successful branch chief were personal wealth and free time. A well-to-do leader not only had the community status necessary to command cooperation, he also had the means to make the necessary large personal expenditures and to perform a time-consuming undertaking. The job, if performed conscientiously, was costly, as the Anjō case reveals. The Anjō branch records indicate that branch chiefs made two two-day trips per year, one to Toyohashi and one to Nagoya, and jaunts of three to five days in alternate years to bases as far as Kure in the west and Mishima, Tokyo and Yokosuka in the east to visit Anjō soldiers and sailors on active duty. The branch treasury contributed small amounts to help finance the chief's trips, train fare was free to reservists in uniform on official business, and lodgings were cheap—the *zaigō gunjinkai* itself helped to maintain two low-priced hotels, one in Tokyo's Kudanshita district and one in Osaka's Higashi Ward.[17] Nevertheless, one does not travel four or five days to Tokyo and finance the trip with a few yen from the branch exchequer. Even more expensive than the Anjō branch chief's periodic trips was his entertainment of visiting officers from the Toyohashi regimental area headquarters. Three times every year —for the annual reservist inspection in August, the draft physical examination in September, and the youth training center review in December—a delegation of officers descended on Anjō. On these occasions, the local chief, with only a little financial help from the branch, wined and dined the visitors. It is easy to visualize the high life these regimental officers must have led as they went from party to party throughout the district and the financial burden on the Anjō and neighboring branch chiefs when they provided periodic spreads of food and sake for thirty or forty people. (Each chief entertained all of local officialdom from the mayor down, as well as the visitors.) This expense was not unique to the Toyohashi district. The Ōkamada-

---

16. Fukutake Tadashi, *Japanese Rural Society* (London and New York, 1967), pp. 146–147.

17. Anjō documents, Volume IX, *Jimu nisshi* [A Diary of Official Business], 1933–1944.

Futagawa branch chief believed it cost him twenty to twenty-five yen to entertain once a year at the time of the annual review. The chief in larger Anjō, who was wealthier and could better afford it, entertained three times a year and must have spent considerably more. Branch officials probably hesitated before placing the burden of such an expensive job on someone without the means to pay for it.

The job was time-consuming as well as costly. The branch chief was required to attend every branch meeting, frequent gatherings of the cadre, most important community events, every military funeral (not only in his own town or village, but often in neighboring ones as well), youth association and youth training center functions, the annual conscription physical examination, and to take long trips to regional meetings or to visit local men on active duty. The volume of the Anjō documents which contains a list of most of the branch's officially sanctioned trips and business records that between April, 1933 and July, 1944, branch chiefs spent almost five hundred days on such official business. The town of Anjō also conducted at least ninety-five public funerals for soldiers between September 8, 1937 and October 22, 1943, all of which the branch chief attended. Moreover, there were sixty recorded annual branch functions in addition to those mentioned above and all of the informal and emergency meetings that the Anjō branch chief of necessity attended.[18] The Anjō branch chief and several other counterparts elsewhere were not exaggerating when they stated that the job took at least half of their work week. Even the Ōkamada-Futagawa chief, who headed a small branch and took no trips to visit soldiers at the barracks, reported that he spent one-third of his time on the job. The reservists who selected chiefs and other branch leaders had to be assured that their choice had the wealth to work half time and still support his family.

The selectors also looked for a man who was available to take on the leadership task. Most men who were wealthy and prestigious enough to hold the branch chief's position were already involved in other community leadership posts since a history of community service was an important prerequisite for the reservist post. Thus, the candi-

18. Anjō documents, Volume VI, *Sembyōshisha oyobi izoku meibo* [A Register of Those Who Died in War and Their Survivors]. This document lists 155 Anjō men who died on active duty between September 8, 1937, and October 22, 1943. It records date and place killed or died, plus rank, name, hamlet, and survivor. In 95 cases, the register records the date on which a town funeral was held. If, as is possible, town funerals were held, but not recorded in any of the other 60 cases, the branch chief attended even more than fifteen or sixteen funerals per year. Volume X, *Jigyō yotei oyobi jisshihyō tsuzuri*, records branch activities for 1926–1933, 1935, 1937–1938, 1941, and 1943. Volume IX, *Jimu nisshi*.

date had to be willing to resign from at least some of the positions he already held, or be temporarily out of a job. Two of the most successful of the local reservist branch chiefs in our sample were middle-school educated, reserve officer, wealthy, and activist landlords who had not served their communities for several years because of illness. They had every qualification to serve including free time, and threw themselves into their new reservist tasks wholeheartedly.

In spite of the costs in money and time, serving as branch chief was not without its compensations. The job brought the holder an honored position in the town or village. Interviews with former members, and local history and newspaper reports of town and village functions show that the reserve branch chief held one of his community's top posts.[19] Only the mayor and school principals consistently ranked ahead of the branch chief, and he generally rated with the fire chief, agricultural cooperative head, and president of the village assembly as one of the three or four most important second-level leaders. For a man like the Anjō chief this reinforced the importance of his family in the town's hierarchy. For one like the Ōkamada-Futagawa leader it was an avenue of upward mobility; by becoming branch chief, he proved his reliability, became an honored member of the community, and earned himself a respect that helped bring him postwar success both as prosperous farmer and community leader.

COMMUNITY ACTIVITIES

The branch officials also looked for reservist chiefs and other top leaders with long histories of community activism, men who would be trustworthy, and hard working once in office. Community pressure ensured that no one refused the branch chief's job once elected, but it did not guarantee a strong commitment to service. A number of nonofficer chiefs, when asked why the officers in their communities did not take the branch's top job, answered that the officers did not feel

---

19. A report of an Isurugi Town ceremony held on March 10, 1936, in honor of the twentieth anniversary of the local youth association, for example, lists the following honored guests in order of precedence: 1. the Toyama regimental area commander, 2. the mayor, 3. the town's police chief, 4. the girls' school principal, 5. the elementary school principal, 6. the county youth association chief, 7. the county reservist chief, 8. the town's reservist branch chief, 9. six town council members, 10. the head of the agricultural cooperative, 11. the managers of the town's banks, and 12. all local men who had won medals on active duty. The reservist branch chief ranked only after the mayor, police chief, and school principals among town leaders; and military and reservist figures ranked first, seventh, eighth, and twelfth in order of precedence at a civilian ceremony. *Toyama-ken Nishi Tonami-gun Isurugi seinen-danshi* (Kanazawa, 1935), p. 365.

an obligation to perform the job well. The branch chief was required, as one respondent said, "to gather up the feelings of the members, put them together, and then act." Gathering the members' feelings—that is, building a consensus—was time consuming; only a man dedicated to spending that time made a good branch chief.

The best way to determine whether or not a man had the necessary commitment was to look at his past record of service to the *zaigō gunjinkai* and community. Most of our twenty-one branch chief-respondents had outstanding records of service before becoming local reservist heads. All of them performed official jobs in the reservist branch; almost every man in the sample was a former assistant chief, director, or hamlet-level leader. But over and above that, at least eleven of the twenty-one had held town and village posts of varying kinds. Our sample includes one farm cooperative head, two school teachers, two village office officials (one of whom was also fire chief), two village assembly members, a hamlet chief, and at least three youth association officials.[20] Men who had already held town and village posts had proven their dependability; they tended to be selected as reservist branch chiefs.

The early careers of four of the top six leaders of the Anjō reservist branch between 1940 and 1943 show how important activism was in the selection of leaders and how intertwined the leadership of the various civil and military community organizations became. These men—the chief, an assistant chief, and two of three directors, all interviewed by the author—held at least seven reservist, eleven youth association, and five other town offices before taking over the reserve branch's war time leadership. Among them, they had served as reservist assistant chief (1), director (1), school district level reservist head (2), and hamlet level chief (3); they had functioned as youth association chief (1), assistant chief (1), treasurer (1), school-district level chief (1), assistant chief (1), hamlet level chief (1), hamlet-level treasurer (1), and youth drill instructor (4); and they served as town fire chief (1), block association head (*chōnaikaichō*) (1), military affairs clerk (1), hamlet treasurer (1), and school teacher (1). In other words, these four men held a total of at least twenty-seven important community posts (including the final four in 1940–1943) between 1926 and 1943, beginning with the youth association ones while still in their early twenties, and

---

20. This information was drawn from question number five of the questionnaires, and from interviews. The biographical section of *Taishō Yamanashi-ken shi* [A History of Yamanashi Prefecture in the Taishō Era] (Kofu, 1927), pp. 481–558, contains numerous examples of activists who became reservist chiefs and then went on to other important community positions.

working up to the reservist and town ones later. All four became the reserve association's top leaders after careers of active service to their hamlet and their town which dated back to their earlier success while on active duty in the army. Moreover, after the war's end in 1945, the men continued to serve their community. One became a city assembly member and later chief assistant to the mayor, and he and one other were honored in the 1960s as "meritorious contributors to local autonomy" (jichi kōrōsha).[21]

HAMLET BALANCE

The selectors had one more requirement to consider in choosing a new branch chief—hamlet balance. Branch chiefs directed a village or town-wide organization and drew on reservists from each of the community's subdivisions. No successful branch could afford to continually draw its leaders from the same part of its jurisdiction because if they did the hamlet oriented farmer-members might not cooperate. The Anjō evidence, which includes our only complete list of all branch officials, their ranks, terms of office, and hamlets of residence, supports this contention. Anjō's reserve branch had thirteen branch chiefs between 1910 and 1945. They represented ten of the town's nineteen hamlets, and only two of the largest subdivisions provided more than one chief. The twenty-seven assistant chiefs came from fourteen hamlets including seven of the nine that had provided no branch chiefs. This balance was even more fundamental among the leaders of the five school district subdivisions. Three districts alternated their top positions from year to year among the subordinate hamlets. The other two, although they did not change leaders annually from hamlet to hamlet, nevertheless made certain that none of these subdivisions were left unrepresented for long. In selecting school-district level and town branch leadership, hamlet symmetry was almost perfectly preserved. In fact, there was only one condition that modified this balance. Hamlets with many reservists provided more officials than those with few. Thus the two hamlets that never provided a chief or assistant chief were two of the four with the fewest members; conversely, the three that provided the greatest number of leaders with one exception had the greatest reservist population. The same was true at the school district level; the fifth district contained three hamlets, but alternated the top position among the two most populous ones, and allowed a leader from

21. Anjō documents, Volume V, *Yakuin meibo; Anjō-machi seinendanshi*, I, pp. 190–215; *Anjō-shi seinendanshi*, (Anjō, 1962) II, pp. 36–49; *Anjō-shi shi* [The History of Anjō City] (Anjō, 1973), II, p. 770.

tiny Chaya into the highest position only once.[22] The men who chose
the top branch officials had to consider hamlet balance and membership population in choosing their leaders if the army was to maintain branch harmony and cooperation.

THREE BRANCH CHIEF CASE STUDIES

Not every branch found a leader who met all of the criteria outlined
here for branch chief selection. Some men were such powerful landlords, or so wealthy, or so intensely active in community affairs that
these qualities more than outweighed shortcomings in other areas.
If the son of the village's richest landlord became branch chief without
having had a career of active community service, it did not necessarily
jeopardize the reservists' local acceptance as a community organization. On the other hand, occasionally a man who did not fill all of the
criteria became branch chief because there was no one else available
who was more highly qualified or more enthusiastic about taking the
job. In such instances, the *zaigō gunjinkai* could fall short of achieving
its purposes completely. In order to illustrate how branches balanced
the six criteria is selecting a chief, and to clarify the degree to which
their fulfillment could affect the army's local acceptance, I will present
briefly case studies of three branch chiefs, two who directed very successful branches and one who led a branch less highly integrated into
his village.

The first case is that of A, who directed a branch in the farm village
of Mitsue in Yamanashi's Naka-Koma County. A met the first two
criteria perfectly. He had had a successful military career by becoming
an officer through the one-year volunteer system in 1919, and he was
one of the two best-educated reservists in the sample of 177. A studied
at Meiji University in Tokyo. A met the third and fourth qualities
also. His father was not only one of Mitsue's largest landowners, but
also a successful rural entrepreneur who ran a cotton (*wata*) manufacturing company, and was a director of many other firms. The elder
A also served as mayor as did three other relatives between 1890 and
1940. Young A clearly had the military success, rank, education, social
status, and wealth to become a successful branch chief. A also had the
free time to become Mitsue's number one reservist because he became
branch chief in 1920 at the age of 22, immediately after he returned
from active service and before he had involved himself in other
community tasks. Thus A, who met the first four criteria, had never

22. Anjō documents, Volume V, *Yakuin meibo*. In 1941, Chaya hamlet had only
17 reservists, but neighboring Ima hamlet had 252.

served his community. A, however, did not need a history of village activism to become branch chief. His family was one of Mitsue's most important, and their activism proved that the son would be a reliable leader. When Lieutenant A took command of the Mitsue *zaigō gunjinkai* in 1920, he was clearly the "young master" taking his rightful position in the village.

The A family's power in Mitsue was so strong that the son continued to control the village's reservist branch even after he moved for business reasons to the nearby city of Kofu in 1922. The family continued as absentee landlords, and Lieutenant A continued as branch chief, running the branch from the village office and his Kofu residence ten miles away. In 1931 he stepped down as branch chief and, although he no longer lived in the county, became county-wide consolidated branch chief. The branch chiefs who chose him must have reasoned that after eight years as Mitsue's branch chief he now met all the criteria, including activism, and he still owned land and thus exerted influence in Naka-Koma.

A's post-reservist career of active regional service is also important, for it indicates that he was the powerful local "man of stature" Tanaka wanted in *zaigō gunjinkai* branch leadership. A's first foray into nonreservist leadership came during the Pacific War. In 1942 he became the county chief, and then the prefectural assistant chief of the civilian Greater Japan Imperial Rule Men's Association (*Dainihon yokusan sōnendan*), an organization which, according to Satogami Ryūhei, became the Japanese equivalent of the Nazi storm troopers in 1942.[23] After the war, A was "purged" by the American military authorities, a fate he viewed as an honor. As he told the author, "I did my duty and felt only pride." After the government lifted this ban on holding office, A renewed his commitment to public service (and to his prewar political views) by becoming a member of the Kofu City, and later, the prefectural, boards of education. "I was glad to be chosen," he stated, "because it allowed me to continue my fight against Communism by opposing the Japan Teachers' Union. Every village board had at least one former reservist on it; this luckily saved the day for postwar Japanese education." A ended his career of community activism by serving as the president of the Kofu chapter of Rotary International; today he lives in comfortable semiretirement and contributes his influence to some local causes. Yamanashi government officials still refer to him as a "regional man of influence" (*chihō*

---

23. Satogami Ryūhei, "Dainihon yokusan sōnendan" [Greater Japan Imperial Rule Men's Association] in Tokinoya Katsu, ed., *Nihon kindaishi jiten* (Tokyo, 1960) p. 354.

no kenryokusha). A was born to lead; thus it seems natural that he became village *zaigō gunjinkai* chief at age twenty-two and fulfilled Tanaka's vision of the ideal branch chief.

The second branch chief, B, led the Anjō branch from 1940 until 1945, and fulfilled every requirement for top leadership. He was assuredly a good soldier. B went on active duty as a one-year volunteer in 1921, served in Nagoya and Manchuria as a sergeant officer candidate, received his commission as a second lieutenant in 1922, and was later recalled to active duty six times, four times for additional training and twice during the Pacific War. He was also a member of the nation's and Anjō's educational elite. Although he did not matriculate in a university like A, B did graduate from middle school, and this placed him in the upper 12 percent of the Anjō questionnaire sample. Most important, B belonged to one of the most prestigious and wealthiest families in Sato, the fifth largest hamlet in Anjō. Although he was not as wealthy as A, B was a landlord who owned 12½ acres, and his father and elder brother owned even more land than he. B and his family's landholdings and prestige guaranteed him the social status, wealth, and free time necessary for a branch chief. He, like A, was available for the job when he was asked to serve in 1940. A had been free to take the job because he was only twenty-two years old at the time and held no local positions. B was free because in 1936 when he took over as a youth association assistant branch chief, he had just recovered from a serious illness which had forced him to resign as a school teacher several years earlier. He moved from the *seinendan* position to reservist assistant branch chief in 1937 to branch chief in 1940. Although he and his family did not have quite the prestige and wealth of A, they did excel in local activism. B had been a youth drill instructor, hamlet government treasurer, and elementary school teacher before becoming assistant chief of the youth and then the reservist branch. His elder brother had been a *zaigō gunjinkai* director and Sato hamlet civil government chief. B also served as Anjō's Imperial Rule Men's Association head during the war, and was chosen in 1968 as "meritorious contributor to local autonomy." Finally, when he became Anjō's twelfth branch chief, B was the first Sato man to hold the post. Sato was one of the town's largest subdivisions; it was obviously time for one of its sons to become reservist branch chief. B had every qualification to become an excellent branch chief, and Anjō maintained a very large and successful branch.

The third branch chief, C, the reservist leader in Ōkamada-Futagawa during the closing years of the Pacific War, was a totally different type of branch chief from A and B. If B was a "hamlet-town power," and A a "regional power" branch chief, C was a "middle level, upwardly mobile" *zaigō gunjinkai* leader. The two landlord chiefs utilized their reservist positions to reinforce their families' local power. C's family did not have that kind of power to reinforce; he gained a reputation of being a village "doer" through his service to the reservist branch, so that his fellow villagers later chose him to fill important nonmilitary posts.

Although C did not become an officer, he did have a successful military career and brought honor to his community. An early graduate of the Ōkamada-Futagawa Youth Training Center, C served only one and a half years on active duty and came home as a superior private in 1931. Rarely did a soldier become a superior private without the extra half year of service, and C was immediately selected as a youth training center drill instructor on his return, a position he held until 1945. His education was the "typical" one for a rural youth and thus inferior to that of A and B. C graduated from higher elementary school and the army's local training center. He alone among the three chiefs was not a landlord with high social status and wealth. C owned and cultivated a farm of over two acres, an average sized farm, and rented and cultivated another acre and a quarter to supplement his income as an owner-farmer. His landownership did not put him in the villages' elite, but it did place him well above average in highly stratified Ōkamada and Futagawa. C was the fourth largest landowner among the twenty farmers in the two villages' reservist questionnaire sample.

C's strongest quality was his commitment to village activism. Not only did he serve for fourteen years as a youth school drill instructor (most drill teachers resigned after three or four years), but he became a director of the Ōkamada-Futagawa farmers' association, and an official, and then the local head, of the villages' Imperial Rule Men's Association. His prewar and wartime activism won C so much respect that after the war he was selected for leadership posts in a number of community farm and civic organizations despite his being barred from holding public office by the American authorities between 1945 and 1951. C did not have the military rank, education, landholdings, and wealth to compare with the first two examples or to allow us to conclude that the branch was led by a member of the village elite; nevertheless, his social position and reputation as a diligent farmer were solid enough to command respect, and C had solid military and community service credentials.[24]

---

24. These biographies are based on questionnaires, interviews with the three leaders, the Anjō reservist documents and youth histories in the case of B; and on interviews and conversations with other reservists, community officials, and neigh-

The evidence indicates that the Anjō reservist branch played more of a community role and won for the army a comparatively greater acceptance than did the Ōkamada-Futagawa branch, and that this may have been related to the difference in leadership. In Anjō, an agricultural town with a relatively low degree of tenancy and stratification, the branch chief in our sample was a middle-school educated, officer-landlord. The other twelve branch chiefs before and after him were either commissioned or noncommissioned officers, most of whom were either doctors or products of the one-year volunteer program, thus at least middle school graduates and well-to-do. Anjō's reserve branch's tentacles extended into virtually every area of the town's life. Anjō reservists led youth group members in military drill, patriotic education, and athletics, carried out extensive public works enterprises, functioned as the mainstays of the fire department, performed disaster relief, and carried out a wide range of other educational and community services with larger than military implications. Anjō reservists acted as if they served in a town and hamlet organization.

In Ōkamada and Futagawa, villages with extensive tenancy, on the other hand, the one branch chief in our sample was an owner-tenant farmer, and the reservist-interview respondents perceived of their local village role differently from their Anjō counterparts. The various community and educational activities which Anjōites considered branch duties, Ōkamada-Futagawa reservists sometimes did not. They too performed disaster relief, carried out public works, fought fires, etc., but they generally did so as hamlet and village residents, not as reservists. In a rare exception to the nationwide *zaigō gunjinkai* obligation to provide instructors for the local youth training center after 1926, the village office did not assign men because of their membership in the reservist branch. All of the instructors belonged to the *zaigō gunjinkai*, but their formal selection as instructors had no official connection with that membership.

The difference in the degree of integration of the reservists' branches into the communities in Anjō and Ōkamada-Futagawa is also reflected in the self-perceptions of the members in the two communities. The four interview respondents in Anjō reported that they perceived of the reserve branch there primarily as a community organization and secondarily as a military one; their three Ōkamada-Futagawa counterparts viewed their former role in reverse order. Eighty-three percent of the questionnaire respondents in Anjō stated that they felt their neighbors respected them as reservists; only 53 percent of the Ōka-

bors in all three areas. Also *Yamanashi jinji kōshinroku* [A Directory of Yamanashi People] (Kofu, 1940), pp. 1135–1136, and *Anjō-shi shi*, II, p. 770.

madans agreed. (Eighty-nine percent of the rest of the respondents felt respected.) [25] It would appear that the Anjō reserve branch was more of a community organization, and that its members earned greater respect (or at least the belief that they were respected) than in Ōkamada-Futagawa. Interpreting the relationship between *zaigō gunjinkai* branch leadership, local acceptance and respect presents us with a "chicken and egg" dilemma. Can we attribute Anjō's comparatively greater success to its leadership, or vice versa? But we need not decide which, if either, was cause and which was effect. It is sufficient to conclude that the evidence indicates that Tanaka was correct: branches with leaders of high community status were more successful in attaining the army's goals. Reservists in Ōkamada-Futagawa alone of the dozen or more communities for which we have leadership information did not achieve total local acceptance. Success at local integration, however, must be viewed on a comparative scale, and even in Ōkamada-Futagawa the army had at least moderate success.

OTHER RESERVIST BRANCH OFFICIALS

Available evidence on subbranch chief officials of the reservist association suggests that lower ranking branch leaders tended to have the same qualities, only to a lesser degree, than chiefs. As one might expect, the upper level leaders generally held higher military rank and therefore reflected greater success while on active duty than the lower ones, who in turn held higher rank and reflected greater success than the members in general. In Anjō for example, all branch chiefs and assistant chiefs held the rank of corporal or above, compared to 74 percent of directors and auditors, 36 percent of the school district leaders, 17 percent of the hamlet or hamlet cluster chiefs, and only 3 percent of the rest of the membership. Moreover, all but one of the chiefs, assistant chiefs, directors, auditors, and school district leaders had served on active duty, and only 28 untrained men were ranked among the 489 hamlet level chiefs. Since in 1927, 51 percent of the membership had never served on active duty, but less than 5 percent

---

25. The question, number 55, reads as follows:
"Were reservists respected by local people?
a. respected
b. not respected
c. no special feeling"
Of the 169 respondents who answered, 140 (82.8 percent) stated "respected," 29 (17.2 percent) "no special feeling," and none "not respected". This broke down to 12–10 (53 percent) for Ōkamada-Futagawa, 35–7 (83 percent) for Anjō, and 93–12 (89 percent) for Katsunuma and the Yamanashi-wide sample.

Table 19

BREAKDOWN OF LEADERS BY RANK, ANJŌ RESERVIST BRANCH, 1910–1945 [a]

	Total	Total data	Officers		Non-commissioned Officers		Enlisted men		Untrained members	
Branch chief/Assistant chief	45	44	22	50.0%	22	50.0%	0	0.0%	0	0.0%
Director/Accountant	59	57	15	26.2%	27	47.4%	14	24.6%	1	1.8%
School district level chief	101	96	0	0.0%	34	35.6%	62	64.6%	0	0.0%
Hamlet level chief	534	489	0	0.0%	81	16.6%	380	77.7%	28	5.7%

[a] Anjō documents, Volume V, *Yakuin meibo;* Vol. X, *Jigyō yotei oyobi jisshihyō tsuzuri; Anjō-chōshi,* (Anjō, 1919),, pp. 123–124.

of the branch officials had received no training, Anjō branch leaders not only held higher rank, but also were more likely to have served on active duty (and therefore to have been more successful) than the reservist rank and file. (See Tables 19 and 20.)

The questionnaire and interview data indicate that there was no difference between subbranch chief officials and members in only one category, that of education. Branch chiefs tended to be better educated middle school graduates, but most of the other reservists in our sample (141 of the 155 who answered) completed no more than the compulsory elementary education, and in most cases the subsequent part-time youth center, vocational, or youth school training. (See Table 13.) There are two reasons for the similarity in the education of officials below the rank of chief and of the members in general. Men who graduated from middle school but did not become one-year volunteers and then officers, lacked interest in military affairs. Many were conscripted, served their two years on active duty, and then migrated to the city to find work commensurate with their education. If they returned home to the village, they joined the zaigō gunjinkai; everyone did. But their lack of enthusiasm in volunteering for officer's rank usually precluded their being singled out as reservist leaders. Moreover, a number of the educated reservists were replacement soldiers who had never served on active duty. As we have seen, only 29 of the 686 Anjō leaders in Table 19 came from replacement soldier ranks, and 20 of these men lived in the town's four smallest hamlets where the reservist branch subunits found a dearth of qualified leaders. A number of middle school graduates fell into the ranks of the untrained replacement soldiers because this was a category determined by one's rating on the conscription physical examination. Needless to say, the best-educated youths were not necessarily the healthiest.

Table 20
BREAKDOWN OF NON-LEADERS BY RANK, ANJŌ RESERVIST
BRANCH, 1918, 1927 [a]

Year	Non-leader members	Officers and non-commissioned officers		Enlisted men		Untrained members	
1918	1,046	32	3.1%		1,014		96.9%
1927	998	29	2.9%	459	46.0%	510	51.1%

[a] Anjō documents, Volume V, *Yakuin meibo;* Volume X, *Jigyō yotei oyobi jisshihyō tsuzuri; Anjō-chōshi,* pp. 123–124.

Middle level branch leaders tended to be socially more prestigious and wealthier than the members in general. Our questionnaire information indicates that among the 128 farmer-member respondents —16 branch chiefs, 69 officials, and 43 members—the higher a man's branch position, the more likely he was to be a landlord or owner-farmer. Seventy-five percent of the chiefs, 65.2 percent of the officials, and 53.4 percent of the members functioned without having to cultivate tenanted land. In comparatively egalitarian Anjō, 100 percent (1), 77.3 percent (22), and 62.5 percent (8) of the respondents in each of the three categories were landlords or owner-farmers. Moreover, although high social status was important to a reservist leader's success, wealth was not a major requirement for subbranch chief officials. Almost all of the traveling and entertainment expenses fell on the branch chief's shoulders.

The Anjō evidence also indicates that reservist leaders tended to play a more active role in community affairs prior to serving in official *zaigō gunjinkai* positions than the membership in general. By comparing reservist and youth association leadership rosters for the 1915–1945 period, the three decades when both organizations existed simultaneously, we find that 80 percent (8 of 10) of the branch chiefs, and 52.7 percent (264 of 501) of the other reservist officials appear on both lists. These 272 men represented 18 percent of the youth branch's 1,500 leaders during these thirty years. The remaining 82 percent—about 1,200 to 1,250 positions—were filled by the other 7,700 20–25-year-olds who served in the youth association's Anjō branch between 1915 and 1945.[26] In other words, reservist officials at all levels were three or four times more likely to have been youth branch leaders than men who did not become *zaigō gunjinkai* officials. Community activism between the ages of twenty and twenty-five, the age limits for *seinendan* leaders, prepared men for later reservist leadership; more important, it proved to local officials and *zaigō gunjinkai* members that the activist was dependable. Finally, as we saw in the section on branch chief selection, hamlet balance was an important consideration in choosing all of the Anjō branch's leaders.

RESERVIST LEADERSHIP CONCLUSION

In communities where the army was able to recruit "natural" leaders to run the reservist association, as in Mitsue and especially in Anjō, it had its greatest success at achieving local acceptance and winning pop-

---

26. Anjō documents, Volume V, *Yakuin meibo*; *Anjō-machi seinendanshi*, I, pp. 190–215; *Anjō-shi seinendanshi*, II, pp. 36–49.

ular support for the army. Those chiefs who best met the six criteria and thus reflected both military rank and skill, and local commitment, status, wealth, activism, availability, and hamlet balance, were able to make their branches the central organizations of their communities. The army attained this goal in six of the seven communities for which we have detailed interview and questionnaire data—in Tsubota, Anjō, Mitsue, Fuchū, Katsunuma, and Iwai, men of moderate to high status were in control, and the branches were successful. One can add to this the patterns of success revealed in the questionnaires distributed to Yamanashi Prefecture reservists from twelve different communities, and conclude that only Ōkamada-Futagawa was not a typical case.

One must also remember that even in Ōkamada-Futagawa the army did not fail. The reservist association helped the army attain its goals of local acceptance and popularity there as well as elsewhere. The difference between reservists in these two villages and in the others, Anjō, for example, was not that the Ōkamada-Futagawa "soldiers" performed fewer community functions. The difference was that in Anjō they always carried them out as reservists, and in Ōkamada-Futagawa they sometimes did not. But Ōkamada-Futagawa men still performed essential community services while they simultaneously belonged to the reservist branch, and thus they served as model citizens and "grass roots" soldiers at the same time. They too became the mainstays (chūken) of their villages, and identified military values with community services.

YOUTH ASSOCIATION LEADERSHIP

The reservist association was the army's channel to local Japan and allowed the military to influence the youth association without direct military manipulation. Tanaka and Ugaki, rather than attempt the impossible and organize nonmilitary types from the Army Ministry in Tokyo, cooperated with national-level civil ministries and, more important, with local-level civil and reservist leaders, to exert influence on the youths. Local reservist branches not only became the model by which the teenagers chose their leaders, but also provided many of them.

The army was able to influence the local youth association both because reservists actually held many of the youth branch's leadership posts and because the reservist branch and its adult members traditionally dominated the younger villagers. To begin with, each community's reservist branch chief automatically became an assistant youth association chief. Tanaka and his Home and Education Ministry colleagues established in 1915, as we have seen, a maximum age limit of twenty years old, and believed that teenage youth were too immature to lead themselves properly. The national leaders decided that the mayor of each village and town automatically would be *seinendan* chief, and that the deputy mayor, the local elementary school principal, and the reservist branch chief would be his assistants.

In 1920, when the Tokyo central leadership abolished this age limit and allowed each prefecture to determine its own maximum requirement, Tanaka and the other central officials also gave local branches the option of continuing to draw their leaders from the four village-town officials, or from among the members. The Tokyo leaders believed the newly enlisted "over twenties" (all prefectures revised the age limit upwards) had the maturity to serve as officials. Despite the new regulations, however, not all communities moved to electing their own branch officials. The Anjō reservist chief, for example, remained a top youth association leader until 1936, and even in those communities that changed to the new system, the reservist leader remained a youth association adviser.[27] The reservist influence did not decline, but actually increased, after member-chiefs began to head the young men's organization. In Anjō, for example, the first three elected youth branch chiefs were ex-soldiers who became reservist leaders, and the last two, both reservists, did not become *zaigō gunjinkai* officials only because the army recalled them to active duty during the post-1937 China War. One of the wartime reservist directors mentioned above in our discussion of the importance of village activism to reservist leadership served as the first elected youth branch chief and as hamlet-level reservist chief (and youth school military drill instructor and town office military affairs' clerk) in 1937.[28]

Reservists also played a major role at the subbranch chief youth association level, both before and after the 1920 revision of the regulations. The selection process for subbranch chief leaders in most communities exactly paralleled the reservist process. Hamlet members chose their hamlet chiefs, and these officials in turn selected the directors, secretaries, and—after 1920, in an increasing number of communities—the branch chief and assistant branch chiefs. Virtually all

27. *Anjō-machi seinendanshi*, I, pp. 190–191; *Anjō-shi seinendanshi*, II, pp. 36–39; *Toyama-ken Higashi Tonami-gun Higashi Nojiri-mura seinendanshi* (Kanazawa, 1935), p. 74; *Nagano-ken seinen hattatsushi* (Nagano, 1935), p. 35; *Zenkoku seinendan kihon chōsa* (Tokyo, 1935), pp. 25, 32.
28. *Anjō-shi seinendanshi*, II, pp. 37–38. The author interviewed this youth-reservist leader.

(99.6 percent) of the officials were from the number of members over twenty years old, approximately 40 percent of the membership at any one time. These men had already taken their conscription physical examination, often had served on active duty, and usually belonged to both the youth and reservist associations at the same time.

Rural youth association members usually elected reservists as *seinendan* leaders because most young men between the ages of twenty and twenty-five were members of the *zaigō gunjinkai*. As we have seen, 60 to 70 percent of the eligibles passed the conscription physical examination and became potential reservists; as we have also seen, practically everyone who passed in rural Japan did in fact join the *zaigō gunjinkai*. Thus we can assume that at least two-thirds of the men in any community's potential youth branch leadership pool belonged simultaneously to the reservist association.[29]

The Anjō evidence, moreover, indicates that reservists with the most outstanding active duty records—i.e., reservist leaders-to-be—tended to hold youth association official positions out of proportion with their actual numbers. As we discussed above, over half of the *zaigō gunjinkai* leaders in Anjō had served as youth branch cadre, and reservist officials of the future were three or four times more likely to become youth branch leaders than other *seinendan* "elders." It appears that the outstanding soldier, on his return from the barracks, was the type of villager most likely to be elected to a *seinendan* office. His military success and youth group activism, in turn, made him a good candidate for reservist leadership. The fittest, most active, best soldiers tended to run both organizations. In Anjō, at least, Tanaka's goal of making reservists mainstays (*chūken*) of their communities by involving them in extra-reservist and especially youth affairs was certainly fulfilled.

In addition, the *zaigō gunjinkai* officially led the youth association in many of its important local activities, especially at the subvillage hamlet level. Reservists in eleven of the twelve areas for which we have detailed evidence drilled youth group members, gave them patriotic lectures, sponsored athletic meets, overnight hikes, and "maneuvers" for them, and directed them in building schools, repairing roads, fighting fires, tilling the fields of families of soldiers on active duty, preparing for and conducting soldiers' funerals, and a host of other "joint" activities. Reservist squad leaders in each Anjō hamlet conducted weekly drill sessions and monthly patriotic ceremonies and agricultural seminars for local youth branch members and led them in

---

29. *Anjō-shi seinendanshi*, II, p. 35.

periodic aid to soldiers' families; Isurugi reservists and youth association members "cooperated" to build a garden for a local school, to perform disaster relief, to clear roads in the winter, to carry out physical training, and to see off and greet servicemen; Higashi Nojiri reservists directed their youthful fellow villagers in constructing a local school, in agricultural improvement, in military and physical training, in funerals for soldiers, and in many patriotic activities; and this is to mention only a few.[30] In these cases, the reservists did not serve as actual member-leaders of the *seinendan*. Instead the village or town office and hamlet officials delegated overall responsibility and command in the performance of the tasks to the reservist branch. Its leaders in turn gave immediate direction to the younger men, often their own brothers or sons. One might say that the 15–20-year-old youths provided the brawn, the 20–25-year-old *seinendan-zaigō gunjinkai* members more muscle and the intermediate leadership, and the older reservists the top direction. In some communities where the maximum youth association age limit was over twenty-five, local practice required that the nonreservist members remain in the *seinendan* until they reached the maximum age. Men who joined the local reservist branch, however, left the youth group at age twenty-five and served in only one "age group" organization. As a result the healthier elite of ex-servicemen and reservists received the authority to direct their own age-group peers, those "youths," often in their late twenties or even early thirties who had failed the conscription physical examination and of necessity remained members of the local young men's association.[31]

One can conclude, I believe, that with this one exception for the unfit, the reservist and youth branches took on the character of unofficial village and hamlet age-group organizations. Even when the community's government did not specifically delegate leadership authority over youths to reservists, the military group took that leadership because its members were the community's fittest men in the physical prime of their lives, and the youths fell into a younger and less experienced age bracket. In Ōkamada-Futagawa, for example, the one village in which the reservists and youths were officially independent, the village and hamlet fire departments chose reservists as lead-

---

30. See Chapter V, Table 26 and footnote 1. *Anjō-machi seinendanshi*, I, pp. 126–131; *Anjō-shi seinendanshi*, II, pp. 168–169, 248; *Isurugi seinendanshi*, pp. 60, 78, 91, 95, 112, 130, 137, 208, 211, 270, 273, 311–312, 324–327, 360, 451, etc.; *Higashi Nojiri-mura seinendanshi*, pp. 80, 84, 89, 91, 126, 136–137, 141–150, 155–157, 169–171, 181, etc.

31. Tsubota Village on Miyake Island is an example. Men who passed the conscription examination left the *seinendan* at age 25; those who failed left at age 30.

ers and *seinendan* members as firemen. They did this because all healthy 20–40-year-old "leaders" served as reservists, and all of the teenage "followers" joined the youth association. Both officially and unofficially, each community's *zaigō gunjinkai* led each *seinendan* in patriotic and physical training and in many community service functions. Tanaka and the army could disregard expanding military influence over the youths at the national level because the reservists provided most of the youth leadership in the village and town.

YOUTH TRAINING CENTERS AND YOUTH SCHOOLS

The army's reservists also provided a large share of the leadership of the youth training centers–youth schools after they were established in 1926. Although the Education Ministry (albeit, at the army's behest), created the new schools, the nature of their curriculum demanded close civil-military cooperation at both the national and the local level. The schools, which enrolled the same 15–19-year-olds who served as the *seinendan's* rank and file, taught in four areas: vocational, particularly agriculture skills; academic disciplines, with an emphasis on the national language and everyday mathematics; ethical training, with special attention on inculcating nationalism; and military drill. Drill consumed over half of the male students' time before 1935, and more than one-third afterward.

The youth schools called on three groups to provide the administrators and teachers necessary to train their expanding number of students. The elementary school principal in the corresponding elementary school district automatically became training center–youth school principal. Since the Education Ministry took responsibility for the new system, the youth school districts coincided exactly with the compulsory education school districts, and the youth classes were normally held in the elementary school building or on its athletic field. The area's elementary school teachers taught vocational and academic subjects and ethics. Reservists provided all of the drill instruction. In 1934, 37 percent of the nation's 112,000 youth training center teachers and principals came from the ranks of the nation's reserve association members, and these 40,937 men represented only the official reservist youth school instructors; another 80,000 to 100,000 *zaigō gunjin* assisted.[32]

Both the youth training center–youth school drill instructors and their assistants were selected for service by the local community's re-

32. Ishikawa Ken, ed., *Kindai Nihon kyōiku seidō shiryō* (Tokyo, 1956), III, p. 555.

servist branch leaders. The leaders in all seven communities where interviews were conducted selected the teachers from among each year's returned servicemen with the most outstanding active duty records. Thus the branch officials tended to select their own successors, the same "activists" who directed the *seinendan* and later rose to the top of the reservist branch and to other village or town offices. In Anjō, for example, the thirty-two branch officials chose the top six soldiers as drill instructors, and a number of others as their assistants, on the basis of reports from the soldiers' active duty commanders. The system was similar in Fuchū, Tsubota, Katsunuma, Iwai, Wakakusa, and even unofficially in Ōkamada-Futagawa. All three interview respondents from Ōkamada-Futagawa served as reservist leaders and youth drill instructors and helped select the latter.

The young men invariably accepted their appointment as drill instructors although the job placed a momentarily unrewarding and time-consuming burden on them. Each teacher and assistant was required to teach between 90 and 120 hours per year, usually three times a week (except during June and October, the busy months of the agricultural year) for an hour or two before dawn or in the evening. The drill instructors received only five or ten yen per year for their efforts, hardly enough to cover their expenses, and the assistants received no recompense at all. Yet when asked why they assumed the job for such limited monetary return, the fourteen interview respondents, all of whom served as drill instructors, answered that they did so out of a sense of obligation to the nation and to the local community. Drill for teenagers, they all stated, served primarily as spiritual and physical (*shinshin no tanren*), not military, training, and this benefited the hamlet's, the village's, and the nation's unity and productivity. One respondent echoed the sentiments of all the others when he justified drill and his role as an instructor as follows:

Military drill in the youth schools was for the good of our local youths. It helped to make them physically and spiritually strong, and allowed them to overcome personal desires and work cooperatively for both the village and the nation. Present day [1969] youths could use more of it. The backbone of our community today are former youth school students. We have a sense of responsibility, but postwar youths don't. Duty, manners, and decorum are important to those of us educated before 1945. And patriotism is important too. Status may have been overemphasized before 1945, but it is definitely underemphasized now.

In other words, their views showed that these men associated the hamlet's, the village's, the army's, and the national good.

The make-up of the youth school cadre, like that of the *seinendan*, again demonstrates the tight integration of the military and the civil at the rural community level. The teachers were drawn from the Education Ministry's principals and teachers on the one hand, and the army and community's reservists on the other. The students had studied with the same civil teachers during elementary school and served under the leadership of the same newly returned ex-servicemen reservists both in the youth association and at the training centers. Teenage subordination to reservists through the two organizations in village and town was like a double pyramid topped by the reservist branch chief, responsible to the army's regimental area commander and the Army Ministry, and by the mayor, responsible to the prefectural government and the Home Ministry. In other words, while the Home, Education and Army Ministries operated independently and often competitively at the national level, their rural representatives cooperated fully in working for Tanaka's military goals and in bolstering the existing community order.

THE NATIONAL DEFENSE WOMEN'S ASSOCIATION

The data we have on the leadership of the National Defense Women's Association, from interviews, from the Tokushima newspaper for 1935, the year the organization began operations there, and from some local histories, indicate that the wives of village, town and city officials almost always held the highest women's branch posts. Because the army established the organization in the first place, and because military leaders depended on reservist aid in soliciting members, one might expect that most of the women who led the new organization would be somehow related (as wives, for example) to *zaigō gunjinkai* officials. Although we do have scattered references to this phenomenon in Tokushima and in Gumma Prefecture's Yamada County, for a series of very important reasons the wives of reservist branch chiefs usually did not take over the organization's local leadership.[33] The principal explanation is that the defense women's association branch functioned as an organization of all of the community's women over sixteen years old, not just of reservists' or servicemen's wives. Thus it was only natural that the wife of one of the top village officials, particularly of the mayor or school principal, took the job. The reservist branch chief's wife, probably five or six years younger than her

---

33. *Yamada-gunshi* (Maebashi, 1939), pp. 782–783, 792–794; *Tokushima nichinichi shimpō*, February 26, 1935, p. 2; March 3, p. 2; March 8, p. 2; March 11, p. 1; April 16, p. 2; April 21, p. 1; April 27, p. 2; May 29, p. 2.

husband, was likely to be at most in her late twenties or early thirties, and not old enough to be out from under her mother-in-law's tyranny, much less to lead an organization of all of the village's women. Most interview respondents reiterated John Embree's remark about the women of Suyemura, that they never met nor acted on their own initiative.[34] In order to organize the local women, and to motivate them to action once organized, it was essential to place older women and the wives of the community's leaders in official posts. In this way, the women leaders could enlist the prestige and support of their office-holder husbands for the good of the organization. Few young rural Japanese women, no matter what their family connections, could have led all the local women in the male-dominated, status- and seniority-conscious, prewar Japanese villages. Secondarily, in some communities —Hiroshima's Kakemachi, for example—when the village or town established the defense women's association, it did so by giving a new name and a few new activities to the existing local women's organization. This is what John Embree meant when he said that the national organization made official an unofficial system.[35] In these cases, the officials of the existing group, probably the wives of the village office and school officials, continued to lead the kokubō fujinkai.

The army showed no concern with the leadership trend described above, but actually encouraged it. It ensured the defense women's association close connections with the community's power structure in which local reservists provided important leadership. Evidence from many sources indicates that the defense women's leaders did not actually lead the organization, but operated like the seinendan under the overall guidance of the village or town office, and the immediate leadership of the reservists, in many primary activities. The questionnaire and interview respondents answered overwhelmingly that the reservists led the women in performing such essential military and community duties as comforting local soldiers on active duty, helping their families, aiding in preparations for funerals of the war dead, seeing off and greeting soldiers to and from the barracks, carrying out various public services like irrigation system repairs, and military drill. In almost every case the town or village office provided the original initiative and funds, the reservists the actual leadership, and the reservists, youth branch members, and defense women the labor. One example, the case of the funeral of a soldier killed in action from one "interview village," illustrates how this leadership functioned. The

---

34. John Embree, *Suyemura: A Japanese Village* (Chicago, 1964), p. 168.
35. *Kakemachi-shi* [The History of Kake Town] (Hiroshima, 1961) I, pp. 521–522; Embree, Suyemura, p. 171.

funeral process began when word came to the family and the military affairs clerk of the town office that the ashes of a local soldier were being returned to the community on a set day in the near future. Immediately, the mayor ordered a "town funeral," which was to be performed as a community ceremony, paid for with local government funds. He did not specifically contribute money for the funeral at this time, however, because the town office had already added an increment at the beginning of the fiscal year to its annual allocation to the reservist branch to cover all of the year's funeral expenses for soldiers. In other words, while the town paid for the costs of funerals for all its sons killed in combat, it did so through the organization which actually directed the funeral, the reservist branch. On the day the urn with the soldier's remains arrived, his family, the mayor, the reservist branch chief, the youth association head, and reservists from the deceased man's hamlet went to the railroad station to receive it. Meanwhile hamlet reservists, youth association members and defense women, under reservist direction, cleaned and readied the grave site, and other defense women from the hamlet helped the dead soldier's family make the other necessary preparations, particularly those at his home, for the next day's services. On the following day, a procession of the family, mayor, reservist and youth branch chiefs from the town, and reservists, youth association members and defense women from the hamlet went to the elementary school for the service and to the grave site for the burial. Traffic was regulated along the route by members of the town association (*chōnaikai*), whose head was the town's reservist assistant branch chief, and whose members were largely the town's women, that is, its defense women. Afterward, the men returned to the home of the deceased for food and drink which had been prepared by the women of the soldier's family and the hamlet's defense women. And, of course, the deceased soldier's mother, sisters, and wife were also defense women themselves. Hamlet women had helped each other make funeral preparations for generations and, moreover, they had done it by cooperating with their husbands and other hamlet men. But after 1910–1915, when soldiers died, the men readied, cleaned, and guided as reservists and *seinendan* members; after 1935, women cooked and prepared as defense women's association branch members. In other words, reservists led defense women not so much because the two organizations were interrelated at the national level, but more because the community's "soldiers" had directed women in these and many other activities long before the birth of the *kokubō fujinkai*. This is why John Embree could say that, "it is difficult to distinguish between the woman as a member of her *buraku* and the woman as member of the Women's Patriotic Association." [36] The army encouraged the local organizers of the new women's association to choose wives of village leaders as officials, and urged reservists to provide the real leadership, because they saw the defense women's group as one more way of identifying themselves with the traditional, cooperative rural village-town order. The army enlisted the women in their system after 1935 with hardly a change in their style of life. And so Tokutomi Sohrō could conclude that "the villages are the army's electoral constituency." [37]

THE LOCAL FINANCING OF THE ORGANIZATIONS

As did the leadership, the local financing of the organizations reflected the extent to which organizations merged into the structure of the village and town. Local officials and elite members underwrote a large part of the costs for all of the groups' local branches, although for three of the four, village and town government had no obligation to do so. The Education Ministry established the youth training centers–youth schools as one element of its national system; local officials of necessity financed them because the government funded schools and all other bureaucratically controlled local operations in this way. The reservist, youth, and defense women's associations, on the other hand, were legally private organizations; local government need not have contributed money to them at all. Substantial village and town funding, therefore, became like elite leadership an indicator that the communities accepted the branches of the three organizations as essential to local well being. The greater the local government's and elite's financial support of the branches, the deeper their penetration into the community and the greater the army's success.

THE MAJOR SOURCE OF FUNDS: LOCAL GOVERNMENT

The most important single source of money for the reservist and youth branches was the village, town, ward, or city office. It was an exceptional branch that did not draw some of its financial support from local government. In 1926, 82.7 percent (10,916) of the nation's 13,119 geographically established reservist branches received local government support, and 15.2 percent (2,093) based their activities on

36. Embree, *Suyemura*, p. 167. For a description of a funeral, see *Ryūōsonshi* [The History of Ryūō Village] (Kofu, 1955), pp. 960–966.

37. Ronald P. Dore and Tsutomu Ōuchi, "Rural Origins of Japanese Fascism," in James W. Morley, ed., *Dilemmas of Growth in Prewar Japan* (Princeton, 1971), p. 197.

Table 21

BALANCE SHEET FOR ALL RESERVIST BRANCHES, 1926 [a]

Income		
Government and organizational support	1,455,518 yen	35%
Earnings and income from investments and holdings	1,100,126	27%
Dues	918,666	22%
Gifts	684,429	16%
Total	4,158,739	100%
Expenditures	3,805,728 yen	——

[a] *Teikoku zaigō gunjinkai gyōmu shishin,* p. 473.

allocations from organizations funded by local government. Most of these local groups supporting the reserve association were village and town military societies of one sort or another, although a few were the companies that sponsored factory branches. According to the *Model Branch History* in 1926, 225 of 236 branches reporting on their finances received at least one-quarter of their funds from either local government or its organizations. The three factory branches among the 225 received their support from the company, the functional equivalent in these cases of local government. Thirty-five percent of the funds of all of the nation's reservist branches in the same year came from local government, related organizations, and in the case of factory branches, the company. (See Table 21.) [38]

The Anjō reservist branch received almost all of its funds from the town office and the local martial society (*shōbukai*). In 1918, the martial society provided 98 percent of the reservist branch's official funds (that is, excluding money spent unofficially by branch leaders). In 1926, this percentage rose slightly to 98.1 percent. By 1937, the *shōbukai* gave the branch only 49 percent of the annual budget; the town office provided almost all of the rest (See Tables 22, 23, and 24.). Thus, the government underwrote the whole operation in 1918, 1927, and 1937—the distinction between the town office and the martial society is academic. The *shōbukai* was a semiofficial organization headed by the mayor and the town council's members. It gathered

38. *Teikoku zaigō gunjinkai gyōmu shishin* (Tokyo, 1929), pp. 473, 480–485; Murata Kikugorō, ed., *Teikoku zaigō gunjinkai mohan bunkaishi* (Kawagoe, 1927), *passim.*

Table 22

BALANCE SHEET FOR ANJŌ RESERVIST BRANCH, 1918 [a]

Income		
Martial society contribution	878 yen	98%
Interest on investments	20	2%
Balance from 1917	1	
Total	899	100%
Expenditures	899 yen	——

a *Anjō-chōshi*, pp. 124–126.

Table 23

BALANCE SHEET FOR ANJŌ RESERVIST BRANCH, 1926 [a]

Income		
Martial society contribution	1,612 yen	98.1%
Interest on investments	30	1.9%
Total	1,642 yen	100.0%
Expenditures	1,464 yen	

a Anjō documents, Volume X, *Jigyō yotei oyobi jisshihyō tsuzuri*.

most of its funds from its right to levy taxes on all Anjō households and had as its only other source of funds the town government itself. In 1916, for example, the martial society raised almost 1,500 yen by taxing every Anjō household just under 50 sen each. In other words, the martial society was in reality an official arm of the Anjō government, and when it funded the reservist branch it did so as the town office's agent.[39]

Not only did at least four-fifths of the reservist branches (and 16 of 19 of the interview-questionnaire branches) receive local governmental financial support between 1910 and 1945, but they received it in in-

39. *Anjō-machi shōbukai kyōikukai eiseikai ketsugi tsuzuri* [A Notebook of Anjō Town Martial, Educational, and Hygienic Society Resolutions], 1916.

Table 24
ANJŌ RESERVIST BRANCH BUDGET, 1937 [a]

Income

Balance from 1936	1 yen	
Interest	2	
Martial society contribution	1,130	49%
Town government contribution	600	26%
Town government contribution for funeral expenses	415	18%
Miscellaneous	160	7%
Total	2,308 yen	100%

Expenditures

Equipment	7
Expendables	3
Transportation	8
Pocket money for advisers	30
Pocket money for messengers	27
Pocket money for branch officials	123
Travel money for branch officials	200
Cost of meetings	374
Condolence money for servicemen	299
Encouragement money	142
Lectures	58
Training of untrained members	82
Printing	53
Books and magazines	171
Festival expenditures	162
Service bag supplements	42
Awards	5
Entertainment	13
Reserve fund	4
Preparatory costs for men recalled to service	43
Funeral costs	390
Miscellaneous	44
Total	2,280 yen
Balance	28 yen

[a] Anjō documents, Volume XI, *Yosan kessansho tsuzuri.*

creasing numbers and amounts. In the *Model Branch History,* the number of branches financed by local government and the amounts received expanded year by year before 1926. It is likely that the increases continued after that year as well. Villages and towns probably supplied most of the local reservist branch's funds by the time the China War broke out.

Youth association branches were also financed primarily by local government offices and their satellite organizations. The Anjō *seinendan,* for example, received all of its 1929 funds from two sources, the town office and the town's educational society (*kyōikukai*). In 1936, ·86 percent of its money came from the educational society and the other 14 percent from members' donations and the preceding year's balance, while in 1941, 100 percent came from the town. (See Table 25.) The Anjō educational society, like the martial society, was a semiofficial organization. It was also headed by the mayor and town assembly members, funded by the town government, and could levy taxes on all the town's households if necessary. The Anjō youth branch's dependence on local government for funding was not exceptional. During the same time period, the Isurugi youth branch and all ten branches in Gumma Prefecture's Yamada County received funds from local government. In Isurugi, almost half came from the village and the rest from gifts of well-to-do supporters. In Yamada County, village and town offices provided all of the funds. Thus, in Anjō, Isurugi, and Yamada County, local government officials, by providing the bulk of the money for youth branch needs, proved their commitment to the local success of this nationally centralized "private" organization.[40]

Even more conclusive is the evidence from Shimo-Ina County in Nagano Prefecture, the nation's hotbed of antigovernment, radical youth activity. In the 1920s and early 1930s, a controversy raged throughout the county over whether or not local *seinendan* branches should break away from the national and prefectural organization. The major argument against establishing an independent Nagano youth organization was that in doing so the branches would lose their local support and become destitute. In fact, these fears were overly pessimistic. In most of the hamlets, villages, and towns where the local youth groups seceded from the national organization, the *seinendan* subbranches and branches continued to function locally and to receive village funds exactly as before.[41] It appears that even in this radical stronghold local financial support was very important to the

---

40. *Anjō-machi seinendanshi,* I, p. 176; *Anjō-shi seinendanshi,* II, pp. 13, 16; *Isurugi seinendanshi,* p. 526; *Yamada-gunshi,* pp. 673–679.

41. *Nagano-ken seinen hattatsushi,* pp. 161–162; 222–224.

Table 25

ANJŌ YOUTH ASSOCIATION BUDGET, 1936 [a]

Income		
Educational society contribution	1,100 yen	86%
Contributions from members	150	12%
Balance from 1935	25	2%
Total	1,275 yen	100%

Expenditures	
Branch meetings	70 yen
Seminars	100
Lectures	50
Swordfighting instructor	60
Patriotic ceremonies	70
Arts and crafts	60
Athletic and martial arts meets	210
Agricultural research	30
Military drill	150
Athletic equipment	70
Dispatch of athletes to county meets	30
Field trips	20
Condolence money for servicemen	15
Branch officials' meetings	30
Printing	10
Expendables	10
Disbursement to subordinate units	250
Miscellaneous	40
Total	1,275 yen

[a] *Anjō-shi seinendanshi*, II, pp. 13–14.

hamlet and village youth associations because local officials considered the subbranches and branches to be primarily hamlet and village organizations.

Some readers may find it unusual that in order to document local integration of the army's *seinendan* into the hamlet and village order, I present evidence indicating the success of radicals in withdrawing local youth branches from the army's system and simultaneously continuing to receive community financial support. I do so because even this extremist success was based on traditional social relationships. The radical Shimo-ina youth leaders, mostly the sons of landlords, used traditional techniques to organize their fathers' tenants' sons. Thus, they garnered the benefits of the community's social order, including village funding. Moreover, even under radical leadership, the youth continued to perform important local tasks like fire fighting and disaster relief. In other words, the young men's group, whether under conservative or radical leadership, was an important hamlet-village organization. Luckily for the army, radical "success stories" were rare and short-lived; the local importance of the *seinendan* almost always worked to the military's benefit. With the exception of this one area in southern Nagano Prefecture, and even there for all but seven or eight years, youth branches functioned within the army's system.[42] If the village and town governments patronized and funded the youth organs under radical control, it is hard to imagine their not supporting those which functioned under more acceptable leadership.

The defense women's association also supported itself financially from local governmental sources, but not as overtly as the other two organizations. The women's group, one composed of all of a community's women, performed most of its activities in conjunction with and under the leadership of other village and town organizations, particularly the reservists' branch. It financed most of its activities through village and town contributions to the other organizations. Anjō, for example, sponsored thirteen funerals for the war dead in 1937; all of the costs were underwritten by the town government. But, rather than disperse this money directly from town hall to each of the organizations involved, Anjō officials funded the reservists and they, in turn, redistributed the cash to the others. Thus, in 1937, in Anjō, the women's branch carried out its funeral activities under the ultimate direction and funding of the town hall, but with the immediate leadership and money provided by the reservist branch. Most other women's group activities were also financed in this way. Thus the *kokubō fujinkai* branch in Anjō had a very small annual budget of its own, largely collected through dues, but provided much of the "women's" labor—cooking, sewing, etc.—necessary for the wartime activities of the town and the reservist and youth association branches. All three of the organizations received a large share of their needed financial resources from local government; they cost the army and navy themselves practically nothing. The degree to which local govern-

---

42. *Nagano-ken seinen hattatsushi,* pp. 207–208, 228–232; Hirayama Kazuhiko, "Chihō seinen undō no tenkai," in Furushima Toshio et al., *Meiji Taishō kyōdoshi kenkyūhō* (Tokyo, 1970), pp. 261–262.

ment took over this monetary burden is evidence of the services' skill in creating an inexpensive rural outlet for military information and values, and of their success in achieving local acceptance. The reservist, youth and defense women's association branches were so much a part of rural Japan by the time the China War began that rural Japan was willing to pay for them.

ANOTHER SOURCE OF FUNDS: INCOME AND EARNINGS

The second major source of funds for the reservists, 27 percent of the total in 1926, was income from investments and savings and earning from branch lands. (See Table 21.) These sources provide further evidence of the importance of official and elite support to the organization. Tanaka encouraged savings from the beginning of his connection with the *zaigō gunjinkai* in 1910, and most branches followed his advice by investing large sums of money in postal savings, stocks, and bonds. The 13,000 branches had a total monetary investment of over fifteen million yen in 1926, and over twenty million yen less than ten years later. The *Model Branch History* indicates that virtually every branch in the nation must have had money invested. All 287 branches reporting on their finances maintained branch savings accounts, and 73 reported investments in securities and bonds. If these branches are typical, one can infer that almost every branch in Japan and abroad drew interest from some kind of investment.[43]

Reservist branches also owned large areas of land which yielded handsome returns. The branches owned over 7,000 acres of land of various kinds in 1926, and over 13,000 acres by 1931. The land was of three kinds: paddy fields, dry crop fields, and timber land. The statistics, unfortunately, do not indicate what percentage of the land fell into each category. According to the *Model Branch History*, however, 64 of its 293 branches owned land; about 3 to 4 percent was paddy, 10 percent dry crop, and the rest forest land. If this ratio held true for all 13,000 acres, the reservist association in 1931 had 400 to 500 acres of wet rice, and 1,300 acres of dry crop fields. The ownership of this land was not insignificant. Ronald Dore reports that in the same period only 3,000 landlords in Japan owned 125 acres or more. The returns from marketing the rice, vegetables, and timber produced in these fields must have brought the branches with large holdings a sizeable profit.[44]

---

43. *Teikoku zaigō gunjinkai gyōmu shishin*, pp. 474–479; *Mohan bunkaishi*, passim.

44. *Teikoku zaigō gunjinkai gyōmu shishin*, pp. 474–479; Matsumura Shōin, "Teikoku zaigō gunjinkai kiyaku kaisei ni tsuite," *Kaikōsha kiji*, April 1933, p.

The source of most of the investment capital and lands, local non-reservists and community government, underlines the interrelationship of the reservist branches and the local communities. Branches received gifts in the amount of 700,000 yen, 16 percent of the annual budget in 1925 and 1926. (See Table 21.) Fifty-one of the "model branches" reported that they received their original investment funds or real estate as gifts from important nonreservist members of the local community; these branches represented more than half of those which reported the original sources of their holdings. One of the twenty-two volumes of Anjō reservist documents includes a list of all contributors to the branch between 1911 and 1943; the notebook contains the names of many of the town's most prestigious families. The reservist branch in Nishio, south of Anjō, was able to raise just over 16,000 yen in contributions in a 1921 fund raising drive. Although the average donation was only 11 yen per contributor, the town's leading family gave 700 yen and 14 other families, companies, and banks donated over 120 yen each. The well-to-do in many of Japan's villages and towns believed the reservist branch important enough to the community to make valuable donations. The village and town office also made "permanent" loans from their holdings, usually timber or firewood land, to the zaigō gunjinkai branch. The reservists received the right to use the land rent free, and whatever returns they earned from their efforts they could use as they pleased. In most cases, the land simply reverted to village ownership after the reservist association's demise at the end of World War II. An interview respondent in Iwai Village, part of present-day Katsunuma, reported that his branch received, used, and returned village timber land in this way. Village and town governments, like some of the rich, patronized the reservist branches as if they were important local organizations.[45]

There is no evidence that the youth associations' or defense women's branches owned any land, or had large investments of their own. The young men did, however, help reservists exploit the latter's holdings to raise funds for joint enterprises. The Iwai reservists, for example, directed seinendan members in harvesting timber on the zaigō gunjinkai's "mountain"; and in Tsubota Village in the Izu Islands, reservists organized youths to harvest agar-agar (tengusa) to sell jointly. The reservist branch, as parent organization, owned the land; the

130; Mohan bunkaishi, passim; Ronald P. Dore, Land Reform in Japan (London, 1959), p. 29.

45. Anjō documents, Volume XXI, Kihonkin [Endowment Fund]; Teikoku zaigō gunjinkai Nishio-machi bunkaishi [The History of the Nishio Town Imperial Military Reservist Association Branch] (Nishio, 1930), pp. 20–29.

youth association, as child group, owned no land of its own, but helped exploit the *zaigō gunjinkai's* land under parental control. This relationship reinforced the village office-rich farmers-reservist-youth hierarchy of rural Japan.

DUES AS A SOURCE OF ORGANIZATIONAL FUNDS

The third major local source of funds for the army's organizations was dues. Although the youth branches, most heavily dependent on town and village support, did not charge dues, the systematic assessment of members became a useful method of financial support for the reservists, and especially for the defense women. Because the army imposed the *zaigō gunjinkai* from outside the community early in the century, it depended to a large extent on funds raised within the branches themselves rather than on community support for its first few years of existence. As late as 1926, 22 percent of reservist funds still came from dues. (See Table 21.) The more a community absorbed a reservist branch into the village or town order, however, the more that branch could forego collecting dues and depend on local governmental and elite aid to fund itself. By the 1930s, reservist branch dues collection became a sign of the absence of complete local acceptance.

When the army first established the organization in 1910, the branches faced severe financial problems, which caused the reservists no end of trouble. The original bylaws of the association declared that the operating expenses of the local branches should be covered by gifts, dues, and the income from organizational activities. But dues proved inadequate to cover all of the branches' needs, and many branches found themselves in difficulty because of the members' over-zealous solicitation of gifts or raising money from "improper" activities. Dues were inadequate because most members could not afford to pay much. Although the dues scales were graduated so that officers paid more than enlisted men, most members were not officers. In 1930, in the semiurban branch of Shinagawa Town, general officers paid thirty sen, field grade officers twenty sen, other officers ten sen, and enlisted men five sen per month. Over 98 percent of the members were not officers and the branch gathered only about forty yen, one-third of its total budget in this way.[46]

Dues became less and less important in financing reservist branches,

---

46. Reservist bylaws, *Senyū*, 1 (1910), pp. 56–61. For examples and reports of financial difficulties or improper solicitation of funds, see *Senyū*, 13 (1911), pp. 56–59; 16 (1912), pp. 56–57; 18 (1912), pp. 56–57; and *Teikoku zaigō gunjinkai sanjūnenshi* (Tokyo, 1944), pp. 58–59, 67, 73–74; *Shinagawa-chōshi* [The History of Shinagawa Town] (Tokyo, 1932), pp. 548–549.

and local governmental and elite contributions became more and more important after 1915. Although some town and village offices helped finance reservist activities even in 1910–1911, it was not until the 1920s that this kind of aid became widespread. In 1915, for example, only thirty-six Aichi Prefecture village and town branches received annual local governmental aid; but by 1926 virtually every community's government provided financial support for reservist branches. In 1915, no Aichi cities supported local reservist branches at all, and even in 1926 the per member contribution of the Nagoya and Toyohashi city governments, the prefecture's major urban communities, was low compared to towns and villages.[47] It was in tightly knit agricultural communities where dues were less necessary and where local government support came first and in the greatest amounts.

The relationship of dues collection, local support, and reservist success is seen nowhere more clearly than in the cases of our two archetypal rural reservist branches, Ōkamada-Futagawa and Anjō. The former branch collected dues—twenty sen per year per member—and received only five yen per year from the village government. The branch was forced to operate on a very small annual budget of about .4 yen per member and confined itself to more narrowly military activities than most branches. The Anjō branch collected no dues but received a constantly increasing amount of support from the local government and martial society. The branch operated on a comparatively large budget of 1.5 to 2 yen per member, and carried out wide ranging non-military activities for the benefit of the local community. The degree of the government's support of the reservists is an indicator of the extent to which the branches had become local organizations.

Dues collection in the defense women's association was based on an entirely different rationale than in the zaigō gunjinkai. The men's group had been founded twenty-five years earlier and had fought and won the battle of community acceptance for both organizations by 1935. The women's group's collection of dues, therefore, did not reflect the weakness of its integration into the local village or town order, but its success. While the reservist branch enlisted only qualified males, the women's organization enrolled all local women whatever their ages or qualifications. Thus the kokubō fujinkai collected dues in the manner of the martial and educational societies when it assessed its members. Every household in the town or village participated in the organization and therefore contributed to support it. Paying dues

47. The 1915 Aichi data were found among documents in a collection of unpublished Aichi Prefecture materials housed in the repository of the Ministry of Education in Tokyo. *Teikoku zaigō gunjinkai gyōmu shishin*, pp. 480–485.

to the defense women's association was like paying part of one's local taxes. Reservist dues collection indicated a relative lack of integration into the local community, but women's association dues collection reflected total integration. The women joined as villagers, paid dues as villagers, and followed the village office and reservists (their husbands and sons) as villagers.

The financing of the branches of the reservist, youth and defense women's organizations must be viewed as a success story in the army's attempt to infiltrate rural Japanese communities. Not only did the local funding of the branches reflect that the army's organizations became basic community units, an important step on the road to building a social basis for militarism, but it also meant the army could save its own money. Not only, as one might expect, did the women's association and the Home Ministry's youth association cost the army practically nothing; but the reservists also placed very little financial burden on the military. It is true that the army provided a number of fringe benefits—active duty officers as central and intermediate headquarters' officials, cheap hotel accommodations in Tokyo and Osaka, low cost train fares for reservists on official business, and printing facilities for reservist magazines—but the officers in the headquarters received no additional salary or pension for their reservist activities, the hotels and printing facilities were self-supporting operations, and the national railroads bore the burden of cheap train fares. Moreover, the army provided no money at all for any of the lower level headquarters. Even the county and city level consolidated branches depended on financial aid from subordinate branches, not from the army. The army saved money and, ironically, by doing so, won rural acceptance in the 1910–1945 period.

YOUTH TRAINING CENTER–YOUTH SCHOOL FUNDING

The youth training centers and youth schools were the only part of the system with any significant central financial support, but even in this case there was no burden on the army because the Education Ministry provided all of the national funds for the system. Moreover, operating the system was not very expensive, even for the Education Ministry. In the 1929–1930 school year, the centers' budget totalled less than 6,000,000 yen, compared to over 300,000,000 for the elementary schools; and while youth school spending increased much more rapidly than any other educational expenditure after 1930, it remained insignificant when compared to other Education Ministry spending. In addition, over 80 percent of the costs of the youth centers and schools depended on local taxes; in 1929–1930, the ministry disbursed only 1,000,000 yen to this post-compulsory education system.[48] The youth system was inexpensive because the centers used the local elementary schools and their teachers and principals; the government had no building, no maintenance, and no teachers' salary expenditures to make for the youth centers and schools.

Although the system cost the Education Ministry one or two million yen per year between 1930 and 1940, it cost the army nothing. Even the burden of the token payments to reservist drill instructors fell on the reserve branch and local government, not the army. The system enabled the army, through the reservists, to give drill instruction to millions of teenage Japanese without spending a yen, and the system cost the cooperating Education Ministry very little. The youth training centers and schools aimed at spreading military values to young men, and particularly rural young men, and again the main financial burden fell on the local communities. Youth drill, like reservist, *seinendan,* and defense women's activities became such an integral part of rural Japan that rural Japan gladly paid for it.

CONCLUSION

As the nature of the local leadership and the financing of the four organizations indicates, the army succeeded in integrating its organizations into the structure and order of the rural community. Since the community's "prominent stratum" tended to lead, and the local elite and officials to finance, the organizations, one can conclude that they considered the branches to be local as well as national groups. In leadership as in membership the branches became microcosms of the village or town as a whole. In financial matters, the local government took over the burden of supporting them. Even in those communities like Ōkamada-Futagawa where members of the local elite did not always lead, and where the government did not contribute significant amounts of money to the four organizations, this lack of integration did not work counter to the army's efforts. The members of the *zaigō gunjinkai* performed most of the necessary social service functions in these communities as well, and their organizations received some village money. If the local elite did not become the official leaders of the groups, they generally supported them unofficially by making

48. Hugh L. Keenleyside and A. F. Thomas, *History of Japanese Education and Present Educational System* (Tokyo, 1937), pp. 163–164; *Kakemachi-shi,* pp. 456–457; *Yamada-gunshi,* pp. 673–679.

contributions of land, money, and moral support. The more a branch enlisted leaders from among the community's elite, however, the more it received local government and elite funding, the better it tended to serve the army's needs. Most branches succeeded in both areas, and they became solidly entrenched local groups through which the army, as we shall see in Chapter V, educated members and their neighbors in military and nationalistic values.

V

THE ACTIVITIES OF THE
FOUR ORGANIZATIONS

The activities of the four organizations and the high degree of participation in them provide the strongest evidence for arguing that the
army successfully integrated itself into rural Japan. The nature of the
membership, leadership, and financing indicated that the organizations
had become accepted parts of the local community's structure; the
activities not only solidified these army-local ties, but also spread the
military and nationalistic values and ideas the army wanted to inculcate in rural Japan. There were three interrelated types of activities: community service, military, and patriotic (See Tables 26 and
27). Of these three, community service activities, above all, reflected
the organizations' integration into the local community. Most of the
community activities had venerable local histories dating back into
the premodern era; after 1910–1915, they became duties of the military's reservist-led "age groups." The military activities directed by reservist leaders for their members, particularly those with no active duty
experience, and for youths and women, introduced military practices
and values into the communities. These activities inculcated and reinforced discipline and group-centered values important to both the
army and the rural community. These again were a mark of the army's
local acceptance since a number of them were traditional by nature
and became "the army's" only after the establishment of the *zaigō
gunjinkai* in 1910. The patriotic functions provided the national focus
of the four groups' education. Through patriotic activities emphasizing
the emperor, identification with national values, foreign threats, and
the glories of empire and war, the army created its "national villagers."

With all three types of activity the reservists integrated community, army, and nation, because they, the reservists, were the local representatives of martial and national values. They alone had left the village for the outside world to serve the army and Japan; they brought home to the locally financed, locally led, and locally structured organizations a military and broader national outlook.[1]

---

1. The activities to be discussed in this chapter are mentioned so frequently in so many different sources that it seems safe to conclude that most of them were carried out nationwide. Therefore, rather than repeat dozens of references when describing each activity of the four organizations, I shall introduce all of the sources here. Subsequently, I shall refer to individual sources only when footnoting specific examples or pointing out exceptional cases. Much material for describing the activities of all of the organizations is found in the pages of local histories. See for example, *Fujino-sonshi* [The History of Fujino Village] (Okayama, 1953), pp. 602–603; *Ryūō-sonshi* (Kofu, 1955) pp. 960–966; *Miyomi-sonshi* [The History of Miyomi Village] (Kofu, 1938), pp. 612–614, 645–652; *Sakurai-sonshi* [The History of Sakurai Village] (Nara, 1954), pp. 432–435; *Anjō-chōshi* (Anjō, 1919), pp. 121–123; *Kawai-mura kyōdoshi* (Morioka, 1962), I, pp. 339–347, 1092–1096; II, pp. 818–825; *Tatsuoka-sonshi* [The History of Tatsuoka Village] (Tokyo, 1968), pp. 783, 1143, 1145–1146, 1167–1172, 1180–1181; *Hongō-kushi* (Tokyo, 1937), pp. 975–976. Other descriptions of reservist activities are found in the Anjō documents, in the "Activities" section of any issue of *Comrades in Arms,* in the pages of *Rikukaigun gunji nenkan,* 1937–1941 editions, in the Nishio and Isshiki reservist branch histories, and in my interviews and questionnaires.

Local youth association histories provide the best source of information on the duties of *seinendan* branches and reservist-youth branch cooperation. See the *Anjō-machi seinendanshi* (Anjō, 1936), *Anjō-shi seinendanshi* (Anjō, 1962), *Toyama-ken Nishi Tonami-gun Isurugi seinendanshi* (Kanazawa, 1937), *Toyama-ken Higashi Tonami-gun Higashi Nojiri-mura seinendanshi* (Kanazawa, 1935), *Nagano-ken seinen hattatsushi* (Nagano, 1935), *Utsunomiya seinendan no hattatsu* [The Development of the Utsunomiya Youth Association] (Utsunomiya, 1934), *Yamashima-mura seinendan keiei jirei dai isshū* [A First Collection of Examples of Yamashima Village Youth Association Management] (Tokyo, 1936), *Tsukitsu-mura seinendan keiei jirei dai sanshū* [A Third Collection of Examples of Tsukitsu Village Youth Association Management] (Tokyo, 1936). Good examples of youth training center–youth school curriculum can be found in Ishikawa Ken, ed., *Kindai Nihon kyōiku seidō shiryō* (Tokyo, 1956), III, pp. 553–557; *Seinen gakkō kyōrenka kyōkasho* [Youth School Drill Manual] (Tokyo, 1940), *Nagoya-shi seinen gakkō yōran* [A Survey of Nagoya Youth Schools] (Gifu, 1938), and *Saishin seinen gakkō kyōin hikkei* [The Newest Manual for Youth School Instructors] (Tokyo, 1939). Defense women's activities are best described in local histories, interviews, questionnaires, and in the *Rikukaigun gunji nenkan,* especially 1939, pp. 596–607.

Other useful sources are *Kaikōsha kiji,* April 1937, pp. 84–87; Tanaka Giichi, "Gun rengō zaigō gunjinkai no jigyō" [The Activities of County Consolidated Reservist Branches] in *Tanaka chūjō kōenshū* (Tokyo, 1916), pp. 241–249; and two regional newspapers, the *Tokushima nichinichi shimpō* and the *Yamagata shimbun,* which were searched systematically for the period 1930–1935 for all references to the organizations under study.

COMMUNITY SERVICE DUTIES

The reservist, youth and defense women's branches performed a wide range of community service activities and thus made the organizations indispensable to the hamlet, village, and town. The army-led or -influenced branches, and especially the crucial leadership group, the *zaigō gunjinkai,* absorbed traditional, nonmilitary, public service activities and fulfilled Tanaka's desire that they become the "mainstays" of the

Table 26

RESERVIST ACTIVITIES BY FREQUENCY OF
QUESTIONNAIRE RESPONDENTS' ANSWERS [a]

Complete questionnaires		162
Reservist activities		
Youth training center–youth school		
drill leadership (patriotic)		140
Labor aid to families of men on		
active duty		136
Youth association leadership		108
Drill (patriotic)	85	
Patriotic education	34	
Fire department	12	
Patriotic ceremonies	8	
Funerals for war dead (patriotic)		102
Defense Women's Association leadership		96
Lectures on soldier's ethos (patriotic)		92
Military drill for members (patriotic)		84
Bayonet competition (patriotic)		83
Help to local community		81
Patrolling at time of emergency		60
Disaster aid and relief		54
Teaching ethics at youth school (patriotic)		32
Service as volunteer fire department		31
Rifle training (patriotic)		26
Road and canal repairs		23
Social gatherings		23
Movies and plays (patriotic)		6

[a] The word "patriotic" in parentheses next to an activity indicates that it had a high degree of patriotic content.

Table 27

NAGANO PREFECTURE YOUTH ASSOCIATION BRANCH ACTIVITIES
BY FREQUENCY OF OCCURRENCE, 1930 [a]

Branches: 417	Members: 86,418 (1934)
Lectures (patriotic)	9,656
Track and field meet	7,893
Road repair	5,361
Military sports meet (patriotic)	4,459
Sports meet (*undōkai*)	3,666
Discussion meeting (patriotic)	3,293
Other sports	2,762
Agricultural competition	2,718
Seminars (patriotic)	2,481
Trial fields	2,266
Parties	2,206
Field trip	2,164
Movies (patriotic)	1,945
Shrine and temple maintenance	1,943
Night patrol and police assistance	1,821
See off, greet soldiers and aid their families (patriotic)	1,795
Sumo wrestling	1,617
Agricultural study trip	1,541
Mountain climbing	1,504
Aid to youth training center (patriotic)	1,453
Respect for aged meeting	1,398
Patriotic meeting	1,213
Labor aid within community	1,163
Agricultural lecture	1,140
Reclamation of land	1,093
Fire department	847
School repairs	662

[a] One major problem in interpreting these figures is understanding what the counters are in each case. For example, did youth association members reclaim 1,093 fields, or work at reclamation on 1,093 days? Another problem is determining which activities youths performed with or under the direction of reservists. It is clear from the chart, however, that Nagano Prefecture *seinendan* members performed the same kinds of activities as Anjō youths; it makes sense, therefore, to assume that reservists worked with the youths at least in some of the fire departments, road repairs, seminars and discussion meetings, athletic meets, etc. The word "patriotic" written in parentheses next to an activity indicates that it normally had a high degree of patriotic content. Source: *Nagano-ken seinen hattatsushi,* pp. 320–324.

local community and raise army prestige. Hamlet "age groups" had maintained local order, aided needy families, performed public works and disaster relief, from at least the Tokugawa era. When villagers performed these functions after the establishment of the four organizations, they did so both as reservists, youth group members, and defense women, and as community "age group" members. In other words, the army's local acceptance was insured by its organizations' ability to absorb these traditional activities as its own. The reservists (and their youthful and female followers) were "mainstays" both because of their organization affiliation and because they were members of age groups which had long traditions as local "mainstays."

MAINTENANCE OF PUBLIC ORDER

After 1910–1915, the reservists' and youth associations' local branches officially absorbed the task of patrolling the community to protect public order. In so doing, they served the purposes of the national army officers and the official and unofficial local elite by helping to maintain the village's and town's status quo. The local young men's group had a long history of patrolling and protecting the hamlet under the direction of the older youths. After 1915, they continued this kind of activity as members of the national organization's local branches under the leadership of the same people who had become members of the national reservist association's local branch. Policing the village or town normally took the politically neutral form of protecting the community from thievery or other petty crimes by outsiders, but on occasion it had a "class struggle" coloration; and it was here that it most benefitted the rulers. Reservists and young men helped to suppress their own neighbors' participation in the infrequent rural tenancy disputes that erupted between 1920 and 1940, and in urban strikes and riots.

There are a number of documented examples of reservists (and to a lesser degree, youths) helping to maintain local order against political, social, and economic unrest. Seta Kaku reported in a 1932 article critical of the army and the reservists that *zaigō gunjinkai* branches were active nationwide in suppressing tenant uprisings. A proreservist Army Ministry staff officer, writing in an army journal a few years later, reiterated this point. Shiota Shōbē describes one such case, a violent incident in Akita Prefecture during which reservists and youth group members protected the landlord's house against the wrath of his tenants (or, at least, some of his tenants, since one assumes that many of the guards ranked among the landlord's tenants themselves). Tsubota reservists and youths broke the strike by Korean diving women described above. Factory branch reservists played a role in fighting strikes at a steel plant in Muroran, at the famed Yawata Iron Works, and during an Osaka trolley strike. Thousands of reservists took part in suppressing disorder during the 1918 Rice Riots and after the 1923 Tokyo earthquake.[2]

Although urban reservists also participated in the 1918 and 1923 riots, I have found no evidence to indicate that reservists and youth branch members participated in rural disorders. In fact, there is only one report of reservists even joining a tenant union—in Gifu Prefecture in the early 1920s—and there no violence was involved. Only 13 percent of the union members were "grass roots soldiers." Since more than 13 percent of the local adult males belonged to the army's organization, reservists were clearly underrepresented in the antilandlord group.

Scholars studying the disputes have exaggerated the scale of the antilandlord unrest. Farmers' unions at the peak of their organizational activity enrolled only a miniscule segment of the nation's tenants, and most of the reported incidents represent little more than the presentation of petitions to the landlord requesting reduced rents or other concessions. Much has been made, for example, of the figure of 1,700 tenant disputes in 1930, the prewar year with the highest number of incidents. As Dore and Ōuchi point out, however, only 175 of the disputes involved any violence (out of 76,000 hamlets in the country), and only 1,076 persons were arrested (out of five and one-half million agricultural households in that year). Few reservists are reported to have participated in tenant disputes because the incidents rarely reached the level at which reservist participation was noticeable. It is logical that reservist tenants joined their fellow tenants in petitioning landlords for concessions, but when the demands reached the violent stage, the reservists either remained neutral or, as in the cases presented above, worked against their own economic interests by helping to suppress the unrest.

How do we explain this willingness of reservists (and youth branch members) to downgrade or even oppose their own family's economic

2. Seta Kaku, "Zaigō gunjindan no gensei," *Kaizō*, July 1932, pp. 94–95; *Kaikōsha kiji*, April 1937, p. 87; Shiota Shōbē, "Tochi to jiyū o motomete," *Shōwashi no shunkan* (Tokyo, 1966), I, pp. 115, 120; Shinobu Seizaburō, *Taishō demokurashishi* (1954–1959), I, pp. 401, 551; *Higashi-kushi* (Osaka, 1940), p. 1000; Inoue Kiyoshi and Watanabe Tōru, *Kome sōdō no kenkyū* [Studies of the Rice Riots] (Tokyo, 1953), I, p. 328; Yoshikawa Mitsusada, *Iwayuru kome sōdō jiken no kenkyū* [Studies of the So-called Rice Riots' Incident] (Tokyo, 1938), pp. 129–130, 357; *Teikoku zaigō gunjinkai sanjūnenshi* (Tokyo, 1944), pp. 128–130; *Gendaishi shiryō* [Materials in Contemporary History], VI, *Kantō daishinzai to chōsenjin* [The Kanto Disaster and Koreans] (Tokyo, 1963), pp. 145, 151, 164, 166, 171–174, 183.

interests? The reservists' actions are partly attributable to their commitment to Tanaka's cherished national unity, productivity and order.
These young adults, especially the ex-servicemen among them, were
the most "national" of the villagers. This reservist and youth commitment to the maintenance of order helps to explain why rural areas in
"police state" Japan needed far fewer policemen per capita than even
rural England.[3]

AID TO THE FAMILIES OF MEN ON ACTIVE DUTY
AND TO NEEDY HAMLET MEMBERS

The nationally centralized reservist and young men's associations ap-
propriated the hamlet's traditional policing activity and made it their
own, but it was a duty that was performed only on infrequent occasions. The second community service function, aid to community families in need or with sons on active duty, also had a long hamlet history,
and was performed often. The purpose of aiding soldiers' families was
to win their gratitude by compensating them for the absence of their
ablest workers. Generally this help, as the questionnaire respondents
report, took the form of providing labor; on occasion the *zaigō gunjinkai* members and their youthful and female helpers gave money and
produce as well. The labor aid was carried out on an informal, hamlet-
level basis. At the busiest times of the agricultural year—rice transplanting and harvest times in particular—three or four reservists, often
a few *seinendan* members, and several women from the soldier's *buraku*
would give a day or two of farm work help to each family. The
women's help was particularly important because one of the major
agricultural chores, the back-breaking rice transplanting, was normally
a female task.

Labor aid also went to needy hamlet members who had no connection with the army or the reservist branch. *Comrades in Arms*
cites a number of such examples. Reservists and their wives in one
Akita Prefecture village helped a family transplant and weed its rice
paddies when all of its members were attacked by food poisoning and
two died. Reservists aided a family in a Kyushu village in cultivating
its fields when the husband, whose wife was blind, broke his leg. In
still another, reservists' families helped transplant rice for a family
with six sick members. And in one more, a doctor-reservist gave free

3. Barbara Ann Lardner Waswo, *Landlords and Social Change in Prewar Japan*
(Ann Arbor, 1970), p. 129; Ronald P. Dore and Tsutomu Ōuchi, "Rural Origins of
Japanese Fascism," in James W. Morley, ed., *Dilemmas of Growth in Prewar Japan*
(Princeton, 1971), pp. 186–187.

treatment to two poor families, to three families of widows, and to all local active duty families. In all of these cases, and such examples are rife in the pages of *Comrades in Arms,* the *zaigō gunjinkai* members sacrificed time for the good of their neighbors, and certainly won some local gratitude at the same time.[4]

All of the interview respondents emphasized the great importance of the labor aid, and added that nonlabor help, money, and produce were important also. At the time of the Japanese attack on the German positions in Tsingtao in China in 1915, for example, monetary assistance was significant. Even though most local branches had not yet become wealthy enough to provide large-scale financial aid to indigent locals, 4,042 families in 596 communities received aid. These monetary contributions were as high as fifty yen per family per soldier (more than a month's income for a poor farm family) and averaged over twenty yen. Families also received the usual labor assistance and rice contributions as large as half a bushel per family.[5]

Some labor, material, and monetary aid came at the time of national crisis, but most of it was provided regularly when local men were drafted or recalled to active duty or when families were in need. A special section in *Comrades in Arms* lists dozens of cases of local assistance, and the questionnaire and interview responses and the Anjō documents report such aid as a regular phenomenon. A few of many typical examples give one an idea of this reservist-youth-women's function. The reserve branch in Kamo Town in Niigata Prefecture set up an investment fund in 1912 and used the interest to help thirty-seven widows and their children, the survivors of local men killed in combat. A group of reservists and their wives (pre–defense women's association) from a village in Gifu Prefecture, ran the farm of a fatherless family in which the elder brother had died and the mother fallen ill while the older brother was on active duty. A Seoul, Korea reservist branch (the members were Japanese residents there) contributed over twenty yen to a sick, poor member.[6]

The impact of this local aid to the families of soldiers and the needy is not difficult to surmise; as one interview respondent said, "People were overjoyed when we came around to help them." The reservists, youth, and women's group leaders were usually "prominent" villagers or their wives, and the recipients were invariably from relatively poorer families; these benevolent and almost paternalistic acts

---

4. *Senyū,* 19 (1912), pp. 54–55; 25 (1912), pp. 92–93.
5. Tanaka, "Seitō kōgeki to zaigō gunjinkai" [The Tsingtao Attack and the Reservist Association], *Tanaka chūjō kōenshū,* pp. 223–227.
6. *Senyū,* 16 (1912), pp. 82–83; 26 (1912), p. 90.

made the owner-tenant and tenant-farmers more and more dependent on the local elite, or at least on the collective community which all of the organizations represented.

Aid to needy families had long been carried out in rural Japan, even before the army established the reservist association; since the village and its elite allowed the reservist branch (and later, the youth and women's groups as well) to assume responsibility for part of the village's aid to the indigent, one can conclude that the village and its elite perceived of the organizations as part and parcel of the local scene. Moreover, the organizations' success in this area underlines the trust the powerful village and town families placed in them. If these families, which had long exchanged relief to the needy for the recipient's loyalty and subservience, were willing to give part of that function (albeit, often unpleasant labor) and its rewards to the army's organizations, they must have either led them, trusted them, or both.

PUBLIC WORKS

Public works, another long-standing activity, also directly benefitted and involved all members of the community. Members of the three organizations repaired roads, reclaimed land, developed mulberry fields, formed cooperatives, worked at forest conservation, ran test farms, planted timber, built schools, contributed free medical care, sponsored lectures on agricultural affairs and disease (especially trachoma and venereal disease) prevention, mediated in tenant disputes, and formed fire departments, both at the hamlet and administrative community levels. Again, examples are rife. Reservists and *seinendan* members in Higashi-Nojiri built the local elementary school in 1923–1924, the farm association's warehouse in 1926, and repaired roads and cleared them of snow every year. Members of the two groups in Isurugi also kept the local roads open during the winter, and in Anjō and Isurugi they repaired them in the spring. Reservists in one city, Hirosaki in Aomori Prefecture, even cultivated fish crops in the castle moat to raise money for community needs.[7]

The pre-1915, local, decentralized youth groups had long performed this type of function. Prior to national centralization young men supplied communal labor under the direction of their elders for the good of the hamlet. After 1910, their elders generally served in the *zaigō gunjinkai*. Thus, under ultimate village or town office direction, the reservists in many places officially assumed the hamlet level leader-

7. *Senyū*, 17 (1912), pp. 51–52; *Higashi Nojiri-mura seinendanshi*, pp. 155–157, 169–171; *Anjō-machi seinendanshi*, I, pp. 133–137; *Isurugi seinendanshi, passim.*

ship role in the performance of many public works. Women by tradition had also fulfilled local community labor needs; after 1935, the defense women's branch, as an organization of all of the hamlet's women workers, naturally absorbed these duties. Even when branch members of reservists, youth, and women did not officially assume responsibility, they still provided the bulk of the activists. The Anjō fire department, for example, drew almost all of its leaders from among the reservists, and all of its firemen from among reservists and *seinendan* members, although the affiliation was unofficial. In the words of the historian of Anjō's youth association, "just as the reservists are intimately tied to the fire department, so too the town's youth branch members have an inseparable relationship with fire fighting. The reservists function as the leaders, and the youths make up well over half of the members." Anjō's wartime fire chief, one of the fourteen interview respondents, was a former youth association official, a youth school teacher and, while head of the fire department, a director of the *zaigō gunjinkai*.[8]

DISASTER RELIEF

Like aid to the indigent and public works, disaster relief was normally performed at the hamlet level but, like public works, under village or town office direction. It was also a traditional function that worked for the army's benefit. Again, the members of the organizations showed themselves to be local mainstays and model citizens (*mura no mohan*) and ensured community acceptance of the army's organizations. Reservists and youth association members carried out disaster relief both during a calamity and after it had struck. They filled sandbags to build dikes, cleared avalanches and snow drifts, fought fires, rowed in rough seas to rescue sailors from sinking ships, distributed food and money, opened their homes to victims, and provided medical expertise and facilities. The pages of *Comrades in Arms* and the various youth branch and local histories abound with cases of heroism, strenuous effort, and great sacrifice on the part of reservists and *seinendan* members when floods, fires, storms, accidents, landslides, and epidemics occurred.

Most of these crises were handled by the action of local branch members within their own communities, but some calamities caused such widespread or intense damage that authorities requested the collective action of many branches over large areas. There were two forms to

8. *Anjō-machi seinendanshi*, I, p. 137; John Embree, *Suyemura: A Japanese Village* (Chicago, 1964), p. 171.

this relief, labor mobilization for service outside their own community by the older male reservists, and fund raising campaigns and financial relief at home by all of the organizations. When a typhoon struck the Tokyo area in September 1917, for example, officials mobilized over 1,000 local reservists and another 1,400 from outside the area to distribute food, clothing, and money. They guarded the area against looting and helped rebuild damaged dikes along the neighboring rivers.[9]

The most striking case of reservist–youth association disaster relief occurred in September, 1923, when the Kantō Earthquake destroyed much of the Tokyo-Yokohama area. During September and October the *zaigō gunjinkai* officially distributed over 3,500 bushels of rice, 180,000 pieces of clothing, 7,000 blankets, vast amounts of food and fuel, and over 300,000 yen, much of which was sent into the head-quarters from branches all over the empire. Over 8,300 reservists, some from as far away as Hokkaidō, Nagasaki, China, and Manchuria, worked under central headquarters' direction to house members who had suffered, to distribute money and clothing, to collect money to send to the stricken area, to patrol against looting, to set up relief centers, and to find jobs for members whose means of support had been destroyed. Reservist officials believed at the time that the number of men from the organization who participated in the efforts was three or four times more than the reported figure. The 8,300 total quoted represented only the number of men who had registered with the central headquarters.

These large-scale assistance activities added national prestige to the army and its hamlet representatives, but also depended on the coopera-tive activities of the organizations at home. During the 1923 disaster, local *seinendan* members aided the reservists by producing a film on the disaster and circulating it around the nation in a successful effort to raise money for earthquake relief.[10] The youth branch in Higashi Nojiri also raised money for earthquake relief during this disaster. And in 1925 Isurugi *seinendan* members, local women, elementary school students, and city officials cooperated under reservist direction to collect money for typhoon victims from western Japan.[11] In these and other cases, aid to disaster victims depended on a combination of local collectivity and cooperation with national efforts for success.

---

9. *Senyū*, 90 (1917), pp. 51–55.
10. *Sanjūnenshi*, pp. 146–147; *Taishō kōron*, III, 10 (1923), pp. 132–133; Kumagai Tatsujirō, *Dainihon seinendanshi* (Tokyo, 1942), pp. 165–166.
11. *Isurugi seinendanshi*, p. 78; *Higashi Nojiri-mura seinendanshi*, pp. 158–159.

MILITARY ACTIVITIES

The army's four organizations carried out six activities which can be best labelled military. Two of them, seeing off and greeting local soldiers, and comforting men on active duty, had pre-1910 histories and were like community service duties. But they were also military since the army benefited directly from them. They raised troop morale and allowed company commanders to use hamlet-village social pressure to ensure the obedience of rural soldiers. The second activities, the reservist-led military drill and martial arts training, enabled the army to mold obedient, disciplined, healthy, and cooperative youths for the local village and guaranteed the army that it would get pretrained, submissive rural recruits. The last two activities—assistance at the annual draft examination and the performance of the reservists' annual inspection—had the short-range military goal of creating a more efficient army. Community pressures were used to guarantee an orderly physical examination attended by all eligible local twenty year olds, to ensure a successful inspection participated in by all local reservists, and to allow the army to depend on the level of training of reservists when they were recalled to active duty. But since the whole community participated in these events and was brought into direct contact with the visiting regular army officers from the regimental district, the events also symbolized cooperation between the army and rural Japan.

SEEING OFF, GREETING, AND COMFORTING SERVICEMEN

Seeing off and greeting soldiers to and from active duty, and comforting local men already in the service were a combination of military and community duties in which women as well as men participated. Every community made a ritual of the events surrounding a soldier's departure. The night before the draftee left, his family held a party in his honor. Hamlet defense women joined in the preparations, and village and school officials, the reservist branch chiefs, and some male hamlet neighbors and reservists attended. The next day, defense women's members donned their white aprons with white shoulder bands inscribed "Greater Japan National Defense Women's Association" and joined an entourage of village or town civil and reservist officials, hamlet fellow reservists, and youth group members. They marched with the recruit to the local shrine to pray for his safety and then proceeded to the railroad station or bus stop to see him off.

When the recruit returned, a similar ceremony was held. He was met again by reservists, youth branch members, and defense women in "uniform." Even the school children from his hamlet came out to join the procession that escorted him back to his home and another party.[12] If the recruit died while serving in the army, the community was also involved in the performance of funerals. Reservists, youth branch members, and local women received the necessary funds from the village and town office and divided the labor among themselves. The reservists were the leaders and shared the heavy physical labor with the young men; the women prepared the dead soldier's home and necessary food for the occasion.

Between the soldier's departure and return, his community's officials, reservists, and defense women maintained contact with him. Village officials and reservist leaders visited local men at the barracks to "encourage" them and took to them personal items, letters, and spending money from home. Defense women often prepared the presents to be taken or sent to servicemen from the community. The women were particularly renowned for assembling "comfort bags" (*imon bukuro*) filled with cigarettes, candy, daily needs, and other amenities, and for sponsoring letter-writing campaigns for men on active duty.

After the outbreak of war in 1937, women's comfort activities expanded even further and included another custom that dated back to the Sino–Japanese War. It was common in these early war years to see defense women and young girls going from house to house, or standing in front of the local railroad station, soliciting neighbors or passers-by to add a stitch to the "one-thousand stitch" cloths (*sennin bari*).[13] These well-known good-luck charms were sent to soldiers who wore them close to their bodies. Hino Ashihei describes their use in his wartime novel *Grain and Soldiers:*

> The soldiers, their rifles stacked, sat under the eaves on both sides of the road, waiting for their unit to move out. Every soldier wore a sweat-yellowed thousand stitch cloth wrapped around his body. . . . The soldiers tried to shade themselves from the blazing mid-summer sun by draping towels or handkerchiefs under their service caps. Many tried to stay cool with Chinese fans, or wiped away the flowing sweat with filthy towels.[14]

Although every infantry man seemed to have a story about the efficacy of the *sennin bari*, they certainly did not serve their reputed function of saving soldiers' lives by warding off bullets. They did serve to comfort the soldiers, however, and made them feel that loved ones and friends in the community cared for them.

---

12. See Embree, *Suyemura*, pp. 195–203, for descriptions of these events.
13. Katō Hidetoshi, "Yume wa kokyō o . . ." [Dreams of Home], *Shōwashi no shunkan*, I, pp. 326–328.
14. Hino Ashihei, *Mugi to heitai* [Grain and Soldiers] (Tokyo, 1960), p. 107.

Comforting soldiers and sending "thousand stitch cloths" and "comfort bags" had a long prereservist, pre–defense women's history. Thus, as World War II approached and finally erupted, members of the army's new women's organization were carrying out the same functions that they had already performed under another guise. In this way, the army made official an unofficial system, and confirmed its commitment to "comfort" and its close ties with the rural community.

Comfort in another form was less innocuous than the activities of the defense women. When reservists visited soldiers on active duty to "comfort" or "encourage" them, that encouragement sometimes was in the form of pressure or praise for recalcitrance or success as a recruit. The visitors stimulated lethargic recruits by warning them against shaming their village, hamlet, and family, or even by threatening sanctions against their families at home. Needless to say, this form of "comfort" enhanced the army's effectiveness, but it also reinforced the army-village contacts previously established through correspondence between the home community's military affairs clerk and the recruit's battalion adjutant. Through this correspondence the company commander knew every detail of the soldier's background, including his family's wealth, social status, and hereditary illnesses. Through the same correspondence, the village office and reservist branch knew which recruits had excelled on active duty and honored the village and which ones had not.

MILITARY DRILL AND MARTIAL ARTS TRAINING

From the army's and the community's point of view, reservist-led drill and martial arts training for young men was one of the most important of the organization's military activities. The army was not able to conscript and "socialize for death" a generation of prewar Japanese males, as Kazuko Tsurumi says, but it could and did discipline and indoctrinate a very high percentage of rural teenage males through the youth association and the youth centers and schools.[15] The community also stood to and did benefit from the discipline instilled in its young men.

Since their main function was to win community support for the army and to indoctrinate those without active duty experience in military values, the reservists themselves did not perform drill but directed all of the military drill for young men. They used the army's infantry manual or more often a youth school drill textbook based on

---

15. Kazuko Tsurumi, *Social Change and the Individual: Japan Before and After Defeat in World War II* (Princeton, 1970), pp. 99–137.

the manual. By requiring every young man to memorize the fourteen-page rescript *To Soldiers and Sailors* with which the textbook began and to read the rescript *On Education,* the reservists imbued the young Japanese with patriotic and military values. These rescripts were followed in the textbook by sections on why military drill was important and on the technical aspects of the drill itself. For example, the book illustrated how to use a bayonet, throw a grenade, fire a rifle, machine gun, and mortar, how to march in a unit and to attack, and how to scout, use a map and compass, and give first aid. In other words, the manual provided the basic information necessary for a good soldier and militarized citizen, and was of tremendous significance since most males in rural Japan began to receive training based on this textbook when they were thirteen or fourteen years old. By the time the army led Japan into the China and then the Pacific wars, many years had been spent in educating young Japanese in military values and skills.[16]

Reservists began to give drill training to *seinendan* members of many Japanese communities early in the century. In Hekikai County and in Anjō, this activity was being carried out shortly after the Russo–Japanese War. There the youth group held military drill sessions three times a month at the Shinto shrine in each of the 19 hamlets, and quarterly joint sessions on the grounds of the five local schools. These sessions were directed by hamlet reservists and were often attended by the hamlet headman and the school principal. The officials came to "encourage the youths" because they, like the reservists, wanted "to improve the physical strength, cultivate the virtues of perserverance and endurance, abet the development of diligence, and establish a cooperative and disciplined spirit among the youths of the town."

Closely related to the weekly drill meetings were the annual activities of the Cold Weather Drill Club (*kankunrenkai*). Every winter on the thirty traditionally coldest days of the year, beginning shortly after New Years (*kan-no-iri*) (ten days after 1926), the hamlet youths gathered at six o'clock each morning for an hour of drill. Under hamlet reservists' direction, they first bowed toward the imperial palace in Tokyo, then performed calisthenics, and concluded with an hour of drill. Each cold weather "season" included two other activities, one community-oriented and the other military. In the first, the youths from each hamlet paid their respects at least once to the town's war memorial, their hamlet's shrine, and the grave of some family member who had died while serving the nation in the military service. In the other,

---

16. *Seinen gakkō kyōrenka kyōkasho.*

an inspection by active duty officers from the Toyohashi regimental district headquarters was held at the end of the drill.[17]

This reservist-led youth drill training was wide-spread in prewar Japan, but it did not reach every community in the nation until the youth training centers were established in 1926. In the early 1920s, a British military attaché observed that Japanese conscripts amazed foreign observers because, unlike Western draftees, they already looked like soldiers when they marched into the barracks. He attributed this ability to the training they received from reservists in their home communities.[18] In Anjō, moreover, the participation rate in the youth association drill was incredibly high. In 1935, for example, every eligible teenager participated in the annual cold weather drill, and the attendance rate for the whole period was 99 percent in the ten most agricultural hamlets, and 92 percent for the town as a whole. Although only one-third of the questionnaire respondents from communities other than Anjō led youth association members in this kind of drill, by 1941 85 percent of the young men in Japan were receiving 75 to 100 hours of military drill per year through the youth schools.

The centers-schools took over the drill function from the *seinendan* where it already existed and added drill where it did not. Thus, the centers and the existing youth association branches complemented each other. Reservists provided much of the leadership for both, and both received direction from the community's governmental officials and school teachers and principals. The youth association's local leadership, moreover, took upon itself the task of ensuring high attendance at the training centers. In Anjō they did this by distributing the names of those who did not attend regularly to the hamlet level *seinendan* leaders; these young men and the hamlet officials then "encouraged" the lax students to participate more regularly. It is not hard to visualize the hamlet leaders using hamlet and family honor, and even community sanctions, for this encouragement.[19]

Another form of drill training was provided for local young men; the reservist branches conducted prebarracks training for all 20-year-olds called to active duty. This training, at the central headquarter's request, was spiritual and physical, not military. In Anjō, it included forty hours of patriotic education—largely lectures on the *Imperial Rescript to Soldiers and Sailors*—and approximately fifteen hours of

---

17. *Anjō-machi seinendanshi*, I, pp. 101–122, 126–129, 137–138; *Anjō-shi seinendanshi*, II, pp. 12, 27, 153–169.

18. Malcolm Kennedy, *The Military Side of Japanese Life* (Boston and New York, 1924), pp. 160–170.

19. *Anjō-shi seinendanshi*, II, pp. 24, 165; Ishikawa Ken, ed., *Kindai Nihon kyōiku seidō shiryō*, III, pp. 554–557.

military drill. Since the trainees had completed four years of drill training in the youth association and at the local training center or youth school, this activity can best be considered a "polishing" course. It, like the other forms of drill, appears to have pervaded throughout the country. All of the interview respondents said they had taken part themselves and that later they led the drill in their communities.[20]

Closely related to military drill was reservist-directed martial arts training. *Zaigō gunjinkai* leaders gave rifle, bayonet, and sword training to their followers, to youth association members, to youth school students and, on occasion, even to women. Because of difficulty in the procurement of ammunition, most rifle training began with dry firing of the youth school's weapons; the reservists had no more than one or two weapons per branch of their own. After this preliminary practice, most communities held rifle meets once or twice a year to select the best reservists and youths for participation in regional competitions. The bayonet and sword training also prepared the young men to take part in community-wide and district level competitions. The bayonet training (*jūkenjutsu* or *jūkendō*) and competition, in which participants fought with long wooden staves in the shape of rifles with fixed bayonets, was the twentieth century military's addition to Japan's "traditional" martial arts and thus one which virtually disappeared from the sport's scene after 1945. Sword fighting (*kendō*), on the other hand, the martial skill which separated the Tokugawa warrior from his social subordinates, had a long premodern history. All three types of training—rifle, bayonet, and sword—taught young men discipline, imperviousness to pain, controlled violence, and ultimately an ability to rise above the fear of death.

But the importance of the nonmilitary side of this physical training cannot be overlooked; in Anjō, for example, reservists helped direct their own and youth association branch athletics. The regular military drill sessions that reservists conducted for their younger cohorts always began with group calisthenics, and the biannual athletic matches that the two organizations cosponsored with the local elementary schools included most of the track and field events performed in similar meets in the United States and Europe. The calisthenics reinforced collective activity, and the athletic meets and the necessary preparatory training developed the participants' bodily strength. The youth association's physical standards established in the 1930s were

---

20. *Anjō-machi seinendanshi*, I, pp. 387–392; "Shōwa jūyonendo sōtei yoshū kyōiku keikaku yoteihyō" [The Planned Schedule of Preparatory Education for Recruits for 1939], in Anjō documents, Volume X, *Jigyō yotei oyobi jisshihyō tsuzuri*.

extremely rigorous; and, although we have no evidence that demonstrates how many or what percentage of local youths passed, it is difficult to imagine a prewar Japanese community that did not sponsor youth athletic meets of one sort or another.[21] For example, the 417 branches in Nagano Prefecture in 1930 held over 16,000 athletic meets, and 6,000 more if one includes martial arts and sumō wrestling competition. (See Table 27.)

Since the purpose of the drill and martial arts was in part to provide military training for future soldiers, and the army was completely male (with the exception of some nurses), the women were not involved in these military activities. The army created the defense women's association to reinforce the traditional virtues and role of women, not to make them soldiers. Women's role was to cook, bear children, manage frugal households, and to help the army by comforting soldiers and their families and by fighting "subversive" movements like women's suffrage. After 1937, however, when there was a dearth of reservists and teenage males in most communities, the army mobilized the women. Women learned to fight fires caused by incendiary bombs, to give first aid to the victims, and to meet various wartime emergencies. On at least one occasion, the women were trained in military skills. After 1943, the reservists mobilized the women for the famed "bamboo spear" defense groups. Home guard units of women were set up to help defend Japan against the expected invasion.[22] But is was only during this manpower crisis of the last year of the war that the army allowed women to be mobilized for "men's work."

The cumulative effect of the *seinendan,* youth school, and preconscription drill alone was sufficient to aid the army in its efforts to mold better trained and more patriotic young citizens. Hundreds of thousands of teenagers were brought under military tutelage. Seventy to one hundred hours per year of military drill and, in places like Anjō, the additional youth association drill, must have had the desired effect of inculcating and reinforcing the values of discipline, obedience, group identity, frugality, order, and identification with the military. The physical rigor involved, the uniforms which helped break down

---

21. In 1938, the standards were as follows: 2000 meter run in 7 minutes, 4000 meter run in 17 minutes, 5.5 meter broad jump, combined distance of 23 meters right- and left-handed with an 8-pound shot put, 60 kilogram weight carry 50 meters in 15 seconds. In 1939, the shot-put event was replaced with a 45-meter hand-grenade throw requirement. *Nagoya-shi seinendan hattatsushi* [The History of the Development of the Nagoya City Youth Association] (Nagoya, 1940), p. 135.

22. Anjō documents, Volume XX, *Bōeitai ni kansuru tsuzuri* [A Notebook Concerning the Defense Corps].

individuality, the patriotic preachments of the reservist instructors recently returned from active duty, the use of the army's *Infantry Manual* as the textbook, the necessity in close order drill for conformity, and the close interconnections between the drill and the hamlet's and village's social order, all certainly helped the army achieve its goals. Even the early morning or evening hours of drill could have had an impact. As Tanaka wrote, early morning drill "does away with frivolity in the evenings, destroys bad habits, and decreases expenditures," since the teenagers are too tired to go out at night.[23] If they drilled at night, they lost their leisure time altogether.

THE ANNUAL CONSCRIPTION PHYSICAL EXAMINATION

The importance of the drill to the community became apparent on the occasion of the annual physical examination and the annual reservist inspection. These were the occasions on which the effort expended in training local youths brought the army and the community shared benefits. Thorough preparation, both through drill and through ensuring an orderly and efficient examination and inspection, guaranteed the community honor and the army fit draftees and reservists. Community success at the examination or inspection symbolized the degree to which the army had infiltrated the farm town and village through its organizations.

Civil village officials mobilized all of the army's organizations—that is, virtually the whole community—to ensure that the conscription examination worked smoothly. Former soldiers and reservist officials briefed the examinees about the procedure in order to eliminate wasted time and in order to win the favor of the examiners from the local regimental area headquarters. The reservist branch chief, several of his top officials, the mayor and some of his subordinates including the military affairs clerk, and a few local school principals spent the day at the examination center—a school or other community building—to encourage the youths, that is guarantee their obedience. Defense women in their white apron "uniform" provided refreshments for all. In the evening, the reservist branch chief hosted a party for the visitors and the local officials. The juxtaposition of army officers, reservists, village or town and hamlet officials, school leaders, defense women, and examinees both reinforced and demonstrated army-community cooperation and integration.

---

23. Tanaka, "Gun rengō zaigo gunjinkai no jigyō," p. 246.

This integration was underscored by the high attendance rate of rural eligibles at the examination. It was a rare village or town twenty-year-old who did not appear on the scheduled day. Community cohesiveness and sanctions guaranteed near perfect attendance. The only evidence of absenteeism was among the sick or those employed in the city. The emigrants to the city from rural communities were expected to return home for the examination and usually did. High absentee rates were common only in the cities. There the army felt compelled to send military policemen along with the doctors to round up the delinquents. As the interview respondents stated with pride, the army did not send the *kempeitai* to farm communities.

THE ANNUAL INSPECTION

The annual inspection, although superficially a strictly military affair, had a strong patriotic content, and again symbolized and reinforced army-community integration. The inspection was an examination of the level of preparedness for army service of all men with military obligations who were officially registered local inhabitants, whether or not they belonged to the reservist branch, had served on active duty, or actually lived in the village. The event was held under reservist auspices at the time of the summer all souls' festival (*bon*), a season when local men who had migrated to the city often returned home to visit. The performance of the inspection, held concurrently with one of the most important festivals of rural Japan, not only made it easier for emigrant absentees with military obligations to attend, but also gave the army a prominent role in an important village and town event.[24]

---

24. Attendance at the roll call was excellent. Over 98 percent of eligibles in Aichi's Hazu County, for example, participated in the years 1926–1928. Nevertheless, a few men who had migrated to the city apparently attempted to avoid the inspection and its expensive and time-consuming trip home. The Akita *Sakigake*, a regional northern Japan newspaper, reported on October 1, 1930, that eleven Hirata County reservists had failed to report their addresses. The area's regimental area authorities thus requested the Yokote Public Procurator's Office to investigate and charge the men with violation of the military obligation code. One assumes that these men did not report their addresses accurately so as to avoid the annual inspection, membership in the reservist association, and recall to active duty. Only two of the offenders, however, had village addresses, and even they were unlikely to have lived at home. Not only did community pressure compel participation, but each village office employed a military affairs' clerk who could have easily identified the addresses of local eligibles who lived at their families' official residences. Even though the emigrants also could have been influenced by the threat of sanctions against their families at home, they were less susceptible to such pressure than their brothers who stayed behind. *Isshiki bunkai shi* [The History of the Isshiki Branch] (Nishio, 1930), pp. 88–89; Akita *Sakigake*, October 1, 1930, p. 2.

The local reservist branch leaders absorbed responsibility after 1912 for preparing all of the community's participants for the "traditional" event. Two or three days before the inspecting officers arrived from the regimental district headquarters, the branch chief gathered all local "soldiers" for preinspection training. The preparation and inspection required that each soldier have a neat uniform and personal appearance, and forced him to submit to a short, military length haircut, to have the appropriate goods in his service bag (hōkō bukuro), and to answer all of the inspecting officer's questions concerning current events, military ideology, technique, and law, and to know how to act in case of recall. The actual examination was rather formalistic. The closer the soldier's answers matched those in the manual, the higher his score. Thus, if asked the manual's first "current events" question, "What is the destiny of our imperial nation?", the examinee was expected to answer, "Our destiny is to honor the way of the deities, to help realize the imperial mission of 'all the world under one roof,' and thus to guide the world to eternal peace." If asked, "Recite the five central ideals of the Rescript of January 4, 1882," the successful reservist responded, "A soldier must strive to be loyal, a soldier must be decorous, a soldier must revere bravery, a soldier must honor fidelity, a soldier must aim at simplicity." Most of the questions focused on spiritual and patriotic values. The outstanding examinee memorized the answers, especially the Imperial Rescript to Soldiers and Sailors, and spewed them back word for word to the inspecting officer. Many Japanese men over forty-five can recite the rescript even today.[25]

One of the primary objects of the examination was the service bag, which still holds a large share of the memories that Japanese have of the prewar era. The hōkō bukuro, which hung in the most honored place in the reservist's home, the alcove (tokonoma), throughout the year, contained everything a soldier needed to take with him when he went to the barracks. It included his orders, his soldier's notebook (gunjin tetchō), which contained his service records, all his awards and medals, his will, his photograph, his personal daily needs, a cloth wrapper (furoshiki), wrapping paper and string for sending his civilian clothes home from the barracks, his valuables, a lock of hair and finger nail clippings to be used for burial if he died in combat and his remains could not be found, his plan of action if recalled to active

25. The army and reservist association published reference books for participants in the annual inspection. See, for example, Kan'etsu tenko gakka montō no sankō [A Reference Book of Questions and Answers by Subject for the Annual Inspection] (Yamagata, 1943), especially pp. 5, 18. The Anjō reservist documents include a volume containing inspection results from 1921 until 1942. Kan'etsu tenko kōhyō [Reviews of Annual Inspections], 1921–1942.

duty, money to pay his train fare to the barracks, his seal, and his savings' book (*hōkō chokin tsūchō*). The branch chief before the event and the inspecting officer at the roll call examined the bag to ascertain whether all of these contents were included. When the soldier went off to active duty, he took the bag and all of its contents (*hōkō bukuro o sagete iku*) except the hair and clippings and the savings book with him; these he left behind with his family. The *hōkō bukuro* held such an important place in the prewar reservist's milieu that when asked by the inspecting officer "Where do you keep your service bag?", one "grass roots" soldier is reputed to have answered, "I keep my service bag hanging in my heart" (*kokoro ni kakete arimasu*). For this answer he was praised by the inspecting officer.[26]

On the surface, these aspects of the annual inspection make it appear narrowly military and a way of ensuring a high level of preparedness among men with army and navy obligations. This narrow interpretation, however, is inadequate. Not only did hamlet cohesion guarantee that all who should, did attend, but the inspection was a total village affair and participation was not limited to reservists. When the officers and men from the regimental area headquarters arrived, they were greeted not only by reservist officials, but also by the mayor, other local government, school, and organizational officials, and even representatives of the defense women's association wearing their famed white aprons and shoulder bands. All of these same officials (women, of course, excluded) attended the branch chief's party for the visitors and, as one can imagine, the women's organization prepared the food and drink for it. The inspecting officers often reviewed youth school students or youth association members as well while in the village or town, and the officials, reservists, teenagers, and even the elementary school children heard patriotic, "national policy" speeches after the inspection.[27] In other words, this annual event became not only a roll call for men with military obligations, but also a major village-town occasion on which all of the army's organizations, the schools, and civil officials participated. The prominent symbolic position of the service bag in the *tokonoma* of the home of every man with a military obligation must also have had its impact on the other members of his family. The total participation of the village in the inspection and the prominence of the service bag in each home's place of honor served both as symbol of the integration of the village and the army's system and as an educational device for reinforcing this integra-

26. Fukuchi Shigetaka, *Gunkoku Nihon no keisei* (Tokyo, 1959), p. 111.
27. Embree, *Suyemura*, p. 66.

tion in the minds of the villagers. The annual inspection demonstrated the important role the military held in village life. The results of many years of drill, physical and patriotic education, success at the conscription examination and on active duty, were revealed here in either honor or shame for the local community.

ACTIVITIES TO INSTILL PATRIOTISM

The third type of activity, spreading patriotic ideals among the rural population, was the natural concomitant of the first two. Community service duties had as their primary goals popularizing the military and its organizations at the local level and at the same time setting up the members and especially the reservists as model good citizens. Military duties not only directly benefited the military by supplying them with better trained, more physically fit, and happier recruits, but they also helped the army achieve rural acceptance and create a disciplined and militarized civilian population. Activities to instill patriotism integrated all of these other activities by educating villagers to believe that the services and duties were done not only for the good of the local community and the army, but also for the emperor and the nation. Loyalty to landlord, to reservist chief, to school principal, to mayor, and to army commander was from the army's point of view not only related to the citizen's local and defense needs; loyalty in all of these cases was also identified with and reinforced by loyalty to the emperor. He was the apex of the pyramid which integrated the basic local units—family, hamlet, army company, and factory—into a national whole.

Japanese military officers, like many civilian commentators, defined their patriotism by using national terms: "nation" (*kokka*), "national populace" (*kokumin*), and "Japan" (*Nippon*); but most military men also stressed an "imperial" dimension. Officers tended to see Japan and Japanese nationalism as both different from and superior to the West and its form because Japan had a unique imperial family. The following excerpt from a 1924 speech to reservist leaders by Tanaka Giichi expresses well this imperial aspect of the military man's Japanese nationalism:

We who are bathed in the glory of celebrating this felicitous event (the marriage of the crown prince) truly have received the benevolence of the lofty throne. Our exalted nation whose glory glows from its national polity based on an unbroken imperial reign is one which has no parallel in the history of the world. There is no other nation which has been ruled continuously by an unbroken line of emperors for over 2,500 years. Our duty is to protect this national polity, defend this glorious nation, and expand Japan's power and prestige eternally throughout the world.[28]

Officers expressed this sentiment repeatedly in their writings. The reservist journal *Comrades in Arms,* for example, included a monthly "imperial activities section," periodic pictures of the emperor and his family, and a large number of emperor-centered, patriotic articles (110 of 436 in 38 issues between 1910 and 1929). The army officers' journal *Kaikōsha kiji* included many similar essays.[29]

Army officers based their conception of Japanese nationalism on their interpretation of the *Imperial Rescript to Soldiers and Sailors* which, argues the student of Japanese militarism, Takahashi Masae, led army officers to believe that soldiers and sailors held a unique place in an already unique Japanese ethnic group. They were the recipients of a rescript which the emperor presented directly to them, which predated the 1889 Constitution, and which placed the army and navy in a position subordinate only to the emperor and not to the civil government. Military men, Takahashi continues, believed that the pre-1945 Japanese government was based on two almost equally important documents, their rescript and the Constitution. The former, which they considered preeminent because of its spiritual basis, established the military as the sole, strong right arm of the "revealed man deity" (*arahitogami*). The latter, a "mere" legal document, reinforced their faith by allowing the services the "right of supreme command," the power in many situations to ignore the civil government and report directly to the emperor.[30] Officers utilized an "imperial" vocabulary and emphasized the *Imperial Rescript to Soldiers and Sailors* in describing their nationalism because this special relationship with the emperor allowed military leaders to perceive of themselves as legitimate competitors for national power with the civil officials. Men like Tanaka believed even before the crisis of 1930 that they were legally independent of the Prime Minister (they accepted some civilian control in the 1920s only because of the antimilitary milieu), that they

---

28. Tanaka, "Akushisō o korobose," Kawatani Yorio, *Tanaka Giichi den* (Tokyo, 1929), pp. 195–196.

29. See, for example, Ninagawa Arata, "Shisō zendō no ichi kōsatsu" [An Observation on Thought Improvement], *Kaikōsha kiji,* December 1929, pp. 91–96; Nagata Hidejirō, "Waga kokutai" [Our National Polity], January 1930, pp. 85–94; Ōkawa Shūmei, "Nippon seishin no kakuritsu" [The Foundation of the Japanese Spirit], January 1930, pp. 95–104; Hongō Fusatarō, "Seishin rikkoku to butoku no tanren" [The Spiritual Nation and Forging Military Virtues], August 1930, pp. 39–52; Araki Sadao, "Kōgun no seishin" [The Spirit of the Imperial Army], January 1933, pp. 1–5.

30. Takahashi Masae, *Ni niroku jiken* (Tokyo, 1965), pp. 134–141.

had the correct view of Japan's destiny, and that they were not being political in their efforts to educate civilians to agree with them. These educational efforts did not violate the injunction against military involvement in politics because military men believed that they rose above politics by serving the emperor and his "whole" nation rather than "divisive" personal, company, and party "political" interests." [31] This self-perception was based on their "unique" imperial rescript and its concomitant special relationship with the emperor. The rescript and the imperial vocabulary, therefore, were crucial to the officers' nationalism and became an important element in their message and thus in the content of the patriotic activities.

NATIONWIDE LEADERSHIP SEMINARS AND NATIONAL PUBLICATIONS

The reservist and youth associations from their establishment in 1910–1915 sponsored national leadership seminars and publications in order to disseminate standardized patriotic views and military knowledge to local opinion makers and leaders. The reservists' seminars, directed by top army officers like Nagata Tetsuzan, Imamura Hitoshi, Tatekawa Yoshitsugu, and Yoshida Toyohiko, along with key Navy, Education, and Home Ministry officials, covered such topics as the elimination of threatening ideologies, the spread of Japan's superior emperor-centered value system, youth education, total mobilization, the sacred national polity, and the impact of "dangerous" foreign ideas on national defense. The first of many such reservist seminars was held in the youth association's Tokyo headquarters in "democratic" October, 1927, and was attended by 174 reservist youth leaders. The national youth association established the same kind of system and even set up a leadership training center in the outskirts of Tokyo.[32]

The reservists and youth association also published magazines to guide local leaders in providing nationally uniform, patriotic, military, and civil education. Even if the reservists' primary publication, *Comrades in Arms*, never quite attained Tanaka's goal, articulated in a February 2, 1913 letter to General Terauchi, of "serving the immediate need of guiding the nation's people," it did reach a wide enough

31. Suzuki Sōroku, speech to August 27, 1935, national reservist conference, in *Senyū*, 304 (1935), pp. 14–17; Hongō Fusatarō, "Shin ni happu seraretaru guntai kyōikurei no seishin," *Senyū*, 30 (1913), pp. 14–15; Ninagawa Arata, "Zaigō gunjin to senkyōsen" [Reservists and the Election], *Taishō kōron*, IV, no. 6 (1924), pp. 16–18.

32. Kumagai, *Seinendanshi*, pp. 399–404; *Senyū*, 210 (1927), p. 9; 233 (1929), pp. 46–47.

audience to be a potent force in the army's drive to indoctrinate reservists and their neighbors.[33] In keeping with the patriotic and social educational goals of the *zaigō gunjinkai*, the magazine had a strong nonmilitary flavor. An analysis of thirty-eight issues between 1910 and 1929 reveals that of 436 articles, over half dealt with subjects of no immediate military purpose—110 were concerned with patriotic and ideological leadership, 50 with health and agriculture, and only 198 with military matters. Among the latter 198, moreover, only 50 were devoted to narrowly military matters; 35 treated reservist affairs, and 113 gave "historical" accounts of patriotic and loyal military heroes and battles of the past. Tanaka, the original head of the editorial board, and his civilian subordinates, drawn from other ministries and from universities, wrote the magazine's articles in a relatively simple style with a minimum of Chinese characters and a great number of phonetic readings (*furigana*) so that leaders and members with minimal education could receive the common message. The clientele for *Comrades in Arms* included not only local reservist leaders and members, but also non-member village and town officials. The reservist association distributed the magazine without charge to all local mayors and normal, middle, and elementary school principals in the hopes of influencing these important local leaders and educators. The circulation of *Comrades in Arms* reached 75,000 copies per issue, and all the men who received it—local reservist officials in addition to the community leaders—were opinion makers.

The reservist association also edited other journals for different audiences. The headquarters published, for example, the *Taishō Review (Taishō Kōron)*, a magazine for a better educated audience (it contained a more formal style, more characters, less *furigana* and a more nationalistic content than *Comrades in Arms*). The *Taishō Review* featured articles by some of Japan's most famous conservative intellectuals: Mitsui Kōshi, Katō Genchi, the famed scholar of Shintoism, Ōkawa Shūmei, and Ayakawa Takeji, as well as Tanaka, Nagata, and many others of the army's leading "intellectuals." The circulation of this journal never exceeded 7,000 copies, but they were a well-placed 7,000.[34] Another important reservist journal was its women's magazine, *Our Home (Wagaie)*, published first in 1917 (fifteen years before the defense women's association was founded). Its object was

33. Inoue Kiyoshi, "Taishōki no seiji to gumbu," in Inoue Kiyoshi, ed., *Taishōki no seiji to shakai* (Tokyo, 1969), p. 371.

34. Fujiwara Akira, *Gunjishi* (Tokyo, 1961), p. 152; *Sanjūnenshi*, pp. 120, 137–138. The Meiji Newspaper Repository (*Meiji shimbun bunko*) at Tokyo University has a representative collection of both journals.

to "show Japanese women the ethical rather than the easy way to salvation and to teach them the beauties of the traditional Japanese family way of life, the greatness of the Japanese national polity, and how best to serve the imperial nation." The magazine, edited in an even simpler style than *Comrades in Arms,* featured articles about homemaking and health, but placed its greatest emphasis on the dissemination of patriotic values and on educating women to perform their national "military" duty of raising patriotic and hard-working children and serving the nation on the home front. The reservists also published a large series of books on reservist, youth, and women's leadership. One goal of all of the publications was to establish guidelines for patriotic education.[35]

The national youth association also published a series of publications to help "unify and coordinate the 30,000 nationwide youth groups." In 1916, the Tokyo headquarters began distributing the *seinendan's* major monthly publication, *Imperial Youth* (the title was changed to *Youth* in 1923.) Although only one military man served on the original board of editors, that officer, needless to say, was the chief of the reservists' board of publications, Tanaka Giichi. In addition, Okada Ryōhei, the Education Minister who helped establish the youth training centers ten years later, Anjō's Yamazaki Nobuyoshi, and Mizuno Rentarō, Education Minister in the 1928 Tanaka Cabinet, also served on the board or as consultants to *Imperial Youth*. From the personnel involved alone one can discern that the magazine's purpose was to spread a uniform, nationally-oriented patriotic and, to some extent, military set of values to Japan's youth. The other two major *seinendan* publications, *Youth Card,* a short, concise, and easy to carry popular periodical, and *Japan Youth Newspaper,* had purposes similar to those of *Imperial Youth* and *Comrades in Arms.*[36] The three youth periodicals were far less blatantly military in content than the reservists', but all of the magazines and newspapers were patriotically progagandistic.

MOVIES, PLAYS, AND EXHIBITIONS

Another type of activity designed to inculcate the army's brand of imperial patriotism (along with military knowledge) to regional leaders and to citizens in general centered around motion pictures, plays, exhibitions, and lectures sponsored by the army and its organizations.

---

35. *Sanjūnenshi,* pp. 121–122; *Wagaie,* 225 (1935); *Rikukaigun gunji nenkan, 1937,* pp. 769–774; *Senyū,* 261 (1932), pp. i–iv, 72.
36. *Seinendanshi,* pp. 122, 404–407.

Movies were used frequently after the mid-1920s because the technology had developed adequately to make projection equipment available. They were entertaining as well as educational. For example, the moving picture *Madame Shizuko Nogi,* about the loyalty of Madame Nogi and her famous husband when they died to follow the Emperor Meiji to his grave in 1912, was so much in demand in the Yamagata area that it circulated for six months in 1935. Other movies during that year, on such subjects as the imperial family, the nation's naval defenses, and Japan's actions in Manchuria at the time of the 1931 incident, were reported to have attracted 500 persons per showing. The movies were particularly popular in the mountain villages of the prefecture. Similar films drew large crowds in Tokushima Prefecture; 1,100 turned out in Anabuki Town alone in the interior of Shikoku, the smallest of Japan's four major islands. And in the Toyohashi reservist district, the one in which Anjō was located, over 145,000 persons attended reservist-sponsored movies in 1932. As one might expect, the more remote the rural area, the larger the attendance; in Hekikai County's Takaoka Village, 5,000 people turned out for a four-day engagement; in Anjō, 1,750 came to the only showing; and in industrial Kariya, no reservist-sponsored films were shown at all.[37] The good attendance can be attributed both to community cohesiveness and to the relative dearth of entertainment in rural as compared to urban areas. But whatever the motivation, thousands of rural Japanese saw army- and reservist-sponsored patriotic and military movies in the 1930s.

Dramatic presentations were used less frequently than movies for the simple reason that they were more difficult to organize and more expensive. Nevertheless, the army and reservists did present them on occasion. For example, in September, 1935, the Tokushima district reserve headquarters and the local Defense Women's Association organization cosponsored the presentation of four plays by a professional acting group from Osaka. The set combined educational and entertaining pieces. It included a comedy about manipulating one's wife, a military drama entitled *For the Nation,* a historical play about medieval Japanese pirates, and a national defense drama especially for women named *Flowers That Bloom on The Home Front.*[38]

Exhibitions were also held for the express purpose of stimulating patriotism and military values through an entertaining medium. For

---

37. *Senyū,* 232 (1929), p. 50; *Yamagata shimbun,* June 22, 1935, p. 3; September 1, 1935, p. 3; *Tokushima nichinichi shimpō,* September 14, 1935, p. 3; Anjō documents, Volume X, *Jigyō yotei oyobi jisshihyō tsuzuri.*

38. *Tokushima nichinichi shimpō,* September 2, 1935, p. 1.

example, the commemoration of Japan's 1905 victory over Russia was given as the pretext for a fair held at the Yamagata Prefectural Hall and city park in April and May of 1935. This exhibition was sponsored jointly by the Yamagata reservist district, the local youth association, and the city's newspaper—the Yamagata daily supported reservist activities to the extent that it ran a semimonthly *zaigō gunjinkai* page. The aid of the city and prefectural governments, the police, and the regional army headquarters indicated the degree of civil-military-newspaper cooperation in this northern Japan area. The governor officiated at the opening ceremony, and the fair included army and navy displays, calligraphy donated by General Araki Sadao and Prime Minister Admiral Okada Keisuke, and some of the personal effects of General Nogi. The local reservists also used the fair as an occasion to present awards to outstanding members and to nonreservist supporters. The high point of the two weeks came on the opening day when reservists led *seinendan* members and youth training center and elementary school students in a mass war game. One can imagine the impact on subteen and teenage youths of playing war with real soldiers and weapons.[39]

LOCAL PATRIOTIC SEMINARS AND LECTURES

Movies, plays, and fairs had greater glamor, but locally sponsored seminars and lectures were the most common method of spreading patriotic values. Reservist, youth, and women's branches all over Japan sponsored, often jointly, speeches by local and visiting authorities on a plethora of military and patriotic subjects. These educational sessions assumed two forms: nationally sponsored, local ethical societies (*hōtokukai*), presided over by community leaders, and less frequent larger lectures, often addressed by visiting speakers. In Anjō, the reservists of each hamlet or hamlet-cluster organized and directed one *hōtokukai* each month, except at transplanting and harvest time. These seminars were attended by all of the community's reservists and youth branch members, combined agricultural, hygienic, vocational, military, and religious education with patriotic indoctrination, and were presided over by the hamlet's reservist leader. The leader lectured to the gathered hamlet men about one of the two key rescripts, *To Soldiers and Sailors* and *On Education*. This was followed by guests' lectures on practical subjects. Usually, local doctors, priests,

---

39. *Yamagata shimbun*, April 26, 1935, p. 1; April 27, p. 2; April 29, p. 1; May 1, p. 1.

agricultural technicians, elementary school principals and teachers, or instructors from the notable Anjō agricultural school spoke. The purpose of these monthly seminars was to educate youths in three closely related subjects: military values, patriotism, and productivity.[40]

More formal, village- or town-wide lectures also served as a useful way of spreading patriotic ideas to villagers of all ages and sexes. The army, reservist association, and national youth organization maintained lecture bureaus so that they could dispatch speakers when requested by local branches and intermediate headquarters. One finds the most illustrious names in the army, civil bureaucracy, and right wing pantheon giving lectures in the nation's smallest villages and towns in the 1920s and 1930s. Invariably, because of local pressure, the prestige of the speaker and the dearth of local entertainment (a patriotic lecture was more than nothing), lecturers drew large audiences wherever they went. The case of Shimo-Ina County is a revealing one. There the radical wing of the *seinendan* imported lecturers of their own persuasion like Royama Masamichi and Miki Kiyoshi. Their more conservative brethren also brought in a series of speakers; the names read like a roster of the Showa intellectual right wing and army. Between 1924 and 1930, Shimo-Ina youths heard, among many others, Ninagawa Arata, a reservist "house" scholar; Uesugi Shin'kichi, the famous conservative constitutional law professor; Ōkawa Shūmei, the Right's "respectable" intellectual; Nagata Tetsuzan, the army's "brains"; and Araki Sadao, Army Minister in the early 1930s and the most prestigious leader of the "imperial way." Such lecturers circled the country at army, reserve association, and *seinendan* expense in the 1920s and 1930s. In 1931, the reserve association lecture bureau reported sponsoring 590 official lectures by Tokyo-based officers alone. When one adds those sponsored by the *seinendan,* and those given by civilians, by regional army officers not dispatched from Tokyo headquarters, and by locally prominent people like Yamazaki Nobuyoshi in Anjō, or by mayors, school teachers, reservist branch chiefs, and agricultural cooperative heads, the number of speeches must have run into the thousands or tens of thousands each year.[41] Army officers and their supporters probably spent more time "going to the people" in prewar Japan than their opponents on the left.

40. *Anjō-machi seinendanshi,* I, pp. 130–131.
41. *Nagano-ken seinen hattatsushi,* pp. 230–231; *Sanjūnenshi,* pp. 191–192, 195, 211; *Anjō-machi seinendanshi,* I, pp. 392–394; *Anjō-shi seinendanshi,* II, pp. 197–198.

ETHICAL EDUCATION IN YOUTH SCHOOLS

Another source of nationally standardized local patriotic education came through the youth training centers and youth schools and their ethics textbooks, which were uniform nationwide. In addition to the reservist-led 40 to 50 percent of the curriculum which focused on military drill, another 10 to 15 percent centered on ethical education— 100 hours during the four years before 1935, 80 hours afterwards. Ethical education, taught by local elementary school teachers in addition to their regular duties, took the same form and emphasized the same values as that taught in the compulsory primary schools. That is to say, while moral education did not concentrate solely on nationalistic content, a large percentage of it did emphasize the state, the emperor, and the imperial dynasty. A study by the Japanese scholar of education, Karasawa Tomitarō, states that one-fifth to one-third of the material in prewar ethics textbooks emphasized the state. In addition, much of the remaining content was used to teach the importance of such military-supported ideals as respect for teachers and for authority in general, the family as a model for social organization, and the importance of such "homely" virtues as diligence, bravery, loyalty, and frugality.[42] The youth schools' moral education added one more thread to the web of patriotic education in Showa Japan.

VILLAGE AND TOWN PATRIOTIC CEREMONIES

Local reservists intensified the weight of patriotic education by leading their community's youth school students, youth association members, defense women, and elementary school students in a long, annual series of patriotic ceremonies. Each year all or some of the organizations, mobilizing all or some of their members, sponsored parades and speeches on Imperial Founding Day, on the anniversary dates or birthdays of the three modern emperors, at New Year's Day, on Army Day, on Navy Day, on the reservist association's and youth association's founding days. In the 1930s, they also sponsored events on such occasions as the anniversaries of the promulgation of the *Imperial Rescript to Soldiers and Sailors,* of the fall of Mukden in the Russo–Japanese War, of the defeat of the Russian Baltic fleet in the Sea of Japan, of the Manchurian Incident, of the 1937 China Incident, of the 2600th anniversary of the "establishment" of the imperial dynasty,

---

42. Tomitarō Karasawa, "Changes in Japanese Education as Revealed in Textbooks," *Japan Quarterly,* July–September 1955; Robert King Hall, *Shūshin: The Ethics of a Defeated Nation* (New York, 1949), *passim.*

and, after 1941, of the opening of the war with the United States. Most villages and towns held approximately eight to ten of these patriotic ceremonies each year; in Anjō, the number rose from ten in 1929 to thirteen in 1941.[43]

The content of the patriotic meetings was similar throughout the nation. The ceremonies included the singing of the national anthem in praise of the nation's imperial dynasty rather than of the nation, the shouting of three banzais for the emperor, the recitation by the reservist branch chief of the *Imperial Rescript to Soldiers and Sailors,* and usually a speech on an ideological or military subject. The purpose of the military lectures was usually to stimulate patriotic feelings among local citizens as well as to explicate national defense concerns. The following titles of military speeches, a few culled from the pages of local newspapers from 1935, provide examples: "The Clash of Western Ideas with Japan's Ideology," "Threats to Japan's Righteousness in these Dangerous Times," and "The Organ Theory Heresy." Other seemingly nonideological topics included "The Manchurian Railroad and the Soviet Union," on the dangers to the Japanese "spirit" of the spread of Communism; "Japan's Army Compared with Those of the European Powers," on the Japanese military's spiritual superiority; and "The Dangers of the 1935 Disarmament Conference for Japan's National Defense," on the insult to "unique" emperor-centered Japan of the concept of the equality of nations.[44]

MEMORIAL SERVICES FOR THE WAR DEAD

Memorial services in honor of a hamlet's or village's war dead reinforced the same kinds of ideals emphasized in the patriotic ceremonies, and helped tie them into the community's social structure. Once or twice a year in most communities, reservists, youth association members, and defense women (before 1932, hamlet women) spent several days in preparation by cleaning the graves of all local men killed in action (in Anjō, grave maintenance was a monthly function). Then, on the final day, that of the ceremony, the members visited the graves and afterwards held rites for the dead either at the local elementary school or the Buddhist temple. A few years after the establishment of the reservist organization, many branches erected, with village or

43. Fukuchi, *Gunkoku Nihon no keisei,* pp. 112–113; *Anjō-machi seinendanshi,* I, pp. 221–223; *Anjō-shi seinendanshi,* II, pp. 50–52.

44. *Fukuoka nichinichi shimbun* [The Fukuoka Daily Newspaper], April 13, p. 5; September 19, p. 7; July 4, p. 7; *Tokushima nichinichi shimpō,* March 27, p. 2; *Yamagata shimbun,* March 30, p. 3; May 31, p. 1; June 23, p. 1.

town government and martial society (i.e. community) financial support, monuments to their local war dead; from that time on, the local organizations held their annual or biannual rites at these memorial spots. The observances assumed much the same form as the patriotic rallies except that the talks emphasizing patriotism and military values were usually shorter and were almost always eulogies for the brave dead or for Japanese heroes of the past. This activity was one of the most frequently mentioned both in the pages of *Comrades in Arms* and in the local youth association histories.

Fukuchi Shigetaka, in his book *The Formation of Militaristic Japan*, has described these ceremonies and their local impact:

> The reservists held a solemn ceremony for the war dead at the hamlet's war memorial on April 30, the day of the annual ceremony at Yasukuni Shrine in Tokyo. The rite consoled the spirits of all of the local war dead. Village leaders, the soldiers' family survivors, school children, etc., took part. The village government paid most of the expenses. During the ceremony the survivors were praised as "Military Nation Mothers," "Military Nation Wives," or "Yasukuni Children." At the ceremony, seating was arranged according to one's military decorations, pensions, and rank.
>
> These ceremonies as well as the financial and labor help the survivors' received and the grave cleaning appealed to their feelings about the continuity of the spirit of their ancestral line, family prestige, and village honor. *Thus, the rites unconsciously cultivated the connection between the political order and obedience, and reinforced the spirit of mutual assistance.*[45]

The ceremonies helped strengthen the existing political order, Sasaki Ryūji tells us, because the village government and the reservist leaders, representatives of the community's elite, sponsored and led the rites while the men being honored usually came from poor tenant-farmer families. Thus, by honoring their followers, the powerful reinforced their own prestige and built popular support for the army and its nationalistic values as well.[46]

PATRIOTIC CEREMONIES INVOLVING THE IMPERIAL FAMILY

The culmination of the patriotic activities, and that which gave the members of the army's organizations a special relationship with the personification of Japanese nationalism, the emperor, was the right

---

45. Fukuchi, *Gunkoku Nihon no keisei*, p. 113, italics added. Yasukuni Shrine is the national shrine in honor of the war dead.

46. Sasaki Ryūji, "Nihon gunkokushugi no shakaiteki kiban no keisei," *Nihonshi kenkyū*, 68 (1963), pp. 12–13.

to participate in a number of "imperial ceremonies." Reservists, youths, and, finally, women were allowed to take part in imperial coronations, marriages, and funerals, and to view the emperor when he traveled around the country. It was the emperor's custom as commander and chief of the military, for example, to attend and "direct" the annual army grand maneuvers held each year in different sections of the nation. The army arranged the sequence of events so that during his three or four days' visit to an area the emperor reviewed local reservists, youth group members, and youth training center and elementay school children. In 1934, for example, the emperor traveled to Takasaki City in Gumma Prefecture for the annual maneuvers. On the third day of his visit, he inspected 20,000 reservists from the area at the parade grounds of the local infantry regiment, and then drove to the campus of the prefectural teachers' college to review the young people. At the end of the day, the emperor returned to Tokyo by car, and members of these various organizations in the communities between Takasaki and Tokyo stood in formation along the sides of the highway and saluted the imperial person as he passed. This same method of greeting was used when the emperor traveled by railroad. When the train stopped at the local station, the reservists' leaders were allowed to climb the platform and actually welcome the emperor.

Many reservists, youths, and women also participated in imperial coronations, marriages, and funerals between 1910 and 1945. Thousands of reservists from every branch along the Tokyo-Kyoto highway lined the route of the Emperor Meiji's funeral cortege in 1912, and hundreds of thousands more participated in local village and town memorial services. *Comrades in Arms* published a special funeral issue which not only included articles by such figures as Field Marshals Yamagata and Terauchi eulogizing the emperor, but also gave detailed instructions on proper ceremonial procedures. The whole process, albeit on a smaller scale, but with youths included, was repeated in December, 1926, when his son, the Taisho Emperor, died. When the third modern sovereign, the Showa Emperor, was crowned in the fall of 1928, thousands of reservists and *seinendan* members took part. Over 20,000 reservists gathered on one occasion alone on the plaza outside the main entrance to the Imperial Palace; they were reviewed and were granted one of the four imperial rescripts presented to the *zaigō gunjinkai* between 1910 and 1937.[47] The army saw to it that reservists and, to a lesser degree, youths who later became reservists had closer ties with the symbol of military Japan's nationalism than

---

47. *Yamada-gunshi* (Maebashi, 1939), pp. 1659, 1687; *Sanjūnenshi*, pp. 168, 176–179; *Senyū*, 9 (1911), pp. i–ii; 23 (1912), *passim*; 211 (1928), pp. 35–36.

most rural Japanese. It is no wonder that several interview respondents stated proudly that they cried when greeting the emperor at their local railroad stations.

Two of the classic examples of reservist-youth participation in emperor-centered patriotic activity came during the halcyon years of Taisho democracy in the 1920's. One occurred at the time of a nation-wide reservist conference in Osaka in October 1925. After hearing speeches by Prince Kanin, the imperial prince who served as honorary president of the reservist association, the Education Minister, and the Mayor of Osaka, all of the thousands of participants moved to Mo-moyama near Kyoto in eleven special trains for the second day's meeting at the grave of the Emperor Meiji. The occasion turned into a religious and patriotic one in which there was no pretense of con-ducting substantive business. The high point of the meeting came when Field Marshal Kawamura Kageaki, the chairman of the organi-zation, pledged to the spirit of the late emperor in the name of all reservists to strive to spread the soldier's ethos to all Japanese, to up-hold the rescript, to place national goals before personal ones, to in-crease military efficiency, and to work for a national defense state. Several months later the counsellors of the association decided, with Imperial Household Agency approval, to commission Itō Chūta, the famous architect and Tokyo University professor, to build a monument at Momoyama with Kawamura's oath engraved on it. This action made permanent the reservist association's presence at one of Japan's most sacred spots, and it solidified *zaigō gunjinkai* ties to the imperial institution.[48]

The second event occurred three years later in April, 1928. The army and reservist leadership, stimulated by an alleged plot on the emperor's life which led to the arrest of hundreds of Communist Party members by the Tanaka Giichi government, ordered all re-servists to swear a loyalty oath to the emperor. Reservists, regardless of their political preferences, gathered at branch ceremonies on April, 29, the emperor's birthday, and publicly took the following oath:

Although the empire must naturally encounter difficulties, there is nothing more appalling than a rebellious outrage by which an attempt is made to destroy our glorious national polity. We, the members of the Imperial Mili-tary Reserve Association, in honor of the emperor's birthday, pledge the fol-lowing and promise to carry them out with unity and cooperation.
1. We pledge to do our duty and to assume responsibility for the protection of our national polity.

---

48. *Sanjūnenshi*, pp. 162–164, 169.

2. We promise to educate our fellow citizens and to reject deceptive and violent ideologies.

3. We pledge to lead our countrymen and to exalt the Great Principle (*Taigi*) of the founding of our nation.[49]

CONCLUSION

By the 1930s, adult reservists and even reservists-to-be, rural teenagers, were nationalistic. The evidence is compelling. The *zaigō gunjinkai* became the most important mass patriotic pressure group in prewar Japan, and many of the members exceeded even the army's leadership in their fervor. The youth association, although an organization of sub-voting-age young men, also participated in the nationalist movement. Reservists and, to a lesser degree, youths took part in every campaign between 1930 and 1936 to pressure the civilian government to take stronger stands against foreign and domestic "threats." They petitioned and demonstrated against the ratification of the London Naval Treaty in 1930, in favor of the Manchurian settlement in 1931–1932, in favor of the withdrawal from the League of Nations in 1932–1933, in support of leniency for the assassins of Prime Minister Inukai in 1933, and finally against Professor Minobe Tatsukichi and his blasphemous "Organ Theory Heresy" in 1935.[50]

The interview and questionnaire data also indicate that villagers not only continued to focus their loyalty on their hamlet, but also became fervently nationalistic, with deep emotional feelings toward the emperor. They became "national villagers." Eighty-five percent of the questionnaire respondents answered that they "felt pride when they put on their uniforms to attend reservist functions." The reservists' pride was partly an outgrowth of their community status as "mainstays," but the uniforms were those of a national army, not of a distinctly local organization. The grass roots soldiers' pride indicates that they felt respected by their neighbors for being members of the emperor's national army as well as for belonging to its local arm. An interview respondent told the author that the proudest moment of his life was on the day he greeted the emperor at the local railroad station when the monarch's train passed through. The ex-reservist related that he "broke down and cried" after he saluted the emperor

---

49. *Sanjūnenshi*, pp. 174–175.

50. Richard J. Smethurst, *The Social Basis for Japanese Militarism: The Case of the Imperial Military Reserve Association* (Ann Arbor, 1969), pp. 258–292; "The Military Reserve Association and the Minobe Crisis of 1935," in George M. Wilson, ed., *Crisis Politics in Prewar Japan* (Tokyo, 1970), pp. 1–23.

through the train window. The respondent continued by saying that "the emperor was not just the symbol of state, he was absolute (*zettai*). That you Americans didn't force the emperor to abdicate after the war was Japan's salvation. We are extremely grateful (*hijō ni arigatai*) to General MacArthur and to you."

All of the ex-reservists interviewed revealed their emotional attachment to the emperor and the nation in their discussions of the Emperor Organ Theory Crisis of 1935. The theory, which called the emperor an organ of the state, attempted to justify parliamentary government within the framework of a constitution which clearly stated that the emperor alone was sovereign. Some of the reservist association's local headquarters conducted a relentless anti–organ theory campaign in 1935, and all of the local members interviewed rejected the theory as blasphemous and insulting to the emperor. As one respondent said, "I didn't get involved in the attack on Minobe because my duty as a soldier didn't allow political participation. But, he got what he deserved. Minobe called the emperor a mere 'organ' and all patriotic Japanese knew that he was the whole. Today I still revere the emperor."

This respondent and all of the others who discussed their feelings toward the emperor were both emotionally moved and moving when they spoke of him. The depth of their feelings is difficult to describe in words. Perhaps the ex-reservists' emotions can best be conveyed through the observations of an American anthropologist studying in northern Japan in 1971. When the emperor visited the town where the scholar worked, practically everyone in town came out to watch. Many middle-aged and older people lined the roads five hours before the emperor's arrival, and sobbed when they saw him.[51] The emperor was more than a symbol of state to these people, and it would be difficult to believe that they waited and cried only out of a fear of hamlet sanctions.

Such manifestations of imperial and national identification surfaced time after time in the interviews. There is the case of the ex-branch chief mentioned in Chapter IV who felt compelled to fight communism and the teachers' union after 1945. Another respondent continued to display national flags on holidays after Japan's defeat, despite the opposition of his children and younger neighbors who called him "feudalistic." Still another led a postwar drive to have the town erect a memorial to the World War II war dead. In his explanation of why he sponsored the drive, he revealed both his

---

51. The scene was described to the author by L. Keith Brown.

patriotism and a moving compassion for his fellow soldiers. "Over 800 men from our town died for Japan during the war. They were brave and patriotic men. We must remember them in terms of their own values to which they, and we who lived, were then loyal. We can't condemn them because we have changed and society has different values today. And anyway, loyalty to the emperor (*chū*) is still praiseworthy. . . . Some people opposed putting up the monument, but I ignored them." All of the respondents told the interviewer that Japan would be a better place today (summer of 1969, at the height of Japanese campus unrest) if "those punks" (*aitsu,* used consistently to refer to the student radicals) had more respect for the emperor, were more patriotic, and had had military drill as teenagers. "Japan has lacked a central value, the emperor, since the war," one respondent concluded. "I believe the emperor is still the mainstay of the nation and the people. We must build a truly peaceful Japan for his sake."

The interview and questionnaire respondents' answers show that many rural Japanese had become emperor-worshipping nationalists as well as hamlet citizens and remained so even after Japan's defeat. Prewar rural Japanese had superimposed national identity and affiliations over their hamlet orientations. But superimposed is the wrong word to use here. We might better conclude that national villagers believed that the goals of the two were identical. When one served the hamlet, he served the emperor and nation, and when one served the emperor and nation, he served the hamlet—either way, he became a "national villager."

CONCLUSION

Ronald Dore summarizes the political activities of prewar rural Japanese as follows:

1. A submissiveness to authoritarian leadership deriving from an acceptance of hierarchical status distinctions which implied a natural right of those above to rule and a natural duty of those below to obey. (Referred to hereinafter as 'submissiveness.')

2. A willingness to subordinate the individual to the group, to sacrifice individual interests for the good of the family, for the good of the village, and for the good of the nation (it being understood that in the case of incompatibility of these goods, the good of the larger group must come first) combined with a stress on harmony in the family, in the village, and in the nation which held that any threat to unity was morally wrong, and he who created conflict by a challenge to the *status quo* was necessarily the wrongdoer. (Referred to as 'holism.')

3. A tendency to interpret the 'good of the nation' largely in terms of the relative power and prestige of a Japan in aggressive competition with other powers. (Referred to as 'nationalism.') [1]

The army's four organizations played an important role in creating this political edifice and in winning rural support for the army. The nature of the membership recruitment techniques, financing, leadership, and activities helped reinforce submissiveness and family- and village-oriented holism. They provided a major stimulus to the creation of nation-centered holism, and nationalism (both without the emperor, as in Dore's definition, or with him, as in mine) in twentieth-century rural Japan. And, finally, these forces ensured that that nationalism benefited the army.

1. Ronald P. Dore, *Land Reform in Japan* (London, 1959), p. 393.

The Japanese army's efforts to build support for the military, nationalism, and national holism through the use and reinforcement of hamlet submissiveness and family and village holism is in striking contrast to the methods that Germany, Japan's World War II ally, used to build popular support. Many comparisons between wartime Japan and the Nazis are well known. The Japanese in the 1930s propounded no *Führerprinzip*, created no party, no SA or SS, and no new ideology, and added no new groups to the ruling elite. But what is of most interest to us here is the different methods by which the leaders of the two nations appealed to the masses.

The Nazis came to power in a time of world and national crisis in 1933 by playing on the real and imagined grievances of large segments of the German population through tight organization, propaganda and demagogy. Hitler's party offered easy solutions to the problems of large "horizontal" segments of German society. Small shopkeepers feared the loss of business to department stores. Hitler promised to tax and control these large enterprises. Farmers, deeply in debt, were afraid of the loss of their farms. Hitler promised a debt moratorium, government loans, and new inheritance laws. Skilled workers feared increased competition and unemployment. Hitler promised more vigorous requirements for the qualification of artisans and more employment through public works. He then added to these economic appeals, often in fervently emotional speeches, a nationalistic cause, the reestablishment of Germany as a world power and later the creation of an empire, and two bogeymen, the socialists and the Jews. All of these methods combined to gain his party 17 million votes and finally national power in 1933.[2]

Two conclusions can be drawn from Hitler's rise. One is that if there had been no crisis, there would have been no Hitler as dictator. If the Allied powers had not forced a Carthaginian peace on Germany in 1919, if reparations payments, rampant inflation and the world depression had not destroyed the economic security of millions of Germans, and if the Weimar Republic had not lost the confidence of the nation between 1929 and 1933, Hitler would have found the road to power rocky and probably impassable. The other conclusion is that Hitler's appeal was to individuals as members of horizontally organized social classes. Although he preached the creation of an organic state that seemed to resemble a gigantic Japanese hamlet, his attraction was to poor farmers, or to artisans, or to petty bourgeois

---

2. David Schoenbaum, *Hitler's Social Revolution: Class and Status in Nazi Germany 1933–1939* (Garden City, 1966); Karl Dietrich Bracher, *The German Dictatorship* (New York and Washington, D.C., 1970).

shopkeepers, not to vertically organized, stratified groups. Hitler did not appeal to all of the residents of a village, but only to those farmers who felt that he could solve their problems.

The Japanese military built its basis of support, as we have seen, quite differently. The sense of crisis which grew in Japan as in Germany in the 1930s probably solidified the military's rural support, helped develop a more widespread nationalism among Japanese farmers, and had an overwhelming impact on urban Japanese, but the army's success at winning rural followers did not depend on the national leaders' ability to appeal to the grievances of the adherents. There is no doubt that the impact of the world depression, the national sense of persecution and isolation which grew rapidly after 1930, and the corruption of party politicians helped speed the military to its powerful wartime position in Japan. Nevertheless, the army's basic support, its own "electoral constituency," was built both before and then independently of the crisis. Although Hitler's rise to power depended on dislocations and unrest in German society, the Japanese army played a major role in governing Japan during the noncrisis era of "Taisho democracy," and military leaders probably would have increased their influence in the 1930s even if the depression, the Manchurian Incident, and the assassinations of party prime ministers had never taken place. The scholar of modern Germany can make a clear distinction between the eras of the Weimar Republic and Hitler; the student of Japan who draws a clear line between the decade of Taisho democracy and that of Showa militarism overemphasizes the importance of the prime minister's chair, and probably ignores rural society.

The Japanese army neither depended on a national sense of crisis to create a constituency nor won its support by appeals to individuals, classes, or horizontally organized categories of people. Hitler spoke to poor farmers and to artisans and to small shopkeepers; the Japanese army spoke to stratified and authoritarian hamlets in toto, from landlord to poorest tenant. When a rural community "plugged in" to the army's system, it brought with it leadership from the hamlet's prominent stratum, governance by elite consensus, 100 percent membership of eligibles, community duties, and financial support from the village office. The stratified hamlet joined the army as a whole. The tenants at the bottom of this vertical organization enrolled not out of a desire for relief from their capitalist or Jewish or landlord "oppressors" as they did in Germany. Rather, by joining, poor farmers confirmed their subordination to their social and economic superiors. Hitler established as one of his goals the creation of a stratified "organic society" but could never build it. The Japanese army built one almost without trying. Since each of Japan's 70,000 hamlets was a cohesive organic society unto itself, he who amalgamated them into a whole became the "dictator" of rural Japan.

To the Western reader, even to one who lived through the 1930s in Germany, the Japanese military's authoritarian pyramid of support, based on these stratified hamlets, must seem suffocating and restrictive. How many of us would have been willing to subordinate our individuality completely to family, village, and nation? And yet there is no reason to conclude that Japanese who did not belong to the prominent stratum of this organic society believed that they were being suffocated, or dictated to, or if they did, minded it. The economic necessity of following the landlord's lead was certainly one motivation for accepting both his and the army's authority. But L. Keith Brown has pointed out in his study of a postwar hamlet in northern Japan that stratification often continues to exist long after its economic underpinnings have disintegrated. Hierarchical hamlet cohesiveness offers more to his villagers than mere economic security, and, as Chie Nakane and many others have pointed out, both rural and urban Japanese even today willingly enroll in stratified village and company groups.[3] Tenants participated in antilandlord protests in the 1920s and 1930s. But both Fukutake, a member of a school of Japanese scholars who often tend to overestimate tenant-farmers' antilandlord attitudes, and Dore have shown that these disputes rarely disturbed hamlet 'holism.' When they did, Fukutake adds, the hamlet quickly returned to cooperative normalcy after the dispute. Barbara Ann Waswo concludes in her study of landlords and rural unrest in prewar Japan that a major cause of tenant disputes was some landlords' abandonment of their traditional paternalistic leadership role in order to become modern—educated and capitalistic—absentee landlords.[4] Villagers apparently preferred the tightly cohesive organization of the hamlet to a freer but more impersonal one. Our own case studies have shown that the army's organizations were more successful in communities like Anjō, where men of high local status led and elite control was both more personal and to us more suffocating, than in cities where social relationships were freer and more impersonal.

We can draw two conclusions for our purposes from this preference of Japanese farmers for living in cohesive, paternalistic, and authoritarian hamlets. One is that the army leaders could not have been suc-

---

3. Chie Nakane, *Tate shakai no ningen kankei* [Human Relations in a Vertical Society] (Tokyo, 1967), published in English as *Japanese Society* (Berkeley and Los Angeles, 1970).

4. Fukutake Tadashi, *Nihon sonraku no shakai kōzō* (Tokyo, 1959), pp. 459–545; Dore, *Land Reform*, p. 105; Waswo, *Landlords and Social Change in Prewar Japan* (Ann Arbor, 1970), p. 198.

cessful in building rural support for themselves if they had not organized through the existing hierarchical structure of hamlets and villages. The organizations that tried to build a new national consciousness without basing it on "hamletness" had less success. Even the political parties used techniques similar to the army's to gather rural votes. When political commentators wrote that Prime Minister Inukai Tsuyoshi had an "iron constituency," one wonders if they recognized that the very men who voted for him also "voted" for the army simultaneously—and for the same reason, to maintain hamlet cohesion.[5]

The other conclusion is even more important for our understanding of pre-1945 Japan: rural society was little or no more authoritarian during the Pacific War in 1943 than it had been in the era of Taisho democracy fifteen years earlier. Scholars writing on wartime Japan constantly point out that it became increasingly more authoritarian as the war approached, and if one concentrates on the plethora of mobilization laws, arrests of alleged dissidents, antiluxury campaigns, new military-operated economic control boards, and mass organizations like the Imperial Rule Assistance Association (IRAA), it seems that they are right. But urban Japan felt most of the impact of this mobilization. It was here that pre-1930 society was freest and most open and where most of the post-1930 factories for the war effort, suppressed government opponents, and postwar political commentators and scholars were located. Thus to them, wartime Japan seemed and was militaristic and authoritarian. But these same scholars continue their analysis of wartime Japan by concluding that rural Japan also became more tightly controlled from above. To support this contention, they emphasize the creation of the IRAA and of the Imperial Rule Men's Association for mobilization, and the block groups (*tonari gumi*), through which a group of families accepted collective responsibility for each others' acts. But in fact the local branches of the first two organizations rarely got off the ground, and when they did it was generally because of the support of the existing reservist branches. (Several of the branch chiefs interviewed also led their local men's associations, and one stated that the organization proved so ineffective in his community that the reserve branch absorbed most of its duties).[6] Moreover, the block groups, crucial to most scholars' efforts to

5. Nobutaka Ike, *Japanese Politics: An Introductory Survey* (New York: 1957), p. 200.
6. One document indicates that at least 47 reservists and 12 active duty or retired officers served in 256 Aichi Prefecture Imperial Rule Men's Association posts in 1942, and other sources indicate that the list is incomplete. Anjō Town office, *Anjō-machi yokusan sōnendan* [The Anjō Town Imperial Rule Men's Association], 1941–1942.

prove wartime militarism in rural Japan, caused no hamlet hardship at all since few people stepped out of line anyway. The block group simply became one more manifestation of the hamlet pressure for social and political conformity. Such coercion had existed in rural Japan long before World War II, and the block groups brought no basic change to the village.

Finally, the army's rural basis of support remained firm throughout World War II, at the same time that various groups within the urban, bureaucratic, industrial, and even military sectors of the society hindered the war effort by fighting among themselves for power and resources. Although Japan did not become Tanaka's huge, total war machine, it was through no fault of the rural segment of the society. Farm production remained high, farm boys faithfully served their nation and army as soldiers, and rural branches of the army's organizations enthusiastically performed all kinds of wartime mobilization activities. Our interview respondents' branches cleared snow from air fields, dug defensive positions, organized massive condolence and letter-writing campaigns for the soldiers at the front, collected scrap metal and other war effort essentials and, finally, in the war's closing days organized "bamboo spear" units to defend the nation and the village against the impending American invasion. As Chief Petty Officer Kira said to the hero in the short story, *Sakurajima*, "They'll fight! They have bamboo spears! They don't need training! They'll fight with their bodies! Murakami, you've been stationed at a *kamikaze* air base, and you still don't understand that spirit?" [7]

There are many reasons why rural Japan's loyalty never wavered. Urban conditions grew worse as the war progressed, but rural ones did not. Authoritarian mobilization brought a strong sense of wartime hardship to the cities, which had been relatively free before the war. American bombers rained destruction and death on most of Japan's urban centers, but the army's villages did not suffer at all. The rural economy flourished during the war, not only comparatively because the city dwellers lost their livelihoods, but also because labor shortages, increased food prices, and various government policies led to a reduction in farm rents and in tenancy. But another reason is that rural people were better prepared to be loyal. The army's two-pronged success at organizing rural support, in using and reinforcing submissiveness of hamlet members to local and higher authority and in creating nationalistic farmers, built a support which never faltered.

---

7. Umezaki Haruo, *Sakurajima*, in Hirano Ken, ed., *Sensō bungaku zenshū* [A Complete Collection of Wartime Literature] (Tokyo, 1971), Volume 3, p. 118.

ESSAY ON SOURCES

The material that provides the basis for the first two chapters of this study, those dealing with the formation of the army's educational system and with its national structure and leadership, fall into familiar categories for scholars writing modern Japanese history: organizational histories, periodicals, biographies, and memoirs. For example, I depended heavily for chronology on the histories of the reservist, youth, defense women's, and patriotic women's associations, the Education Ministry's publications concerning the youth training centers and youth schools, on the history of the wartime Imperial Rule Assistance movement, and I traced the ideas and actions of the organizations' founders and leaders from their own writings. Fortunately, Tanaka Giichi, the central actor, wrote prolifically in the reservist periodical *Comrades in Arms* and in the youth magazine *Imperial Youth,* published a number of books and collections of essays on reservist and youth affairs, and is the subject of three biographies, all of which contain excerpts from many of his articles and speeches on the two organizations. A collection of papers by and about Tanaka is housed in the Yamaguchi Prefectural Library (and on microfilm in the National Diet Library). The biographies and published writings of other key national figures were also useful for analyzing the central leaders' views and actions. I found particularly informative the biographies, memoirs, and collected writings of four former reservist association chiefs, Generals Terauchi Masatake, Ichinoe Hyoe, Suzuki Sōroku, and Inoue Ikutarō, of the youth center founder, Ugaki Kazushige, and of two youth association leaders, Tazawa Yoshiharu and Yamamoto Takinosuke. Other information on the national structure and officials of the organizations came from the pages of the reservists' *Comrades in Arms* and *Taishō Review,* the army's *Army Officers' Journal* and *Army and Navy Military Affairs Yearbook,* and other army, reservist, and youth association publications. Finally, I obtained extensive background information from the writings of and from conversations with many Japanese scholars, particularly three who specialize in the study of the military and the twentieth century right wing movement, Fujiwara Akira, Matsushita Yoshio, and Takahashi Masae.

I found greater difficulty in tracing the membership, leadership, finances, activities, and community impact of the local reservist, youth, and women's branches and schools. For example, although membership statistics for the youth and defense women's associations, and the youth training centers and schools are available in official published sources, such data does not exist for the reservist association. Thus, I culled the membership data for that organization from some of the hundreds of village, town, county, ward, city, and prefectural histories published in Japan in the present century. Many do not contain local reservist membership statistics, but I was able to find over forty local histories which do. I then compared the membership figures with census data for the appropriate sex and age groups to make comparisons between rural and urban recruitment success.

I used seventy of these community histories, eight local youth organization histories, the reservists' 1927 *Model Branch History,* two local reservist branch histories, unpublished Aichi Prefecture, Yana County documents (for the period before the end of World War I), and a number of official books, pamphlets, and periodicals to draw the broad outlines of local branch leadership, finances, and activities. This information, although detailed, did not provide a precise picture of the functioning of the army's groups in any one community. Thus I singled out four agricultural communities—Anjō Town (now city) in Aichi Prefecture, and Ōkamada-Futagawa Villages (two small villages merged for administrative purposes), Mitsue Village, and Katsunuma Town in Yamanashi Prefecture—for more thorough study. I chose Anjō as a case-study community because its town office published the most thorough and systematic local youth association history, a two-volume documentary collection. This work, which describes the local youth group from Tokugawa times to the post–World War II era, contains a complete roster of branch leaders, sample budgets, membership statistics, extensive lists and detailed descriptions of activities, and accounts of youth branch cooperation with other hamlet and town organizations. I then broadened the scope of the case study with information from interviews with four former leaders of both the reservists' and youth branches, forty-two questionnaires distributed to former members and officials, and twenty-nine notebooks of unpublished reservist branch and town government documents for 1906–1945 housed in the Anjō City Library. These documents contained hundreds of orders and communiques to the branch from the central and regional head-quarters, membership statistics, annual budgets, plans and reports on activities, a roster of all men with reserve obligations in 1918, a volume listing all branch officials by name, rank, period of service, and hamlet of residence, notebooks on martial and education society funding, on annual inspection results, on the dispatching of members on official business, on town-branch sponsored funerals, on the wartime "bamboo spear" defense corps, and even a map of the location of graves of all local war dead.

I chose the three Yamanashi communities because they had more extensive tenancy, landlords with larger holdings, and more frequent tenant disputes in the prewar era than relatively egalitarian Anjō. I was compelled to depend to a greater degree than in Anjō on interviews and questionnaires in these three communities because local youth and reservist branch histories or documents do not exist. I conducted six interviews in the three villages, and distributed twenty-two and thirty-five questionnaires in Ōkamada-Futagawa and Katsunuma, respectively. Research was enhanced in these cases, however, by other materials. The Katsunuma town office published a monumental local history in 1962, and a group of sociologists led by Ariga Kizaemon wrote an unpublished report on social stratification in Ōkamada and Futagawa based on extensive field research.

The published sources and the materials from the four case study communities were supplemented with additional interviews and questionnaires. I conducted three interviews in Tsubota Village on Miyake Island and one in Fuchū City in Tokyo Prefecture. Seventy-four former reservists out of 360 contacted in Yamanashi Prefecture (exclusive of Katsunuma and Ōkamada-Futagawa) returned a questionnaire distributed through the mail with the aid of the Yamanashi Prefectural Board of Education and Veterans' Pension Bureau.

BIBLIOGRAPHY

I. UNPUBLISHED DOCUMENTARY COLLECTIONS

A. Anjō Reservist Branch Documents, 1906–1945.

Kijiroku [Annals], branch records, 1906–1910.

Anjō-machi zaigō gunjinkai bunkai rekishi [The History of the Anjō Town Reservist Association Branch], 1911–1913.

Hatsuraikan tsuzuri [A Notebook of Communications from Higher Headquarters], May 13, 1933–March 23, 1944.

Kunrei kunji tsuzuri [A Notebook of Directives and Instructions from Higher Headquarters], November 4, 1914–May 7, 1932.

Yakuin meibo [A Register of Branch Officials].

Sembyōshisha oyobi izoku meibo [A Register of Those Who Died at War and Their Survivors].

Kan'etsu tenko kōhyō [Reviews of Annual Inspections], 1921–1942.

Shōkonsha setsuritsu shikin kankei tsuzuri [A Notebook Concerning Funds for the Establishment of a Shrine to the War Dead], 1929–1945.

Jimu nisshi [A Diary of Official Business], April, 1933–1944.

Jigyō yotei oyobi jisshihyō tsuzuri [A Notebook of Planned and Completed Activities], 1925–1943.

Yosan kessansho tsuzuri [A Notebook of Proposed and Completed Budgets], 1936–1945.

Eikyū hatsuraikan tsuzuri [A Permanent Notebook of Communications from Higher Headquarters], 1924–1945.

Hyōshō jōshin kankei shorui tsuzuri (A Notebook of Documents Concerning the Reporting of Awards and Decorations to Higher Headquarters], 1924–1945.

Sembyōshisha bohi shozaichi hyō [A Map of the Location of the Grave Markers of the War Dead].

Hatsuraikan tsuzuri (A Notebook of Communications from Higher Headquarters], January 4, 1943–December 28, 1944.

Kyōiku ni kansuru tsuzuri [A Notebook Concerning Education], August 15, 1943–March 5, 1944.

Kunji kokuyu kōhyō tsuzuri [A Notebook of Instructions, Official Directives, and Criticisms from Higher Headquarters], August 8, 1943–1945.

Kaigi ni kansuru tsuzuri [A Notebook Concerning Cadre Meetings and Affairs], branch records, August, 1943–1944.

Gyōji ni kansuru tsuzuri [A Notebook Concerning Branch Functions], August, 1943.

Bōeitai ni kansuru tsuzuri [A Notebook Concerning the Defense Corps], 1944.

Kihonkin [Endowment Fund], 1925–1942.

Hatsuraikan tsuzuri [A Notebook of Communications frim Higher Headquarters], January–March, 1945.

B. Anjō Town Documents, 1916–1945.

Anjō-machi shōbukai kyōikukai eiseikai ketsugi tsuzuri [A Notebook of Anjō Town Martial, Educational and Hygienic Society Resolutions], 1916.

Zaigō gunjin meibo [Register of All Anjō Reservists], 1918.

Ōshūsha kazoku chōsabo [Register of Investigations of Families of Men Recalled to Active Duty], 1939–1940.

Anjō-machi yokusan sōnendan [The Anjō Town Imperial Rule Men's Association], 1941–1942.

Chōshū reijō jūryōroku tsuzuri [A Notebook of Receipts For Orders Calling Men to Active Duty], 1937–1945.

Dai ichi kokuminhei senji meibo [A Register of First National Soldiers for Use in Time of War].

Dai ni kokuminhei meibo [A Register of Second National Soldiers].

C. *Aichi-ken shiryō, heijimon* [Aichi Prefecture Materials, Military Documents], for Yana County until 1916.

D. *Tanaka Giichi kankei bunsho* [Writings Concerning Tanaka Giichi].

II. ORGANIZATIONAL PUBLICATIONS

Aikoku fujinkai yonjūnenshi [The Forty Year History of the Patriotic Women's Association], 2 vols., Tokyo, 1941.

Anjō-machi seinendanshi [A History of the Youth Association of Anjō Town], Volume I, Anjō, 1936.

Anjō-shi seinendanshi [A History of the Anjō City Youth Association], Volume II. Anjō, 1962.

Dainippon kokubō fujinkai jūnenshi [The Ten Year History of the Greater Japan National Defense Women's Association], Tokyo, 1943.

Isshiki bunkai shi [The History of the Isshiki Branch], Nishio, 1930.

Kan'etsu tenko gakka montō no sankō [A Reference Book of Questions and Answers by Subject for the Annual Inspection], Yamagata, 1943.

Kumagai Tatsujirō. *Dainihon seinendanshi* [A History of the Greater Japan Youth Association], Tokyo, 1942.

Mammō mondai shiryō [Materials Dealing with the Manchurian and Mongolian Problem], 1931–1932.

Mombushō. *Gakusei hachijūnenshi* [The Eighty Year History of the Educational System], Tokyo, 1954.

————. *Sōtei kyōiku chōsa gaikyō* [The General Report of a Survey of Preinduction Training for Recruits], Tokyo, 1931.

Murata Kikugorō, ed. *Teikoku zaigō gunjinkai mohan bunkaishi* [A History of the Imperial Military Reserve Association Model Branches], Kawagoe, 1927.

Nagano-ken seinen hattatsushi [A History of the Development of Nagano Prefecture Youth], Nagano, 1935.

Nagoya-shi seinendan hattatsushi [A History of the Development of the Nagoya Youth Association], Nagoya, 1940.

Nagoya-shi seinen gakkō yōran [A Survey of Nagoya Youth Schools], Gifu, 1938.

Saishin seinen gakkō kyōin hikkei [The Newest Manual for Youth School Instructors], Tokyo, 1939.

Seinen [Youth], 1926.

Seinen gakkō kyōrenka kyōkasho [Youth School Drill Manual], Tokyo, 1940.

Senyū [Comrades in Arms], 1910–1935.

Taishō kōron [The Taishō Review], 1921–1928.

Teikoku seinen [Imperial Youth], 1916–1923.

Teikoku zaigō gunjinkai gyōmu shishin [A Directory of Imperial Military Reservist Association Affairs], Tokyo, 1929.

Teikoku zaigō gunjinkai Nishio-machi bunkai shi [The History of the Nishio Town Imperial Military Reservist Association Branch], Nishio, 1930.

Teikoku zaigō gunjinkai sanjūnenshi [The Thirty Year History of the Imperial Military Reservist Association], Tokyo, 1944.

Toyama-ken Higashi Tonami-gun Higashi Nojiri-mura seinendanshi [A History of the Toyama Prefecture Higashi Tonami County Higashi Nojiri Village Youth Association], Kanazawa, 1935.

Toyama-ken Nishi Tonami-gun Isurugi seinendanshi [A History of the Toyama Prefecture Nishi Tonami County Isurugi Youth Association], Kanazawa, 1937.

Tsukitsu-mura seinendan keiei jirei dai sanshū [A Third Collection of Examples of Tsukitsu Village Youth Association Management], Tokyo, 1936.

Utsunomiya seinendan no hattatsu [The Development of the Utsunomiya Youth Association], Utsunomiya, 1934.

Wagaie [Our Family], November, 1935.

Yamashima-mura seinendan keiei jirei dai isshū [A First Collection of Examples of Yamashima Village Youth Association Management], Tokyo, 1936.

III. YEARBOOKS, STATISTICAL AND DOCUMENTARY
COLLECTIONS, AND REFERENCE WORKS

Aichi-ken nōchishi [A History of Agricultural Land in Aichi Prefecture], 2 vols., Nagoya, 1957.

Aichi-ken tōkeisho [Aichi Prefecture Statistical Handbook], 1946.

Asahi nenkan [Asahi Yearbook], 1936.

Gonda Morinosuke, ed. *Nihon kyōiku tōkei* [Japanese Educational Statistics], Tokyo, 1938.

Ijiri Tsuneyoshi, ed. *Rekidai kenkanroku* [A Chronological Record of Officials], Tokyo, 1967.

Inahara, K., ed. *Japan Yearbook, 1934.*

Ishikawa Ken, ed. *Kindai Nihon kyōiku seidō shiryō* [Materials on the Modern Japanese Educational System], Volume III, Tokyo, 1956.

Kantō daishinzai to chōsenjin [The Kantō Disaster and Koreans], *Gendaishi shiryō* [Materials in Contemporary History], Volume VI, Tokyo, 1963.

Kokumin nenkan 1919 [1919 Citizens' Annual].

Kokuseiin. *Nihon teikoku tōkei nenkan* [The Statistical Yearbook of the Japanese Empire], 51 (1932); 57 (1938).

Kyōdo nenkan [The Local Yearbook], Okayama, 1937.

Naikaku kambō kirokuka. *Genkō hōrei shūran* [Collection of Existing Statutes and Laws], 2 vols., Tokyo, 1927.

Naikaku tōkeikyoku. *Kokusei chōsa hōkoku* [The National Census Report], 1920, 1930, 1935, 1950.

Naimushō keibōkyoku. *Shisō geppō* [Monthly Ideology Report], 1933–1939.

Naimushō keibōkyoku. *Shōwa hachi, kyū, jū, jūichi, jūninenchū ni okeru shakai undō jōkyō* [The Circumstances of Social Movements in 1933, 1934, 1935, 1936, 1937].

Naimushō keibōkyoku. *Tokkō geppō* [Monthly Thought Police Report], 1933–1939.

Nōchi kaikaku temmatsu gaiyō [A Summary of the Circumstances of Land Reform], Tokyo, 1951.

Ōtsuka shigakkai. *Shimpan kyōdoshi jiten* [A New Encyclopedia of Local History], Tokyo, 1969.

Rikugun daijin kambō. *Rikugunshō tōkei nempō* [The Annual Army Ministry Statistical Yearbook], 1925–1935.

Rikukaigun gunji nenkan [The Army and Navy Military Affairs Yearbook], 1937–1941.

Teikoku oyobi rekkoku no rikugun [The Armies of the Empire and the Powers], Tokyo, 1936.

Tiedemann, Arthur. *Modern Japan.* New York, 1962.

Tokinoya Katsu, ed. *Nihon kindaishi jiten* [An Encyclopedia of Modern Japanese History], Tokyo, 1960.

Yamanashi jinji kōshinroku [A Directory of Yamanashi People], Kofu, 1940.

Zenkoku shichōsonjimei daikan [A Guide to the Nation's City, Town, Village and Hamlet Names], Tokyo, 1951.

IV. NEWSPAPERS AND OTHER PERIODICALS

Akita Sakigake [The Akita Leader], October, 1930.

Asahi shimbun [The Asahi Newspaper], 1925–1927.

Kaikōsha kiji [The Army Officers' Journal], 1930–1940.

Tokushima nichinichi shimpō [The Tokushima Daily News], 1930–1935.
Yamagata shimbun [The Yamagata Newspaper], 1930–1935.

V. OFFICIAL BIOGRAPHIES, MEMOIRS, AND THE
PUBLISHED WRITINGS OF ORGANIZATIONAL LEADERS

Hagiwara Shunzō et al., ed. *Rikugun taishō Suzuki Sōroku den* [The Biography of Army General Suzuki Sōroku], Tokyo, 1943.
Hori Shika. *Saishō to naru made Tanaka Giichi* [Tanaka Giichi until He Became Prime Minister], Tokyo, 1928.
Hosokawa Ryūgen. *Tanaka Giichi,* Tokyo, 1958.
Kawatani Yorio. *Tanaka Giichi den* [The Biography of Tanaka Giichi], Tokyo, 1929.
Kohara Masatada et al., ed. *Ichinoe Hyoe,* Tokyo, 1932.
Kumagai Tatsujirō, ed. *Yamamoto Takinosuke zenshū* [The Complete Works of Yamamoto Takinosuke], Tokyo, 1931.
Kuroda Kōshirō. *Gensui Terauchi hakushaku den* [A Biography of Field Marshal Count Terauchi], Tokyo, 1920.
Mihara Fukuhei et al., ed. *Inoue Ikutarō den* [The Biography of Inoue Ikutarō], Tokyo, 1966.
Tanaka Giichi. *Shakaiteki kokumin kyōiku* [The Social Education of the Public], Tokyo, 1915.
———. *Taisho kōshoyori* [From a High and Clear Place], Tokyo, 1925.
———. *Tanaka chūjō kōenshū* [The Collected Speeches of Lieutenant General Tanaka], Tokyo, 1916.
Tanaka Giichi denki [The Biography of Tanaka Giichi], 3 vols., Tokyo, 1960.
Tazawa Yoshiharu. *Seinendan no shimei* [The Mission of the Youth Association], Tokyo, 1930.
Tokutomi Iichirō. *Kōshaku Katsura Tarō den* [The Biography of Prince Katsura Tarō], Tokyo, 1917.
Ugaki Kazushige. *Ugaki Kazushige nikki* [The Diary of Ugaki Kazushige], 3 vols.,Tokyo, 1968–1971.
Yabe, Teiji. *Konoe Fumimaro,* 2 vols., Tokyo, 1952.

VI. LOCAL HISTORIES

Aichi-ken Hazu-gunshi [The History of Hazu County in Aichi Prefecture], Nishio Town, 1923.
Akita-kenshi [The History of Akita Prefecture], 15 vols., Tokyo, 1960–1966.
Akita-ken sōgō kyōdo kenkyū [Akita Prefecture Collective Local Research], Akita, 1966.
Anjō-chōshi [The History of Anjō Town], Anjō, 1919.
Anjō-shishi [The History of Anjō City], 2 vols., Anjō, 1971–1973.
Arakawa-kushi [The History of Arakawa Ward], Tokyo, 1936.
Asaguchi-gunshi [The History of Asaguchi County], Takashima Town, 1925.

Ashikaga-shishi [The History of Ashikaga City], 2 vols., Ashikaga, 1928–1929.

Aso-gunshi [The History of Aso County], Kumamoto, 1927.

Atetsu-gunshi [The History of Atetsu County], 2 vols., Niimi Town, 1929–1931.

Azabu-kushi [The History of Azabu Ward], Tokyo, 1941.

Edogawa-kushi [The History of Edogawa Ward], Tokyo, 1955.

Fujino-sonshi [The History of Fujino Village], Okayama, 1953.

Fujita-sonshi [The History of Fujita Village], 4 vols., Fujita, 1936.

Fukui-shishi [The History of Fukui City], 2 vols., Fukui, 1941.

Fukuoka-ken Kurate-gunshi [The History of Kurate County in Fukuoka Prefecture], Fukuoka, 1934.

Gumma-ken Gumma-gunshi [The History of Gumma County in Gumma Prefecture], Tokyo, 1925.

Hakodate-shishi [The History of Hakodate City], Hakodate, 1935.

Hamana-gunshi [The History of Hamana County], Shizuoka, 1926.

Higashi-kushi [The History of Higashi Ward], 5 vols., Osaka, 1939–1941.

Hiroshima-ken Numaguma-gunshi [The History of Numaguma County in Hiroshima Prefecture], Hiroshima, 1923.

Hongō-kushi [The History of Hongō Ward], Tokyo, 1937.

Ichinomiya-shishi [The History of Ichinomiya City], 2 vols., Ichinomiya, 1939.

Iwatsu-chōshi [A History of Iwatsu Town], Iwatsu, 1936.

Kaibara-chōshi [The History of Kaibara Town], Kaibara, 1955.

Kake-chōshi [The History of Kake Town], 4 vols., Hiroshima, 1961–1962.

Kami Katagiri-sonshi [The History of Kami Katagiri Village], Matsukawa Town, 1965.

Kamoto-gunshi [The History of Kamoto County], Kamoto Town, 1923.

Kariya-chōshi [The History of Kariya Town], Kariya, 1932.

Kasai-gunshi [The History of Kasai County], Kobe, 1929.

Katsunuma-chōshi [The History of Katsunuma Town], Kofu, 1962.

Kawai-mura kyōdoshi [The Local History of Kawai Village], 2 vols., Morioka, 1962.

Kita-Koma-gunshi [The History of Kita-Koma County], Kofu, 1930.

Koishikawa-kushi [The History of Koishikawa Ward], Tokyo, 1935.

Kyōbashi-kushi [The History of Kyōbashi Ward], 2 vols., Tokyo, 1937–1942.

Matsumoto-shishi [The History of Matsumoto City], 2 vols., Matsumoto, 1933.

Miwa-sonshi [The History of Miwa Village], Miwa, 1935.

Miyomi-sonshi [The History of Miyomi Village], Kofu, 1938.

Miyoshi-sonshi [The History of Miyoshi Village], Niimi Town, 1961.

Mizusawa-chōshi [The History of Mizusawa Town], Mizusawa, 1931.

Mutsumi-sonshi [The History of Mutsumi Village], Mutsumi, 1926.

Nagoya Naka-kushi [The History of Naka Ward in Nagoya], Kyoto, 1944.

Naka-Koma-gunshi [The History of Naka-Koma County], 2 vols., Kofu, 1926–1928.

Nambu-chōshi [The History of Nambu Town], Kofu, 1964.
Nihombashi-kushi [The History of Nihombashi Ward], 2 vols., Tokyo, 1937.
Nishi-Kamo-gunshi [The History of Nishi-Kamo County], Tokyo, 1926.
Nishio-chōshi [The History of Nishio Town], 2 vols., Nishio, 1933–1934.
Nojiri-sonshi [The History of Nojiri Village], Kanazawa, 1929.
Ogi-gunshi [The History of Ogi County], Saga, 1934.
Owari-kuni Higashi-Kasugai-gunshi [The History of Higashi-Kasugai County in Owari Province], Nagoya, 1923.
Ryūō-sonshi [The History of Ryūō Village], Kofu, 1955.
Sakurai-sonshi [The History of Sakurai Village], 2 vols., Nara, 1954–1957.
Shiba-kushi [The History of Shiba Ward], Tokyo, 1938.
Shimajiri-gunshi [The History of Shimajiri County], Naha, 1937.
Shinagawa-chōshi [The History of Shinagawa Town], Tokyo, 1932.
Shin Ōtsu-shishi [The New History of Ōtsu City], 2 vols., Ōtsu, 1962.
Shiozaki-sonshi [The History of Shiozaki Village], Kofu, 1927.
Shitaya-kushi [The History of Shitaya Ward], 2 vols., Tokyo, 1935–1937.
Shizuoka-shishi [The History of Shizuoka City], 5 vols., Shizuoka, 1930–1932.
Taishō Yamanashi-kenshi [A History of Yamanashi Prefecture in the Taishō Era], Kofu, 1927.
Takawashi-sonshi [The History of Takawashi Village], Takawashi, 1960.
Tatsuoka-sonshi [The History of Tatsuoka Village], Tokyo, 1968.
Tottori-ken Hino-gunshi [The History of Hino County in Tottori Prefecture], 2 vols., Kyoto, 1926.
Tsukubo-gunjishi [The History of Tsukubo County Government], Okayama, 1923.
Tsukude-sonshi [A History of Tsukude Village], Tsukude, 1960.
Yamada-gunshi [The History of Yamada County], Maebashi, 1939.
Yamanashi-ken Kita-Tsuru-gunshi [The History of Kita-Tsuru County in Yamanashi Prefecture], Ohara Village, 1925.
Yana-gunshi [The History of Yana County], Shinshiro Town, 1926.
Yatsuka-gunshi [The History of Yatsuka County], Matsue, 1926.
Yutaka-mura [Yutaka Village], Yutaka, 1960.

VII. OTHER WORKS CITED

Anderson, Ronald S. *Japan: Three Epochs of Modern Education.* Washington, D. C., 1959.
Arendt, Hannah. *The Origins of Totalitarianism.* Cleveland, 1958.
Borton, Hugh. *Japan Since 1931: Its Political and Social Development.* New York, 1940.
Bracher, Karl Dietrich. *The German Dictatorship.* New York and Washington, D.C., 1970.
Crowley, James B. *Japan's Quest for Autonomy: National Security and Foreign Policy, 1903–1938.* Princeton, 1966.
Dore, Ronald P. *Land Reform in Japan.* London, 1959.
———, ed. *Aspects of Social Change in Modern Japan.* Princeton, 1967.

Embree, John. *Suyemura: A Japanese Village*. Chicago, 1964.

Fujiwara Akira. *Gunjishi* [A Military History]. Tokyo, 1961.

Fukuchi Shigetaka. *Gunkoku Nihon no keisei* [The Formation of Militaristic Japan]. Tokyo, 1959.

Fukutake Tadashi. *Nihon sonraku no shakai kōzō* [The Social Structure of Japanese Villages], Tokyo, 1959.

————. *Japanese Rural Society*. London and New York, 1967.

Furushima Toshio et al. *Meiji Taishō kyōdoshi kenkyūhō* [Research Methods in Meiji and Taishō Local History], Tokyo, 1970.

Hackett, Roger F. *Yamagata Aritomo in the Rise of Modern Japan, 1838–1922*. Cambridge, Massachusetts, 1971.

Hall, Robert King. *Shūshin: Ethics of a Defeated Nation*. New York, 1949.

Hata, Ikuhiko. *Gun fashizumu undōshi* [A History of the Military Fascism Movement], Tokyo, 1962.

Horibe Senjin. "Yūryō chōson o miru" [Viewing Superior Towns and Villages], *Shimin* [Good Citizen], XXXI (1936), 79–88.

Hino Ashihei. *Mugi to heitai* [Grain and Soldiers]. Tokyo, 1960.

Iijima Shigeru. *Nihon sempeishi* [A History of Troop Selection in Japan]. Tokyo, 1943.

Inagaki Koreasa. "Anjō shiiku in okeru jinkō kōsatsu" [An Analysis of Population in the Anjō City Area], in *Anjō-shi kenkyū hōkoku* [A Report of Anjō City Research], 3 (1968), 56–67.

Inoue Kiyoshi. *Tennōsei* [The Emperor System]. Tokyo, 1966.

————, ed. *Taishōki no seiji to shakai* [Politics and Society in the Taishō Period], Tokyo, 1969.

————, and Watanabe Tōru. *Kome sōdō no kenkyū* [Studies of the Rice Riots], 5 vols., Tokyo, 1953.

Kaigo, Tokiomi. *Japanese Education: Its Past and Present*. Tokyo, 1968.

Karasawa, Tomitarō. "Changes in Japanese Education as Revealed in Textbooks," *Japan Quarterly*, 2 (1955), 365–383.

Keenleyside, Hugh L., and A. F. Thomas. *History of Japanese Education and Present Educational System*. Tokyo, 1937.

Kennedy, Malcolm. *The Military Side of Japanese Life*. Boston and New York, 1924.

Kinoshita Hanji. *Nihon fashizumushi* [A History of Japanese Fascism], 2 vols., Tokyo, 1949–1951.

Kishimoto Eitarō. *Nihon rōdō undōshi* [Japanese Labor Movement History]. Tokyo, 1950.

Kublin, Hyman. *Asian Revolutionary: The Life of Sen Katayama*. Princeton, 1964.

Kubo Yoshizō. *Nihon fashizumu kyōiku seisakushi* [A History of the Educational Policies of Japanese Fascism], Tokyo, 1969.

Marshall, Byron K. *Capitalism and Nationalism in Prewar Japan: The Ideology of the Business Elite, 1868–1941*. Stanford, 1967.

Maruyama Masao. *Nihon no shisō* [Japanese Thought]. Tokyo, 1961.

Matsushita Yoshio. *Meiji gunsei shiron* [Historical Essays on the Meiji Military System], 2 vols., Tokyo, 1956.

————. *Nihon gunjishi jitsuwa* [True Stories of Japanese Military History]. Tokyo, 1966.

————. *Nihon gumbatsu no kōbō* [The Rise and Fall of the Japanese Military Clique], 3 vols., Tokyo, 1967.

————. *Nihon no gumbatsuzō* [A Portrait of the Japanese Military Clique]. Tokyo, 1969.

Miller, Frank O. *Minobe Tatsukichi: Interpreter of Constitutionalism in Japan.* Berkeley and Los Angeles, 1965.

Morley, James, ed. *Dilemmas of Growth in Prewar Japan.* Princeton, 1971.

Nakane Chie. *Tate shakai no ningen kankei: Tan'itsu shakai no riron* [Human Relations in a Vertical Society: A Theory of a Simple Society]. Tokyo, 1967.

Ōishi Shinzaburō. "Chōheisei to ie" [The Conscription System and the Household]. *Rekishigaku kenkyū* [Studies in Historical Science], 194 (1956), 1–12.

Oka Yoshitake. *Yamagata Aritomo.* Tokyo, 1958.

Okabe Tomio, ed. *Dainihon kyōikushi* [The History of Education in Greater Japan], Tokyo, 1939.

Okamura Seigen et al. *Nihon guntai ni okeru seishin kyōiku* [Spiritual Education in the Japanese Army]. Tokyo, 1960.

Ōkubo Toshiaki. *Nihon zenshi—kindai III* [A Complete History of Japan —Modern III]. Tokyo, 1964.

Passin, Herbert. *Society and Education in Japan.* New York, 1965.

Presseisen, Ernst L. *Before Aggression: Europeans Prepare the Japanese Army.* Tucson, 1965.

Robertson Scott, J. W. *The Foundations of Japan.* London, 1922.

Sasaki Ryūji. "Nihon gunkokushugi no shakaiteki kiban no keisei" [The Formation of the Social Basis of Japanese Militarism]. *Nihonshi kenkyū* [Studies in Japanese History], 68 (1963), 1–30.

Satō Mamoru. *Kindai Nihon seinen shūdanshi kenkyū* [Studies in the History of Modern Japanese Youth Organization]. Tokyo, 1970.

Schoenbaum, David. *Hitler's Social Revolution: Class and Status in Nazi Germany 1933–1939.* Garden City, 1966.

Seta Kaku. "Zaigō gunjindan no gensei" [The Present Status of Reservist Groups]. *Kaizō* [Reconstruction], (July, 1932), 90–97.

Shinobu Seizaburō. *Taishō seijishi* [A Political History of the Taishō Period], 4 vols., 1951–1954.

————. *Taishō demokurashishi* [A History of Taishō Democracy], 3 vols. Tokyo, 1954–1959.

Shōwashi no shunkan [Moments in Shōwa History], 2 vols., Tokyo, 1966.

Shimonaka Yasaburō, ed. *Yokusan kokumin undōshi* [The History of the National Imperial Rule Movement]. Tokyo, 1954.

Smethurst, Richard J. "The Creation of the Imperial Military Reserve

Association in Japan," *Journal of Asian Studies*, XXX, no. 4 (1971), 815–828.

———. *The Social Basis for Japanese Militarism: The Case of the Imperial Military Reserve Association*. Ann Arbor, 1969 (Dissertation).

Smith, Robert. "The Japanese Rural Community: Norms, Sanctions, and Ostracism," in Jack M. Potter et al., eds. *Peasant Society: A Reader*. Boston, 1967, pp. 246–255.

Steiner, Kurt. *Local Government in Japan*. Stanford, 1965.

———. "Popular Political Participation and Political Development in Japan: The Rural Level," in Robert E. Ward, *Political Development in Modern Japan*, Princeton, 1968, pp. 213–247.

Storry, Richard. *The Double Patriots*. London, 1957.

Suzuki Eitarō. *Nihon nōson shakaigaku genri* [Principles of Japanese Rural Sociology]. Tokyo, 1940.

Takahashi Masae. *Ni niroku jiken* [The February 26 Incident]. Tokyo, 1965.

———. *Shōwa no gumbatsu* [The Shōwa Military Clique]. Tokyo, 1969.

Takeda Taijun. *Seijika no bunshō* [The Writings of Politicians]. Tokyo, 1960.

Tsurumi, Kazuko. *Social Change and the Individual: Japan Before and After Defeat in World War II*. Princeton, 1970.

Umezaki Haruo. *Sakurajima* in Hirano Ken et al., eds., *Sensō bungaku zenshū* [A Complete Collection of Wartime Literature], Volume III, Tokyo, 1971, pp. 85–120.

Ward, Robert E., ed. *Political Development in Modern Japan*. Princeton, 1965.

Waseda daigaku shakai kagaku kenkyūjo. *Nihon no fashizumu: keiseiki no kenkyū* [Japanese Fascism: Studies in the Formative Period]. Tokyo, 1970.

Waswo, Barbara Ann Lardner. *Landlords and Social Change in Prewar Japan*. Ann Arbor, 1970 (Dissertation).

Wilson, George M., ed. *Crisis Politics in Prewar Japan*. Tokyo, 1970.

Yoshikawa Mitsusada. *Iwayuru kome sōdō jiken no kenkyū* [Studies of the So-called Rice Riots' Incident]. Tokyo, 1938.

INDEX

Aikoku fujinkai. See Patriotic Women's Association

Anjō, 28, 29, 31, 40, 52, 64, 70, 82, 95, 123, 156, 157; community structure, 55–56; as an agricultural town, 59–63; selection of Reservist Association leadership, 90, 91; expenses and duties of reservist branch chief, 104, 105; community service by reservist chiefs, 107, 108; case study of reservist branch chief, 111, 113; selection of Youth Association leaders, 119, 120; funding of Reservist Association, 128–130, 137; funding of Youth Association, 131, 132; funding of National Defense Women's Association, 133, 137–138

Araki Sadao, 170

Asahi shimbun, 40

Army: Choshu faction, xx, 2, 12; as Tanaka's "final national school," 6, 13; number of peacetime personnel, 6; and education, 11; control of reservist association, 16; influence on youth training centers, 39, 40; domination of National Defense Women's Association, 45, 46; chain of command to "civilian" organizations, 51–53; use made of hamlet structure, xv, 64, 65; organizing efforts in urban areas, 66–69; use of hamlet cohesiveness and social order to recruit for organizations, 81–84; influence on National Youth Association, 118, 119; influence

on youth schools, 122, 123; educational efforts, 165–169

Buraku. See Hamlet

Cold Weather Drill Club, 155

Communist Party, 36–37, 175

Comrades in Arms, 27, 35, 65, 147, 148, 150, 164–167, 173, 174

Conscription, 5–7; physical requirements, 72; eligibility of urban and rural youth compared, 72–74; annual physical examination, 159–160

Factory branches: of Reservist Association, 84–85; of youth training centers, 85–86; of National Defense Women's Association, 86; as urban counterpart of hamlet, 87. *See also* Imperial Military Reserve Association; National Youth Association

Falkenhayn, Erich von, 18

"Familism," 19, 48

Fushimi, Prince, 1

Greater Japan Imperial Rule Men's Association, 110–112

Greater Japan National Defense Women's Association. *See* National Defense Women's Association

Greater Japan National Youth Association. *See* National Youth Association